# "THIS IS NPR"

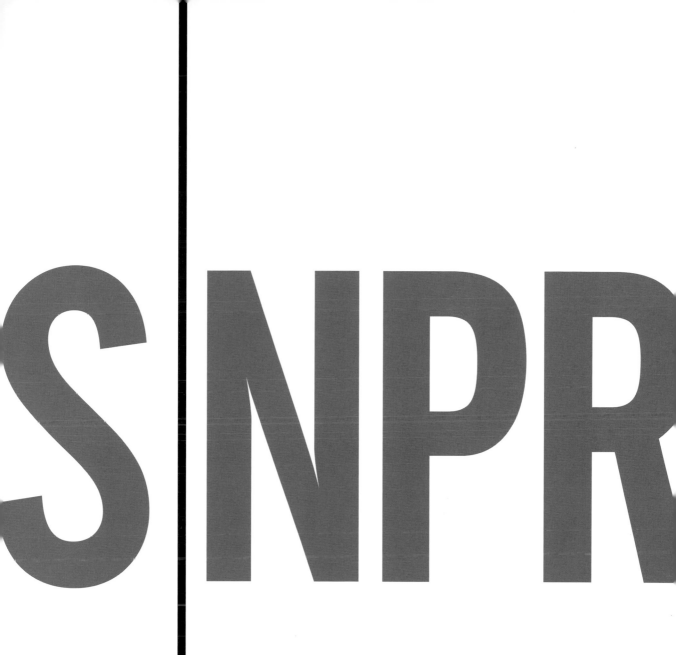

CHRONICLE BOOKS
SAN FRANCISCO

# "

**The mission of NPR** is to work in partnership with member stations to create a more informed public—one challenged and invigorated by a deeper understanding and appreciation of events, ideas, and cultures. To accomplish our mission, we produce, acquire, and distribute programming that meets the highest standards of public service in journalism and cultural expression; we represent our members in matters of their mutual interest; and we provide satellite interconnection for the entire public radio system.

*NPR's mission statement*

# TABLE OF CONTENTS

## 1970s
BY NOAH ADAMS 18

## 1980s
BY JOHN YDSTIE 70

FOREWORD
*by Cokie Roberts* 9

INTRODUCTION
*by Susan Stamberg* 13

AND RADIO 21

CUE THE OPENING THEME 22

TAKE A CHANCE—
GO TO THE NETWORK 28

THE *ATC* DAY 32

RADIO'S MAGIC 40

A MISTAKE HEARD WORLDWIDE 44

NEW LEADERSHIP 48

MORNING COMPETITION 56

BRASS AND CLASS 62

THE EIGHTEEN-HOUR
REPORTER'S SHIFT 64

THE NEWS VERSUS THE MUSE 68

RECORD GROWTH AND
A CLOSE BRUSH WITH DEATH 73

PAINFUL GROWTH 78

THE REAGAN REVOLUTION 82

JOHN LENNON SHOT IN NEW YORK 84

FIRST WOMAN SUPREME
COURT JUSTICE 90

BUILDING NPR'S NATIONAL DESK 96

COWBOY BOOTS 100

*A PRAIRIE HOME COMPANION*
GOES NATIONAL—BUT NOT ON NPR 102

LAYING THE FOUNDATION
FOR NPR'S FOREIGN DESK 104

THE NPR FINANCIAL CRISIS . . .
A NEAR-DEATH EXPERIENCE 112

NPR DEBUTS *WEEKEND EDITION
SATURDAY* WITH SCOTT SIMON 118

INVESTIGATIVE REPORTING 121

BIG CHANGES AT *ALL THINGS
CONSIDERED* 128

A TRIBUTE TO SUSAN STAMBERG 130

*WEEKEND EDITION SUNDAY*
LAUNCHES 132

CHANGES AT THE TOP OF THE
NEWS DEPARTMENT 138

# 1990s
BY RENÉE MONTAGNE    140

# 2000s
BY ARI SHAPIRO    192

NPR TAKES YOU THERE    143

AIR SUPERIORITY    148

WOMEN COVER THE WAR    152

HEARING IS BELIEVING    154

LOOKING WEST    162

ZEROING OUT PUBLIC    166

PUTTING FUN ON THE RADIO—
OR NOT    168

CREATING SHOWS THAT STICK    174

PRELUDE TO A CRISIS    180

END OF A DECADE—
TURN OF A CENTURY    190

THE MOST EXTRAORDINARY STORY    195

WE COULDN'T GO BACK    196

I WAS SUPPOSED TO DIE HERE    210

INVESTIGATIVE REPORTING WAS
ALMOST NONEXISTENT    220

IT CHANGED THE DIMENSIONS
OF HOW PEOPLE THOUGHT
ABOUT THEMSELVES    224

MAKING THE DEMOCRACY BETTER    230

WILCO DID IT    232

YOU DIDN'T NEED TO DO
A RADIO SHOW    240

THE WAY WE APPROACH TELLING
THE STORY WILL BE DIFFERENT    242

THIS IS A TERRIBLE SITUATION    244

THE GROUND IS UNDULATING
UNDER MY FEET    246

WE DID IT IN THE WORST
WAY POSSIBLE    250

EPILOGUE
*by David Folkenflik*    261

INDEX    268

# FOREWORD: RADIO HAS THE BEST PICTURES

by Cokie Roberts

"We're going to talk to our listeners just the way we talk to our friends," Susan Stamberg remembers the legendary Bill Siemering telling his skeleton staff at one of their first meetings. National Public Radio had just been created, and Bill, the brains behind *All Things Considered,* was its first program director. Susan's reflections on the birth of NPR find an echo in David Folkenflik's rumination on the future, as he considers what makes us unique: "People are given the chance to speak in their own voices."

For forty years, it is that sense of the connection and friendship with listeners and with storytellers speaking in their own voices— whether they be servicemen and -women in Afghanistan, students in Atlanta, people devastated by a massive earthquake in China, or senators in Washington—that has served as NPR's hallmark. And what friends we have made over the last four decades! Now some thirty million strong, they not only listen, they give money. They make NPR possible. When people ask why I keep getting up at 5 every Monday for *Morning Edition,* I answer simply, "Because of the listeners." If you want to be heard by young people, farmers, the chief executives of the Fortune 500, members of Congress, players in the media, and especially moms, NPR's the place for you. Those of us who have been around for a long time constantly have the experience of some young—or not so young—person coming up to us and saying, "I grew up listening to you."

(They don't mean it to sound as bad as it does.) And we always joke: "Your mother made you listen in the car, didn't she?" Somewhat to their embarrassment, they admit it's true.

This history chronicles those growing-up years from the Little Radio Network That Could to what's now the major source of news for millions of people around the world. It reminds us of the major events of those years and the people who brought them to us, along with memories of some of the non-news contributors. Longtime listeners will probably find themselves smiling as they remember some of those names, people like Kim Williams and Daniel Schorr. Most of the people in these pages are still with NPR, still connecting to their friends at the other end of the broadcast line, or the Internet, or the iPhone.

In his chapter about the 1970s, Noah Adams recalls Susan Stamberg's Watergate coverage. Reading about the 1980s, no one will have to struggle to remember Linda Wertheimer or Nina Totenberg or Scott Simon as John Ydstie describes the Reagan Revolution, the appointment of the first woman to the Supreme Court, and the fighting in Central America. It might, however, come as a surprise to learn that Robert Siegel was once behind the scenes as an editor and manager long before he took the helm at *All Things Considered.* Other editors, managers, engineers, producers, and support staff have played essential roles over these forty years,

**OPPOSITE** Cokie Roberts covering Congress in 1983 (NPR photo).

especially the two Ellens—Weiss and McDonnell—who came as kids and ended up basically running the place.

Any history of NPR must be more than one of news events and the people who reported them; it must also serve as a salute to quirkiness. Noah Adams playfully provides a list of stories from the 1970s that includes "bed of nails champ," "four-year-old Italian singer," and "Julie Nixon Eisenhower breaks her toe," along with "Mideast turmoil," "national medical health insurance," and "computer dating—five part series." Noah repeats what he calls a mantra of the Siemering era: "Celebrate the human experience." And, as you read through the decades, you realize that's exactly what NPR's been doing all these years.

Along the way, that celebration has earned NPR countless awards, but this isn't a paean to our accomplishments, though some have been significant indeed—Sylvia Poggioli's Peabody Award, for instance, for her coverage of ethnic cleansing in Bosnia. Renée Montagne tells us that what pleased Sylvia wasn't the award, but the fact that her horrific stories about rape as a weapon of war went a long way toward formal recognition of rape and sexual violence as war crimes and crimes against humanity, punishable by an international court. In writing about the 1990s, Renée looks admiringly at the intrepid women like Sylvia, Deb Amos, and Anne Garrels, who rushed to fields of battle, microphones at the ready, to bring us stories of human suffering and triumph from one war zone after another.

As good reporters, we can't avoid NPR's failures—how, in the 1970s, the network decided not to produce Garrison Keillor's wildly popular *A Prairie Home Companion* and, in the 1990s, made a similar dumb move when considering whether to run Ira Glass's *This American Life.* Fortunately, *Wait Wait . . . Don't Tell Me!* came along at the end of the decade to join *Car Talk* as a refuge from traditional NPR earnestness, and we are now treated weekly to an alternative version of Carl Kasell. In looking at our history, there's also no way to avoid painful episodes, like the financial crisis that almost sunk us in 1983, or the abrupt departure of Bob Edwards in 2004, or the economic situation that forced

the cancellation of *News and Notes, The Bryant Park Project,* and *Day to Day* with Alex Chadwick and Madeleine Brand in 2008.

There were plenty of scary moments over the years as well—Bill Drummond under fire in Beirut; Scott Simon hiding from gunfire in El Salvador; Renée Montagne escaping thugs in South Africa; Neal Conan captured during the first Persian Gulf War; Lourdes Garcia-Navarro's rear window, tire, and laptop destroyed by bullets in the second Iraqi war; Ivan Watson barely avoiding a bomb in Baghdad. And there were the horrifying moments. Michael Skoler's description of the scene at a church in the Rwandan countryside during the genocide of 1994 is not one that anyone who

**ABOVE** Ellen McDonnell, Michael Richards, and Nina Totenberg in 1980 (NPR photo).

heard it has ever forgotten. Neither is Melissa Block's 2008 live account of the earthquake that shook Chengdu, China. Both stories, and so many others, make it starkly clear that a picture is not, in fact, worth a thousand words. As Susan Stamberg is fond of saying, radio has the best pictures.

From Susan's essay of remembrance through David's look into the future, the history of National Public Radio merges with the history of American journalism over the last forty years. We look back on the time when NPR relied on journalists from newspapers to bring us eyewitness accounts from across the world and realize that many of those journals no longer can afford foreign bureaus—it's now NPR's reporters around the globe that provide information to other news organizations. We laugh about the days when we cut our audiotape with razor blades and pieced it together with splicing tape and took apart telephones to attach little "alligator clips" in order to file from the field, compared to today's digitized editing and filing. And, as we commemorate the past, we can't help but be concerned about the future. Changes in technology present challenges as well as opportunities, and we don't know where they will lead. But one thing we do know as we march into the decades ahead: We will keep talking to our friends and giving them the chance to say their piece. Together we will celebrate the human spirit.

# INTRODUCTION: IN THE BEGINNING THERE WAS SOUND BUT NO CHAIRS

by Susan Stamberg

"God, I hope they like it."

It's early April, 1971, and I'm sitting on the floor in an office at 1625 I Street, in Northwest Washington, DC. On the floor, because NPR is so new there's not enough furniture—it either hasn't arrived yet or hasn't been ordered because the budget is small. So maybe twelve of us—the very first staffers of National Public Radio—are forcing our bell-bottoms into lotus positions, on the floor, listening to tapes. Bill Siemering, NPR's tall, skinny, and too pale program director, has asked for samples of work we'd done before there was an NPR. Mine is from a series I produced on my earlier (and only) public radio job. I was rather proud of that series—a weekly panel discussion of current affairs, recorded in Washington with the highest-powered experts I could inveigle. When my turn comes, Bill threads up the audio reel, and we hear the deep, stentorian announcer's voice.

"From WAMU-FM in Washington, DC . . . this is 'A Federal Case.'"

Bill looks up. He tilts his head back, and semi-smiles. "That is exactly how we DON'T want to sound!"

I am mortified. What can be wrong? The guy on tape has a great voice—masculine, commanding. He was just a college kid I'd recruited to be my announcer, but he sounded like all the Big Guys on commercial radio. Does Bill think his voice is too young? Too . . . what?

"We want NPR to sound more relaxed," Bill said. "Conversational. We're going to talk to our listeners just the way we talk to our friends—simply, naturally. We don't want to be the all-knowing voices from the top of the mountain."

I'd been working at this brand-new public radio organization for maybe three days and had just learned the first of what would be thousands of lessons—from Bill Siemering, and then so many others—about how to create a fresh, original, inventive kind of broadcasting.

The on-the-floor mortification took place a month before NPR's flagship program, *All Things Considered*, went on the air for the first time. By that first broadcast—May 3, 1971—more furniture had arrived, and all of us had learned a good deal. You could hear that on the air. The first program was raw, visceral, and took listeners to the heart of America's

**OPPOSITE**
Susan Stamberg, who has won every major award in broadcasting, in 1975 (NPR photo).

**ABOVE** Linda Wertheimer was the first director of *All Things Considered*. This 1972 photo was taken at the first *All Things Considered* studio. From left: Renee Chaney, Kati Marton, Linda Wertheimer, and Kris Mortensen (NPR photo).

agonies over the war in Vietnam. On the day of our radio debut, antiwar demonstrators tried to shut down the federal government. Thousands of them—mostly but not exclusively long-haired young people—were in Washington to protest the Nixon administration's policies. Thousands of the demonstrators were arrested. NPR's original staff of five reporters (today there are some 122) took their recorders and microphones onto the streets, and spent all day working the story. Jeff Kamen's report on that first broadcast quickly became a touchstone for our early style and approach.

"Excuse me, Sergeant," Jeff said to a police officer. "Is that a technique? Where the men actually try to drive the motorcycles right into the demonstrators?"

"Naw, it's no technique," the officer replied. "We're trying to go down the road, and the people get in front of you. What are you gonna do? You don't stop on a dime."

It was guerrilla journalism—tough and aggressive. No deep-voiced announcer to be heard. More than seven thousand people were arrested that day. And Kamen and the others caught their rage and dismay—as the wrenching public conflict over Vietnam filled the Capital's streets.

All day long, and uncomfortably close to airtime, in edit booths at 1625 I Street, reporters' tapes were frantically slashed with razor blades, then spliced together with sticky tape, to make them coherent and fit the allotted timeslot. Down the hall, in the NPR control room, the hastily edited reels of tape were flung like Frisbees over to the big playback machines. It was a wild, thrilling scene. Hearts truly pounded faster—lucky we were all young enough to sustain the stress (even though most of us smoked then)! Exhilaration and dedication got us through without lunch—no time for it. Anyway, we had our cigarettes. And when the ninety-minute program was over, Bill Siemering gave a big smile and a nod to his brand new young staff. We grinned our heads off, thrilled we had done it, but terrified, too, because we knew we'd have to do it all over again tomorrow.

"Daily radio programs are like the dishes," *ATC*'s first director, Linda Wertheimer, said. "As soon as you've got them all washed and dried, it's time to eat again." We would come to think of *All Things Considered* as a kind of glorious media monster—massive, mobile, and always demanding dinner.

Ninety minutes a day, five days a week. And a tiny staff to do the catering, when 5 o'clock came (oddly enough, it came relentlessly, every night at precisely the same time!). There were some 65 of us all together at the beginning. And across the country, fewer than 100 member stations were broadcasting our nightly extravaganzas. The 90 stations (today we're carried on some 878 stations) included listeners in places that sounded wildly exotic to a native New Yorker like myself: Murfreesboro, Tennessee; Kankakee, Illinois.

In addition to carrying our program, reporters at those and other stations let America listen in to what was happening in their towns. They interviewed citizens and produced stories on local doings, and their tapes were broadcast on *ATC*.

"What's there to do in Murray, Kentucky, on Saturday night?"

"You go down south 'til eleven-thirty. To Tennessee for beer. Then you come back here and usually you eat. You get a pizza. You drive around town two or three times. Nothin.' You go home. That's it."

"Surely there's more than that?"

"There's nothing else to do in Murray. If there was something else to do, we wouldn't be up there on Saturday night driving up and down the street."

For news from even more exotic places, we relied on reporters from the *Christian Science Monitor*. It was a big, flourishing paper in the '70s, with cadres of reporters stationed all over the world. A deal was made with the *Monitor* that allowed us to phone their ubiquitous reporters whenever there was news in their area and put those conversations on the air. With only five reporters of our own—none stationed overseas—this arrangement let us keep an ear on the world, using seasoned observers who were also good communicators.

That's how it was in the beginning. Puny resources, an abundance of imagination, and the ambition to cover events in a first-rate fashion. Forty years later, the resources are broader, imagination persists, and that ambitious dedication to excellence remains. We continue learning, inventing, striving. Still at it, after all these years.

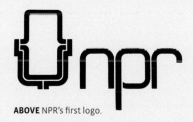

**ABOVE** NPR's first logo.

MARIAN MCPARTLAND PIANO JAZZ

ONLY A GAME MORNING EDIT

JAZZ PROFILES THE DIANE REHM

NPR NEWSCA

LATINO USA ALL THINGS

WORLD OF OPERA WAIT WAIT...DON

FRESH AIR WEEKEN

MOUNTAIN STAGE TALK OF THE

ON THE MEDIA

ION

CAR TALK

SHOW

THE THISTLE & SHAMROCK

STS

ON POINT

WORLD CAFÉ

HEARING VOICES

FROM THE TOP

CONSIDERED*

'T TELL ME !

TELL ME MORE

JAZZSET

D EDITION*

NATION

ALL SONGS CONSIDERED

● Newscasts
● News Magazines
● Talk and Information
● Entertainment
● Music

*Total estimate includes all week and/
or weekend program editions.

SOURCE: ACT1 based on Arbitron
Nationwide, Fall 2009, Persons 12+,
based on program broadcast times,
Mon–Sun midnight–midnight.

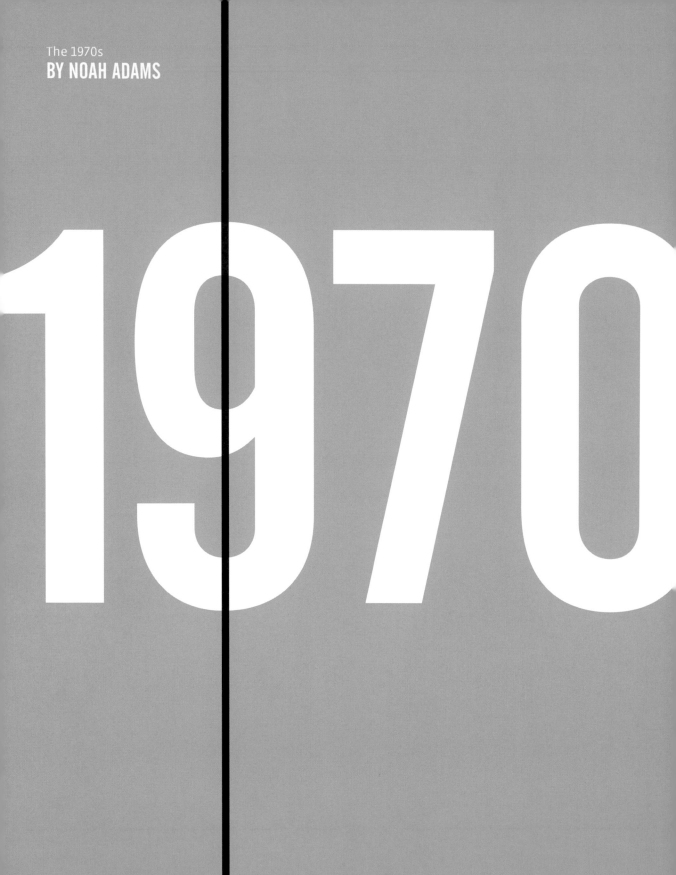

The 1970s
**BY NOAH ADAMS**

1970

1970 1971 1972 1973 1974 1975 1976 1977 1978 1979

**APR 1971**
NPR goes on the air.

**MAY 1971**
*All Things Considered* debuts.

**JUN 1972**
The Watergate scandal breaks.

**OCT 1973**
OPEC proclaims an embargo on oil to the U.S., leading to a domestic oil crisis.

**AUG 1974**
Richard Nixon resigns.

**APR 1975**
Saigon falls, and the Vietnam War comes to an end.

**JAN 1977**
Jimmy Carter is sworn in.

**AUG 1977**
Frank Mankiewicz becomes president of NPR.

**DEC 1978**
Jim Russell, one of the first hosts of *All Things Considered*, leaves NPR.

**MAR 1979**
The partial meltdown of a nuclear reactor at Three Mile Island, in Pennsylvania.

**NOV 1979**
*Morning Edition* debuts the day after 66 Americans are taken hostage at the U.S. Embassy in Iran.

# AND RADIO

"And radio." Without those two words, perhaps we would have never come together as NPR staff, as NPR stations, as NPR listeners. Very late on a winter night in 1967, those words were typed repeatedly, then cut out with scissors and Scotch-taped onto the pages of the Public Television bill that was about to leave the White House and be introduced in Congress. At the last minute, the draft language for the lawmakers was changed to insert "and radio" after every significant mention of television.

Public television? Educational, diverse, and perfect for President Lyndon Johnson's concept of a Great Society. It would be a system of stations in major cities; each of which would be a production center. Radio? Why bother? There was already an array of "educational" radio stations around the country, most of them part-time, poorly funded, and attracting few listeners. But a few of the larger stations were far from dreary, and they decided to push for the federal money and a national system. Broadcast veterans from the University of Michigan led a stealthy incursion into the depths of Washington bureaucracy, adding "and radio" throughout the bill, and stepped up their lobbying until the Public Television Act was changed to the Public Broadcasting Act. National Public Radio was put together the next year to be a central production service. For all that, only 10 percent of the public broadcasting funds approved by Congress would ever go to radio. But that would be enough.

**OPPOSITE**
Noah Adams, contributing correspondent and former long-time cohost of *All Things Considered*, in 2001 (photo by Anthony Nagelmann).

**ABOVE**
NPR Engineering Supervisor Bruce Wahl with the crew as the audio routing switcher racks are being moved into headquarters (photo by Ched Hudson).

# CUE THE OPENING THEME

Ten years after NPR's first program went on the air in April 1971, Charles Kuralt of CBS was able to write: "Day in and day out, *All Things Considered* is the most interesting program on the air . . . beats anything else on radio, television, shortwave, CB, or ship-to-shore."

Kuralt told of traveling with his camera crew in Virginia, driving along in the rain one afternoon. They had found an NPR signal and were "listening to someone explain Lebanon." They stopped at a country store for apples and cheese, and Kuralt recalls, "the man who ran the store and his teenaged daughter were sitting in there in rocking chairs listening to a radio on the shelf. They were listening to *All Things Considered*, too, hearing all about Lebanon while the rain fell on the tin roof of their store on a back road in the Appalachian Mountains."

This is exactly what Bill Siemering had in mind when NPR began to shimmer and take shape as a radio reality. Nine radio station managers were on the founding board of directors, including Siemering who had come from running WBFO in Buffalo, New York. After meetings with his colleagues, he was asked to write the new organization's mission statement. From the opening paragraph:

> *National Public Radio will serve the individual; it will promote personal growth; it will regard the individual differences among men with respect and joy rather than derision and hate; it will celebrate the human experience as infinitely varied rather than vacuous and banal; it will encourage a sense of active constructive participation, rather than apathetic helplessness.*

Bill Siemering hired many of NPR's original staff, including Susan Stamberg, who became one of the cohosts of *All Things Considered*. In December of 1972, with the program a year-and-a-half old, Siemering was called into the president's office and fired. He says, "I was told it was time for me to leave." A few months later *All Things Considered* won a Peabody Award for national news programming.

"There were differences in style," Bill Siemering says now. "They thought I wasn't a good fit,

**LEFT**
Bill Siemering, the first director of programming (photo by Bill Siemering).

wasn't a good organizer. I had a beard; I guess I wore fanciful clothes. Some of the station managers thought I should be hiring more professional-sounding hosts and reporters. But it wasn't about content; it wasn't about the stories."

Siemering was born to radio and was a natural fit for leading NPR's early development. He grew up near Madison, Wisconsin, within sight of the WHA towers. WHA-AM was a powerhouse station started at the University of Wisconsin in 1917, and it grew to reach out across the entire state. In a small schoolhouse, Siemering had listened with his class to the "Wisconsin School of the Air." He graduated from Wisconsin, having earned his way at the radio station as an announcer, newscaster, control board operator—even an actor.

In 1962 he was called to reorganize WBFO at the University at Buffalo. It was a student-run

station that didn't sign on until 5 o'clock in the afternoon. It went off the air during school vacations and the summer. But the university wanted the station to grow, so it hired Siemering, supported him, and left him alone.

Bill Siemering told Buffalo, "The airwaves belong to the people." He experimented with the sounds of the city and found pathways into social issues. WBFO set up a storefront studio in the African American community. And the station had a professional staff in place by 1970 when a student strike exploded across the campus. Part of the coverage included a three-hour show each day, with voices from all sides. It was called *This Is Radio*, and WBFO staffers eventually took this program concept to Philadelphia where it became *Fresh Air*.

ALL THINGS
CONSIDERED:
THE FIRST
BROADCAST

# BILL SIEMERING

*One of the founders of NPR and the first director of programming*

**When we selected May 3, 1971,** for the inaugural broadcast of *All Things Considered*, we could not have predicted that hordes of angry demonstrators would choose this same day to march through the streets of Washington, DC, in what became the largest demonstration against the Vietnam War in the country's capital. The demonstrators filled the roads, blocked the bridges, and stalled the morning commuter traffic, all in an effort to shut down the government. The demonstrators were met with 10,000 federal troops, 5,000 DC police, and 2,000 members of the National Guard. By the end of the day, more than 6,000 had been arrested, the largest mass arrest in U. S. history.

Our staff was small and came from a broad range of backgrounds, from the *New York Times* to NBC, CBS, AP, WHA, and the American Red Cross. It takes time to work effectively as a team, and we had worked together only on mock-ups of the program for two weeks.

But the team flourished under the pressure of the demonstration, and we had the opportunity to achieve some of our goals for National Public Radio. We wanted to capitalize on the sound quality of radio to tell stories, to escape from the sterility of a sound-proof studio, and to give the listener a sense of being present amidst the action.

Reporters fanned out from the Pentagon to the Mall, recording multiple perspectives of the events as they happened. I directed the program that first day, and we hustled to edit the multitude of voices into a cohesive documentary. But at 5:00 P.M. the tape had not yet made its way to the control room. The host, Robert Conley, calmly filled for six minutes, until the documentary was finally cued and ready to roll.

What followed was an extraordinary twenty-four-minute sound portrait of the events as they happened, with the voices of protesters, police, and office workers above the sirens and chopping of helicopters. Yes, there were flaws, and yet it stands as probably the best sound record of that historic day. ■

# DON QUAYLE

*First president of NPR, 1970–1973*

**Prior to beginning our broadcast** of *All Things Considered* on May 3, 1971, our first regularly produced program, we covered the antiwar demonstrations taking place in and around Washington, DC. These were fed to the member stations as news reports they could record and include in their local news programs. Occasionally, we covered real-time events and fed them live for stations to broadcast simultaneously or record for later use.

One day, our news director came into my office with one of our reporters who was complaining that he was not able to participate personally in any of the protests because we insisted that he maintain a reporter's distance and objectivity and not give vent to his personal feelings. He was brought to me to appeal that decision by the news director since I, as president, was the executive in charge. After listening to his appeal, I agreed that he should be able to join in the protest as an individual if that was his choice. I did indicate that he would not be covering the events as an NPR reporter, and I requested that he turn in his press pass. He did make that choice and surrendered his pass.

That evening, I received a phone call from our general counsel suggesting that I turn on the television and watch the local news. I saw coverage of a demonstration that showed the DC police on motorcycles around a circle of demonstrators, some sitting, some standing, focusing on someone in the center of the circle. It turned out to be the chief of police. He was lecturing the demonstrators, trying to get them to be orderly and suggesting that they break up the demonstration and return to their homes. Suddenly one of the demonstrators got up from his sitting position, walked through the other demonstrators to the chief of police, grabbed his badge, and ripped it off his coat. As this happened, I recognized the individual taking that action as our reporter. I was very glad that he was not carrying his NPR press pass. ■

**OPPOSITE** Vietnam veterans opposed to the war assemble on the steps of the Capitol in Washington, April 19, 1971 (AP photo).

## TRANSCRIPT EXCERPT
## *ALL THINGS CONSIDERED*

**SHOW DATE:**
*1971-05-03*
**CAT. TITLE:**
*May Day Demonstrations
in Washington Against
Vietnam War*

**JEFF KAMEN:** One, two, three army helicopters flying surveillance over the small section of Washington's complicated highway system. A line of young people has just come across the highway. Traffic is stopped. Here come the police. One demonstrator knocked down by a motor-scooter policeman . . . Anger now . . . anger of the young people.

**DEMONSTRATOR:** Come on, people.

**KAMEN:** The demonstrators just told a motorcycle sergeant that one of his men did knock one of the demonstrators down.

**POLICEMAN:** All right, let me get an ambulance down here for you. Motor 3 on the Southwest Freeway, have one injured down here. Could you send me an ambulance, please? It's right at Maine Avenue.

**DEMONSTRATOR:** . . . when he hit the kid, he went right through the line.

**POLICEMAN:** . . . got past me and almost knocked me down . . . in the blue . . .

**SECOND DEMONSTRATOR:** Yeah, but it's a policeman we're talking about.

**THIRD DEMONSTRATOR:** Policeman on a motorcycle hit him, not a . . . not a citizen, man . . .

**FOURTH DEMONSTRATOR:** Right there, the man over there. Right there.

**KAMEN:** Sergeant, excuse me, Jeff Kamen, National Public Radio. Is that a technique where the men actually try to drive their bikes right into the demonstrators?

**POLICEMAN:** No, it's no technique. We're trying to go down the road, and the people get in front. What are you going to do? You don't stop on a dime.

**KAMEN:** What happened, officer?

**POLICEMAN:** . . . bricks they don't count.

**KAMEN:** Somebody threw a brick at you, officer?

**POLICEMAN:** Yes, sir.

**KAMEN:** Right here, as you were driving through?

**POLICEMAN:** Right.

**KAMEN:** One of the motorcycle police officers says someone threw a brick at him. I was here at the time. I didn't see anything thrown. Army helicopters coming in low, keeping constant surveillance, keeping the various command posts, military police, and obviously presidential staff advised as to what's going on.

One helicopter now is in real low, military police helicopter, up on the rise of this highway section. Young people are holding an American flag upside down. A handful of police officers has succeeded in clearing at least half of this roadway. Traffic is flowing again.

A Washington, D.C., bus has just arrived. Police officers, wearing white riot helmets, come out of the bus. They snap on their helmets. Integrated police team. The demonstrators are fleeing. The police officers are carrying or wearing their tear gas masks. The tactic this morning, obviously, is to keep the demonstrators on the run.

**STEVEN BANKER AT THE PENTAGON:** Is this your boat?

**DEMONSTRATOR:** Yes.

**BANKER:** Would you describe it.

**DEMONSTRATOR:** It's a one-man kayak.

**BANKER:** It must be pretty hard to get here if you're the only demonstrator in front of the Pentagon and you had to come by kayak.

**DEMONSTRATOR:** No, I'm sure I could have driven a whole lot easier.

**BANKER:** This man is wearing an orange Mae West. Is that what you have on?

**DEMONSTRATOR:** Just a life preserver.

**BANKER:** A life preserver and a white crash helmet. And he carried a green kayak from the Potomac River onto the grounds of the Pentagon. What are you going to do now?

**DEMONSTRATOR:** Go back to the Potomac River. Maybe paddle across and go through the reflecting pool, then back upstream.

**BANKER:** But surely you must have expected to meet a lot of other people here.

**DEMONSTRATOR:** Yes, I did. I'm kind of disappointed.

———————————

**DEMONSTRATOR:** My eyes are burning a little bit. My skin burns. I always react this way to gas.

**SECOND DEMONSTRATOR:** I'm fine, but we're gonna shut the fucking city if it takes all day.

**KAMEN:** Are they going to stop you today?

**THIRD DEMONSTRATOR:** It's—it's just, you know, it's just so disorganized. You know, like I was hoping that we could just, you know, go in en masse somewhere and just sit down and then just, you know, be peacefully arrested. But I don't know, they just—they just, you know, the scare tactics are working. I'm afraid.

**FOURTH DEMONSTRATOR:** I just don't know how much more running we can do and how much more gassing we can take. I really think that we can achieve our tactic by taking a long time to get arrested, without resisting, with being nonviolent.

**FIFTH DEMONSTRATOR:** I was at Washington Square, and when the cop busted me, they put me in the car. I was peaceful. Then when they got me in the car, they said, "You're stupid, kid," and he whacked me with the billy club in the car. Eleven stitches.

**SiXTH DEMONSTRATOR:** The cops jump off the bus, and said, "We going to kill you all, you all damn people." Because like we told them . . . like we didn't want any trouble. He hollerin,' "You're going to get trouble." First he try to run over me with the car. After he get out the car, he going to start beating on me.

There's no room for nonviolence. The only way you're going to beat this doggone man is to use tactics that he use. After spending thirteen months in Vietnam and coming back here and getting my ass kicked . . . I don't need it.

**SEVENTH DEMONSTRATOR:** This is the very thing, you know, you're protesting about, man. They're doing the very thing that, you know, you're trying to end. They're coming and just beating heads. It's done all over the world, and they're doing it at home. They don't really care, you know, who they do it to, as long as they maintain the status quo or whatever, you know.

**EIGHTH DEMONSTRATOR:** Yeah, the cop that busted me said, "How old are you?" I said, "Nineteen." He said, "How come you're not in the army?" I said . . . you know, I didn't say anything. I didn't . . . you know. He said, "You're chicken," and he started hitting me.

**NINTH DEMONSTRATOR:** We were standing down on the corner and a busload of police came up and they seemed to be really pouring out of the bus, and I didn't know what to do, so like, you know, I ran like hell and, like, I was running along. Someone clubbed me in the stomach, but, like, my coat protected me. And then I was running through a parking lot, and someone threw a club at me. ■

# TAKE A CHANCE— GO TO THE NETWORK

I drove into Washington on a Sunday evening in September 1975, crossing Memorial Bridge over the Potomac River. Everything that was a part of my life at that moment was in my car (which I would soon have to sell). The monuments were gleaming, the city handsome. I found NPR's building, across the street from the CBS Bureau, then walked along the streets for a while, understanding that this was a moment all newcomers share: Should I have gone for this? Can I do this work?

Left behind in Kentucky was a solid job. I could have stayed forever. WBKY (now WUKY) at the University of Kentucky had only five full-time staff, and I'd become the chief announcer. I had found public radio after a decade of indecision and frequent failure. But luck found me in a city with an NPR station, and I'd been listening. The voices were welcoming and, above all, sincere. I had five years of experience in commercial radio (not sincere), so I volunteered for air work at WBKY. A bluegrass show came first; I'd help out and sometimes fill in for the regular host. Then, I took over with a three-hour, nightly progressive rock show. I signed off at 2 o'clock in the morning, got a few hours sleep, and had to show up on my construction job—I was a laborer for a company that put up steel buildings—at 7 o'clock. One day, a carpenter on my team asked me if I'd ever heard *All Things Considered*. He said, "Don't tell the other guys I've been listening."

After two years, a full-time job opened at WBKY, and I spent my days at a control board, playing classical music, trying to learn the pronunciations. At 5 o'clock, I'd turn the knob that brought in the

LEFT Noah Adams and Liane Hansen cohosted *All Things Considered* on the weekend (NPR photo).

## 1972: OVER THE FALLS IN A BARREL

# IRA FLATOW

*Host and executive producer,* Talk of the Nation: Science Friday

**That was the idea.** To find out what it was like to go over Niagara Falls in a barrel without actually going over the falls in a barrel. Or at least to hear what it might be like.

The scheme was the brainchild of Mike Waters, one of the first hosts of *All Things Considered*. And I was selected to prepare the tape recorder and affix it to the barrel. Having worked for Mike at WBFO in Buffalo, New York, I had followed him to Washington in 1971 as a production assistant assigned to do anything the important people asked me to do. Get coffee. Cut tape. Throw a barrel over the falls.

It turned out that getting the contraption built was the easy part. Getting it into the Niagara River in the dead of winter—February 1972—and over the falls was something quite a bit more challenging. You see, in the off season, two serious hurdles must be overcome: the 5 feet of ice that turns gentle pathways into treacherous slalom runs and the paucity of water going over the falls. Yes, in the winter the power utility diverts water from the raging river to make electricity, so the falls are not so mighty, nor the rapids so … rapid. (No tourists; no need for a big splash.)

Undaunted, I set the tape recorder to play and sealed up the barrel, and Mike and I heaved it into the river (with the cooperation—and amusement—of the local police). We jumped into Mike's car to race the barrel to the falls, anticipating the mighty plunge. But alas, the barrel was nowhere to be seen. It had found its way to the bank of the shallow river and was bobbing up and down in 2 feet of water, mocking us with tape recorder running.

A Park Service policeman shimmied down into the gorge ("I pull out bodies this way"), picked up the barrel ("It's loose as a goose in there!"), and heaved it again into the once mighty river.

But alas, the barrel, showing good sense, refused to go over. With tape running out, we retrieved the drum, opened it up, and listened to the sound of the river, best summed up by Eyewitness News's Henry Tennenbaum on the scene: "Just sounds like a toilet bowl flush."

Hot cocoa was enjoyed by all. ∎

network, and the bouncy, electronic *All Things Considered* theme would start. I was being paid to listen to people who were becoming friends and to stories that I hadn't thought I'd care about. A career in public radio seemed possible. I had taken out a bank loan and bought an IBM Selectric (thinking I would try again to write short stories), and so the application letter I wrote to Jim Russell, the *All Things Considered* producer, was beautifully typed. He had an opening for a production assistant, who would edit tape and write segment introduction copy. Russell hired me with just that letter and a phone call between us. He told me he liked that I was somewhat older, "I want someone who knows who Solzhenitsyn is." I did know that Alexander Solzhenitsyn was a Soviet dissident, but I had never read any of his work.

My only previous news experience involved UPI wire copy—"rip and read," we called it— and weather forecasts. I had done a single documentary report, about a local environmental issue. I had filed one feature story that ran on the network. I was all too conscious of my inexperience and lack of credentials as I walked into the NPR office that first day. Eventually, I would work in the same *All Things Considered* studio with Linda Wertheimer and Robert Siegel. They had prestigious degrees— Wellesley and Columbia—and both had worked as journalists in New York and London. Despite my insecurities, I was always made welcome at that table, as I was at my first *ATC* editorial meeting. It seemed that if somehow you had made it through the door—in my case with only a year or so of college and a sketchy resume—things would be okay. But you had to be able to do the work, and the broadcast day could move terrifyingly fast.

# SUSAN STAMBERG REMEMBERS

**LEFT** Susan Stamberg in 1975 (NPR photo).

## 1972-07-30: HOW *ATC* GLOWED IN THE DARK

**Science reporter Ira Flatow** wanted to test a theory. So, live, on *ATC*, he took me into a dark closet (we had long microphone cords) so we could see whether Wint-O-Green Life Savers made sparks when you chewed them. We chewed away for quite a while in the closet before we indeed did begin seeing sparks. By then it was time to close the program. Ira held a lit match while I read the closing credits ("Hurry up, the match is starting to burn my finger!"). That night sales of Wint-O-Green Life Savers spiked. ■

## 1971: HOW *ATC* GOT ITS NAME

**There was a staff contest.** Everybody was asked to submit an entry. The winning title came from George Geesey, NPR's first operations manager. In 1979, when *Morning Edition* went on the air, we were asked for ideas. My favorite came from producer Jay Kernis: *Tomorrow We'll Be Better.* ■

**ABOVE** Within Jay Kernis's first year at NPR, his boss suggested that he should cut his hair (NPR photo).

## 1972: CRANBERRY RELISH RECIPE TRADITION

**My first Thanksgiving** as host of *All Things Considered* (1972), I began a tradition that lasts to this day. On the Friday before Thanksgiving, I broadcast my mother-in-law Marjorie Stamberg's outlandish-sounding recipe for cranberry relish. ("The recipe that sounds terrible and tastes terrific!"):

| | |
|---|---|
| 2 cups raw cranberries | 2 tablespoons—this is |
| 1 small onion | the outlandish part— |
| ½ cup sugar | horseradish |
| ¾ cup sour cream | |

Grind the berries and onion together. Add everything else. Mix and freeze. Thaw on Thanksgiving morning for 1½ pints of thick, chunky, Pepto Bismol–colored, utterly delicious, slightly icy relish. Can't have an NPR anniversary book without Mama Stamberg's recipe! ■

**LEFT** Mama Stamberg's famous cranberry relish (photo by Avie Schneider/NPR).

## 1972: PRESIDENTIAL ELECTION NIGHT

**I anchored NPR's first presidential election-night** coverage in 1972. No satellites, no live interconnection between stations. In our Washington studio, when I wanted to ask a panelist in Michigan to interpret some results, I posed my question, paused five seconds while the engineer threw the switch that put Ann Arbor on the air, listened to the answer, then paused another five seconds until the switch put me back on the radio. Talk about instant communications! Those instants felt like hours. ■

# THE *ATC* DAY

**ABOVE** Scott Simon in 1979 (NPR photo).

If you flip back through the *All Things Considered* logbooks, you'll start to understand the quotidian reach of the program, the possibilities that exist in any morning's meeting: What has to be on? What do you really want to hear? What don't we understand? What's making us laugh? But the clock is inexorable, determined, and the program itself—starting no matter what at 5 o'clock—is the art of the possible.

We've always kept large three-ring binders for the *All Things Considered* rundowns—two pages for each program, with brief descriptions of the stories. The earliest rundown entries, quite terse, were handwritten, in cursive, by Linda Wertheimer, who'd agreed to be the director (and therefore after-show record keeper).

Each day, we started with the news and reaction to the news, and then whatever else might come along—sometimes long in the planning, sometimes a matter of serendipity. Here's a sampling of the stories that the program covered from 1971 through 1979, culled from the pages of the old black binders:

*Songs of the Irish Republican Army*

*Violence in Ulster, Ireland*

*Bed of nails champ*

*Four-year-old Italian singer*

*Old-time wheat threshing*

*Mideast turmoil*

*National medical health insurance*

*Sky marshals*

*Reading program in Kansas City ghettos*

*Lifting of very fat men with little effort in English pub*

*Friends of FBI form to counter criticism of J. Edgar Hoover*

*Division in Europe to* Jesus Christ Superstar *movie*

*Wives and mothers of POWs in Vietnam come to the U.N.*

*Hiroshima, parts 1 and 2*

*Pollution of the Great Lakes*

*Julie Nixon Eisenhower breaks her toe*

*Live sex theater owner*

*Riot at Attica*

*Young white radicals and moderates react to Attica*

*Hippie wedding in Michigan*

*Computer dating—five part series*

*Clearwater Pete Seeger effort to restore Hudson River*

*Hobo convention*

*Vegetarians tell how they celebrate Thanksgiving*

*Soviets agree to pay damages to American lobstermen*

*Bob Hope makes his annual Christmas tour of Vietnam*

*Sexual problems handicapped*

*Letcher County coal mining*

*Irish tea drinker takes her milk after her tea*

*Patty Hearst search*

*Fred Rogers—how parents should react to kids fears about Iran*

Then there was Watergate. June 1972–August 1974. Coverage that started with the break-in and continued through to the cover-up, the Senate investigation, the impeachment inquiry, and Nixon's resignation. In her book, *Every Night at Five*, Susan Stamberg calls it

**LEFT** In 1973 hosts Susan Stamberg and Mike Waters discuss a taped segment for *All Things Considered* (NPR photo).

**White:** *You know, Susan, I just have a hell of a time believing all of that. I really think that the guy knew. He maybe didn't know exactly what was happening, but he had to know that there was something being done. If he came right out and said, "Yes, I did know that there was something going on, and I was not in favor of it," or was in favor . . . whatever . . . I would stomach it a whole lot better than his beating around the bush forever. I never have liked that and never will.*

As the events unfolded, White eventually told Susan that he was a *former* Nixon supporter. Richard Larson of Las Cruces, New Mexico, however, remained a loyalist to the end.

**Larson:** *It's going to come around full turn, the events, and we'll find that President Nixon wasn't the culprit everyone is so ready to condemn him for being.*

**Stamberg:** *What evidence do you have for that?*

**Larson:** *He never wavered. He never wavered . . . every time you've got someone that's got a crooked story going, the story changes . . . it never does with him. It's continuous. I'm happy for the man. He's done a good job.*

As the end drew closer, Susan spoke with citizen commentator Jan Saecker of Markesan, Wisconsin, about whether impeachment might threaten the democratic system:

**Saecker:** *No, no. I don't. In fact, I think it would be more of a safeguard. If we don't approach questions of legality openly and honestly, we're in more danger.*

**Stamberg:** *Are you worried about world reaction to an America that might impeach its president?*

**Saecker:** *No. I worry about world reaction to the kind of America we've had in recent years, where there seems to be so much hanky-panky, where we say one thing and support another.*

"the most relentless, longest-running story *All Things Considered* has ever told." A few particular voices became central to the story as it unfolded on *All Things Considered*. At the time, Stamberg developed a style of interviewing "citizen-commentators," which *All Things Considered* used to open up the discussion far beyond the Potomac, including Wade Horton of Augusta, Georgia:

**Wade Horton:** *The fact that you called me about the thing is what makes me so mad, see!!!*

**Stamberg:** *Why?*

**Horton:** *For the simple reason that you media people are trying to create this whole thing. You people are doing this, and you know you're doing it. You have complete control of what you say and what goes on. What I say is not going to come out the same way it goes in.*

The events of the Watergate saga were analyzed as they unfolded, with reports from Senate hearing chambers and the White House pressroom. Then a call might go out to Horton or to Charlie White in Manhattan, Kansas:

These talks with listeners across the country brought a genuine openness to news on the radio in the United States. (In Canada, the CBC evening program *As It Happens* predates *All Things Considered* with its similar approach to connecting with listeners.) Susan Stamberg would phone the housewife in Wisconsin or the rancher-banker in Kansas, and they'd work though developments in the Watergate affair. When we turned on the radio, we joined a community; Susan and familiar voices from across the country came forward to share our convictions and wonderings. The conversations were quiet—in a tone that suggested two chairs close together—but they could tingle with challenge. No one's done this better than Susan Stamberg, before or after.

We also had regular "professional" commentators to help bring faraway places to Washington and therefore back out to a larger world. They were people who had real lives and real accents. Over the years, we would get to know Daniel Pinkwater in the Hudson River Valley, Bailey White from south Georgia, Andrei Codrescu of Romania and New Orleans, Texas's Carmen Delzell, and Donald McCaig, sheep rancher in a far and high Virginia valley. There were many others, usually writers who had strong ties to their home places.

Kim Williams was an early favorite. Kim lived in Missoula, Montana. She was a naturalist, teaching about edible wild foods at the university and leading groups on study hikes. She also wrote essays for KUFM, her home station. They sent us a tape in the hopes that we might use her on a national level. She had a distinctive style that Susan described best: ". . . a sweet bumpy voice, a confidential tone, and sounds like a cross between Edith Bunker, a twelve-year-old, and your favorite Norman Rockwell grandmother." Kim loved laughing, telling of adventures with her husband Mel: "In South America we once ate a dish of spaghetti and, when we looked closer, each piece of spaghetti had a little black eye. It was baby eels." She was often quite adamant, sharing her breadth of knowledge, once warning about the highly poisonous water hemlock after a river guide had died after eating it, thinking he was eating

water parsnip: "Water hemlock grows naturally on the banks of rivers and tubers or roots can come loose from the main plant. That's why I have this new rule. It is: don't eat any root that is wandering around unattached to a plant."

Kim went on to write books and even appeared on the David Letterman show, but she got her start on *All Things Considered,* and she almost wound up in the rejection pile. One day, our producer (we had eight in the first ten years) called several of us into his office, grinning. "I just want you to hear this lady's tape before we send it back." He played Kim's audition. We heard a lively, quite unusual voice. "Isn't that wild?" the producer said. "I've never heard anyone like that." But to a person the rest of us said, "She's great—you've *got* to put her on the radio."

She sent in her commentaries for a decade, and last was heard in 1986 when she told Susan that she was dying of ovarian cancer. She'd foregone radiation and chemotherapy and was "getting ready to move on to new dimensions." Susan and Kim both said their thanks and goodbyes. Neenah Ellis, the production assistant editing the tape, decided to leave in the final sound of Kim's phone hanging up. It was perhaps the single most evocative one-half second of tape that has ever been aired.

# REPORTING WATERGATE

**ABOVE** Richard Nixon says goodbye with a victorious salute to his staff members outside the White House as he boards a helicopter after resigning the presidency on August 9, 1974. Nixon was the first president in American history to resign the nation's highest office (AP photo).

TRANSCRIPT EXCERPT
# *ALL THINGS CONSIDERED*

**SHOW DATE:**
*1972-06-19*
**CAT. TITLE:**
*Watergate: Attempted Wiretapping*

**STAMBERG:** This is certainly a day of intriguing cloak-and-dagger words in the news. First "hijackers" and now "spying" or what the chairman of the Democratic National Committee has called "political espionage," the attempt to bug his party's headquarters in Washington over the weekend, otherwise referred to as the Caper of the Bungled Bugging.

The incident raises a number of serious questions about the credibility of politicians and political groups. Rich Adams raised some of these questions in a conversation today with Richard Strout of the *Christian Science Monitor*.

**ADAMS:** Mr. Strout, to someone who is already somewhat skeptical of the political process and is, perhaps, about willing to give up on organized politics, what effect do you think this kind of cloak-and-dagger activity would have on him?

**STROUT:** Well, I think this deepens the feeling of suspicion, of being unable to believe what's going on here, a credibility factor. This is a raw and flagrant example that captures the headlines, but it's only the latest in a series of them. And I think there's a feeling of frustration and bitterness and cynicism all over the country about Washington, where queer things of this sort can happen.

**ADAMS:** Let's turn back to our imaginary cynic again, who, sitting there watching all of this, must be asking himself: If this is what politicians do to each other, what might they do to the country?

**STROUT:** Well, I think you put your finger on a very important thing. I think that the real issue now is the credibility of Mr. Nixon and his administration, just as it was in the days of Lyndon Johnson.

I don't know what the average listener or reader or viewer can say when a group of five men, one of whom is employed by the Republican National Committee, is arrested at gunpoint in the offices of the Democratic Committee, and they have on them sophisticated electronic and photographic apparatus and they have some sixty-five hundred dollars' worth of new hundred-dollar bills that are serially consecutive.

**ADAMS:** What effect, if any, do you think this whole thing will have on the political scene?

**STROUT:** I don't know. I would say that it would be argued for a long time. I think that what the professional politicians suspect and are rather fearful of is that there is some great new undercurrent and emotional swell going on in the United States that has produced such men as McGovern and George Wallace and given them very large votes in the primaries. There's a great new turnout of youngsters who are coming in. And I think there is a feeling of cynicism about the incumbents, and there may be a turn-the-rascals-out movement. It's too early to know that. ∎

TRANSCRIPT EXCERPT
## *ALL THINGS CONSIDERED*

**SHOW DATE:**
*1973-07-20*
**CAT. TITLE:**
*Nixon/Rose Garden
Staff Pep Talk*

**ROBERT CONLEY:** Back to the White House came the president, home from the Bethesda Naval Medical Center in suburban Maryland. Recovering, but not recovered yet, from viral pneumonia. And once there, the president had the White House staff—one hundred or so—out into the Rose Garden for a pep rally, in a sense, and to display the Nixon grit once more about Watergate.

**NIXON:** I was rather amused by some very well-intentioned people who thought that perhaps the burdens of the office, and, you know, some of the rather rough assaults that any man in this office gets from time to time, brings on an illness. And that after going through such an illness, that I might get so tired that I would consider either slowing down or [laughs] or even, some suggested, resigning.

Well, now, just so we set that to rest, I'm going to use the phrase that my Ohio father used to use. Any suggestion that this president is ever going to slow down while he's president or is ever going to leave this office until he continues to do the job and finishes the job he was elected to do—anyone who suggests that—that's just plain poppycock. We're going to stay on this job until we get the job done.

**CONLEY:** One quirk in all that was the president's own daughter, Julie Nixon Eisenhower, who revealed that the president had asked his family, if only as a talking point, whether they thought he should resign.

**NIXON:** No one in this great office at this time in the world's history can slow down. This office requires a president who will work right up to the hilt all the time. That's what I've been doing. That's what I'm going to continue to do, and I want all of you to do likewise.

Oh, I know, many say, "But then you'll risk your health." Well, the health of a man isn't nearly as important as the health of a nation and the health of the world. I do want you to know that I feel that we have so little time in the positions that all of us hold and so much to do. And what we were elected to do, we are going to do. And let others wallow in Watergate. We're going to do our job.

**CONLEY:** Presidential aides were upset when Julie Nixon Eisenhower first mentioned that resignation talk—a mistake, they said. But she bounced back with the comment, "What do they know?" Now the latest turn: the White House says that Julie Nixon Eisenhower will be making no more public appearances for a while, nor will she be mentioning Watergate. It's rather ridiculous to be repetitious and for her to say the same things over and over, the White House decided. ∎

**ABOVE** Robert Conley, the first host of *All Things Considered* (photo by George Geesey).

# RADIO'S MAGIC

Many listeners will never forget a voice that was privately recorded in 1975 and not broadcast on *All Things Considered* until ten years later. Air Force 2nd Lieutenant Richard van de Geer was a helicopter pilot serving in Southeast Asia. One day at home base in Thailand, he made a cassette to send to his best friend back in the States. Intended for only one person to ever hear, it was an honest communication, his voice drenched with exhaustion and confusion, close to despair but still with a note of hope.

Lt. van de Geer had flown rescue missions into South Vietnam, as the Fall of Saigon became a reality.

"I got back today; I am in bits and pieces, fairly incoherent."

You can hear Armed Forces Radio—'70s rock and announcements—faintly in the background. He's taping in a base dayroom, just talking to Dick back home. The audio quality and the presence of van de Geer's voice is extraordinary. At the beginning, he tells Dick about checking into a Thai hotel after flying an earlier rescue operation in Cambodia.

"So the moment I walked into the room, I told them I wanted flowers in the room, and I wanted some gin, and I wanted the best body massage that Bangkok had to offer and a place and a woman for me . . ."

Then a note was brought to his door.

"The message said there would be a plane waiting at the airport at 1700 . . . I really didn't have a good idea why I was being recalled, but we felt as though it had something to do with Vietnam."

He flew four sorties, evacuating Vietnamese and Americans from the roof of the U. S. Embassy in Saigon. The helicopters were the last hope for those who wanted to leave. The North Vietnamese had shut down most of Tan Son Nhut airport. The AP's Peter Arnett, watching from the roof of the Caravelle Hotel, reported seeing three aircraft fall in flames, hit by rockets.

Van de Geer said the operation went on until 5 o'clock in the morning.

"The night sorties were the worst because we flew lights out. The tracers kept everybody on edge. To see a city burning gives one a strange feeling of insecurity."

Van de Geer closes by saying, "I wish you peace, and I have a great deal of faith that the future has to be ours. Adios, my friend."

**ABOVE** Mountains of exhausted-looking audio tapes, replete with white leader tape to help engineers thread them onto tape recorders (NPR photo).

The Saigon withdrawal was on April 30, 1975. Twelve days later, an American container ship, the *Mayaguez* was captured by the Khmer Rouge off Cambodia. The crew was taken hostage. American Marines were flown to the ship and the island of Koh Tang, and their helicopters were hit by rockets. Van de Geer's craft was among those that crashed into the sea; he was killed along with eighteen others. These were among the last fatalities of the Vietnam conflict, and Lt. Richard van de Geer's is the last name on the Vietnam Veteran's Memorial.

Without NPR, van de Geer's voice would probably have never been heard. It would have stayed in his friend's desk drawer. Art Silverman was the producer who kept on making the phone calls that found the cassette, even though he already had enough material to put together the twenty-minute segment he was working on for the tenth Saigon anniversary. (Art had seen a transcript and figured the tape still existed.)

# KEE MALESKY
*Reference librarian*

**The first person hired** for NPR's original news magazine was not a reporter or a producer. It was a researcher, Carolyn Jensen, who joined the newsroom a year before *ATC* went on the air. Bill Siemering, the program director who made that decision, explained why: "We wanted to ensure that we could provide news of events and ideas in a context that gives them meaning ... We had a strong commitment to NPR as a most responsible enterprise." He knew that the kind of journalism NPR intended to practice would require strong information support.

By 1975, the News Division had a professionally staffed reference collection operating seven days a week. We have grown to four full-time librarians, who in 2009 spent 2,500 hours answering almost 10,000 questions for reporters, hosts, and editors, as well as supporting NPR management, the Ombudsman, and station services. The reference librarians perform background research and fact-checking, find experts and phone numbers, provide guidance in grammar and pronunciation, produce briefing books for major events, and work on investigative projects for NPR on the radio and on the Web.

Starting out with printed books and journals, newspaper clip files, and a typewriter, the NPR reference librarians have embraced every new technological advance, right up to to e-books, blogs, and wiki software. And they're ready for whatever comes next. ■

AFTER THE SHOW IS OVER

# MAUREEN CLEMENTS
*Broadcast librarian*

**When NPR was still in its infancy**, the founding fathers and mothers made the fortuitous decision to archive and preserve all the audio NPR provided for broadcast through its airwaves. Programs were archived not only for historical reasons but for practical purposes. NPR could reuse its own audio, thus making available to reporters a vast treasure trove of sounds and voices. Librarians were hired to catalog each program down to the segment level so that the audio could be found and repurposed. This is how the NPR Broadcast Library was born.

As the network grew, so too did NPR's Broadcast Library. What started as a collection of handwritten roadmaps and less than two hours of daily archival radio programming has turned into a massive library that encompasses the complete aural spectrum. Today, there are eight librarians and two transcript coordinators who care for the collection, which consists of 125,000 hours of NPR programming, 10,000 commercially produced multimedia items, a music library, 28,000 transcripts, and at least one million cataloged records. Did I mention we also answer some 3,000 plus audio-related questions for staff per year? So the next time you hear that wacky Richard Nixon clip or that perfectly placed tune at the end of a story, remember to thank a broadcast librarian. ■

# A MISTAKE
# HEARD
# WORLDWIDE

**"**

**I said, 'Professor Board, this man is yelling something in a foreign language.' Joe almost laughed. 'No, Noah, he's yelling in Swedish. It's *his* language.'**

In December 1976, I got the chance to travel overseas for the first time. Five of the Nobel Prizes had been won by Americans! Among the laureates in Stockholm would be economist Milton Friedman and novelist Saul Bellow. Robert Montiegel, one of NPR's veteran producers, was asked to put together live satellite coverage from Sweden, and he wanted me to come along as the reporter and host. For many nights beforehand, I couldn't sleep. Live! By satellite! The Nobel ceremonies had never before been broadcast outside Sweden, and there we would be, not on a noisy phone line, but in full high-tech fidelity.

I met Montiegel in Stockholm ("Take the bus from the airport," I was told. "The cab's too expensive.") But, we did stay in the Grand Hotel, ate well, and worked a few long days at Sveriges Radio putting together a documentary about Alfred Nobel to run beforehand. It was

dark most of the day in Stockholm, and I was perpetually confused—jet lag being a new mystery. Everything went fine until partway through the award ceremony. Milton Friedman stepped forward to accept his medal from King Carl XVI Gustaf, and a man in the auditorium stood up, blew a whistle, and yelled. Loudly. Friedman's theories about development in the third world were provocative, and I'd seen protestors, but this man's interruption shattered the elegance of the Stockholm Concert Hall.

I turned to our broadcast analyst. Joe Board had come along, on loan from Union College, New York, where he taught Swedish Studies. I said, "Professor Board, this man is yelling something in a foreign language." Joe almost laughed. "No, Noah, he's yelling in Swedish. It's *his* language." Thankfully, back in Washington, no one ever brought it up; if they heard it at all, they probably just laughed.

The following summer, I was offered a cohosting spot with Jackie Judd on the new hour-long Saturday and Sunday editions of *All Things Considered*. There had been a Saturday "best-of-the-week" program, and then a thirty-minute version of *All Things Considered* on both weekend days, with part-time staff, but this was a determined, well-budgeted move to establish a seven-day service.

# JIM ANDERSON

*Broadcast technician, 1974–1980*

**Producing a two-hour weekly** "live-on-tape" (what would it be called now? live-on-hard-disc?) music program is no simple task. Production staff, audio engineers, and musical talent are the raw ingredients, but occasionally, the clichés "a little bit of luck" and "being at the right place at the right time" can help get a new series "off on the right foot."

The right place was New Orleans, the right time was the spring of 1977—and the opening night performance of Ella Fitzgerald at the New Orleans Jazz and Heritage Festival would establish the new NPR show *Jazz Alive!* with footing. It was never explained to me why I, the junior recording engineer on the crew, was assigned to make a recording of such an important and prestigious concert, but I wasn't going to look a "gift horse..." (ok, enough with the clichés).

The legendary NPR Winnebago recording truck (legendary? imagine a 22-foot camping van turned into a recording studio that's how legends are made) was parked outside of the New Orleans Municipal Auditorium, and audio lines were run into the hall for the evening's concert. (There was no closed circuit video!) For reference, the Municipal Auditorium is the same hall where the King of Mardi Gras, Rex, has been crowned for generations.

The reigning Queen of Jazz wouldn't be available for an afternoon sound check; the first time I'd hear her would be in the evening when she stepped on stage for her set. It wouldn't be the first, nor the last, time we'd begin recording live to two-track stereo, with no multitrack backup, without the benefit of a rehearsal, but, hey, that's live radio for you. I felt confident we'd have a successful evening of recording because, for insurance, I had an experienced ringer with me in the van, jazz producer Michael Cuscuna.

With the tune "Too Close for Comfort," the concert began. The hall was packed with vocal admirers, shouting for their favorites. Ella dodged a couple of requests, "A-Tisket, a-Tasket" and "Lady Be Good," but relented with "Mr. Paganini" and "How High the Moon." Toward the end of the hour, Ella sang a new song, "Summer Soft" from Stevie Wonder's hit album *Songs in the Key of Life*. Like her classic Berlin rendition of "Mack the Knife," where she can't remember the lyric and scats her own, Miss Fitzgerald's final chorus of "Summer Soft" was an improvised apology to Stevie Wonder for not being able to recall his words. Instead of singing the song's final lyric "and he's gone, winter's gone ...," she finished the tune with "he's here, Stevie's here." Upon conclusion of the song, audience member Stevie Wonder went on stage to join Ella Fitzgerald. The first word spoken by a breathless Stevie Wonder was "Wow ..." and the audience went wild at the first meeting of the two singers. After a bit of bona fide banter, there was no way that Stevie would be allowed to leave the stage that evening without singing and, luckily, Ella had been performing "You Are the Sunshine of My Life" in her recent shows (remember "the bit of luck"?). Ella's backing band, the Tommy Flanagan Trio, started "Sunshine's" familiar opening, and the crowd realized that they were in for some moments of musical magic.

> Ella sang: "You are the sunshine of my life..."
> *(the audience clapped appropriately on two and four, very hip)*
> "... that's why I'll always be around."

Stevie sang the next line, with the appropriate Stevie Wonder nuance:

> "You are the apple of my eye..."
> *(the audience, still clapping, also screamed)*
> "... forever you'll stay in my heart."

At the start of the next line, both performers forgot themselves in the tune and, together, sang:

> "If..." *(Ella, Stevie, and the audience shared a genuine laugh at the "mistake")*
>
> And Ella graciously finished the line "... feel like this is the beginning."

With that genuine moment between Ella and Stevie, it was the beginning for NPR's *Jazz Alive!*

P.S. The performance of Ella and Stevie singing "You Are the Sunshine of My Life" was commercially released in 2007 on the Verve tribute album *We All Love Ella*. The liner notes contained the credit line "Recorded Live in New Orleans 1977" without giving acknowledgment to me, Michael, NPR, or *Jazz Alive!* But, hey, that's the music business. To this day, I take a special pride in playing "my first serious jazz recording" for my NYU students, and it just happens to be a live recording of Ella Fitzgerald and Stevie Wonder. Right place, right time, and a bit of luck. ∎

**LEFT** Susan Stamberg and Bob Edwards in 1978 (NPR photo).

**OPPOSITE** Jay Kernis sitting in an edit booth. The editor would put physical marks on the back of the ¼-inch recording tape with a grease pencil, place the tape in an edit block, cut what was not needed with a razor blade, and attach the tape ends with splicing tape. They'd hold on to the reels and rock the tape back and forth across the tape machine's playback head, listening for distinct sounds, breaths, or musical notes. Sometimes they'd put out-takes on a separate reel, sometimes they hung small phrases or breaths or pauses on the edit room wall. Given today's digital technology, tape editing seems like a crude, mechanical process. But the great tape editors were like accomplished surgeons (NPR photo).

## 1976: DIFFERENCES BETWEEN 1976 AND TODAY

# ROBERT SIEGEL

*Senior host,* All Things Considered

**Here's how different it was** in December 1976, when I came to work as a newscaster. There was no newscast booth. When I read the newscasts for *All Things Considered*, I sat in the studio with the hosts. Bob Edwards would smoke (as did I and many others—the studios stank from tobacco), and Susan Stamberg would draw with colored pencils and then give me a grade at the end of the newscast. She graded me better for content than for posture. Save for one reporter in New York, the entire news department worked in Washington and could fit in a single conference room. When I hosted our nine-minute morning show, *A Closer Look*, the morning newscaster, Jacki Judd, one newscast producer, and I were the only three news staffers who were at work before 8 A.M.

This was before we sent out programs to the stations by satellite; they went out over landlines, and the longer the distance, the lower the fidelity. We used to listen to our stations in Washington where our programs sounded crystal clear, but by the time the signal made it to the Baltimore station, it had looped through the entire Northeast and sounded like a long-distance phone call. When we distributed programs that required good audio quality—concerts, for example—we made multiple, high-speed copies on heavy 12-inch metal reels of ¼-inch tape that we mailed to the stations: a dozen machines whirring at once. I used to take visitors to watch the copies being made; it was the best show in the building, sort of an audio Laundromat. Our budget did not permit much reporting in the field, but by the standards of the radio stations I had worked at, we were pampered. When I applied for the job, I heard *All Things Considered* interview a reporter in Beijing by telephone. I was used to getting grief, or permission, for calls outside the area code.

What's the same? Then, as now, *All Things Considered* sounded remarkably live despite being the most recorded, edited radio show I had ever seen. Then, as now, we started the program with producers still working on the pieces that would air at the end of the show. And, then, as now, an unusually purposeful, uncynical attitude pervaded the place, as if this was the radio program WE would listen to even if we didn't work on it. ∎

# NEW LEADERSHIP

On August 1, 1977, a sturdy, lively, gray-haired man walked through the front doors and into the lobby of the building on M Street where NPR had its studios and offices. This was Frank Mankiewicz. He was the new president, come to save the day. NPR had established a national audience. Talented reporters were being hired, and the member stations were doing well, many setting up their own first-rate news operations. Music and cultural programs seemed to have a secure future. But in the wide, real world, especially in the politico-media power centers of Washington and New York—NPR hardly mattered.

Frank Mankiewicz had visibility, energy, and style—he drove a Mustang convertible around Washington, and when he walked into NPR that first morning, he was carrying the biggest Rolodex I had ever seen. "That's why we hired this guy," I remember thinking.

Mankiewicz knew New York *and* Hollywood. He was born in Beverly Hills and his screenwriter father cowrote *Citizen Kane*. He studied political science at UCLA, earned a master's in journalism from Columbia, plus a UC-Berkeley law degree. He had been in Latin America with the Peace Corps and ran George McGovern's presidential campaign in 1972. He is perhaps best known, and sadly remembered, as the press secretary who, in 1968, told the world that Bobby Kennedy had died from an assassin's gunfire.

*Raconteur* is, and was, the Frank Mankiewicz label. He loved the phone calls to Capitol Hill, LA, Wall Street; loved the laughter and the threats and trading gossip. He loved the deal—and the best one he made at NPR was for the Panama Canal.

NPR's live broadcasts of the Panama Canal Treaty debate from the floor of the Senate brought the network both credibility and acclaim. There had, of course, been live coverage from Senate hearing rooms, but the main chamber of the Senate was sacrosanct, and why should that be violated? Why should the "world's greatest deliberative body" be heard actually deliberating whether the canal should be turned over to its home country?

Well, mostly because Frank Mankiewicz thought of it and started lobbying for the broadcasts. He wanted Linda Wertheimer, by then a congressional correspondent, in a booth in the room with a microphone. The senators couldn't find a good

reason not to allow this, and there was another, more idiosyncratic factor: the Senate Majority Leader, Robert Byrd. Byrd had grown up with old-time music in West Virginia and was an accomplished fiddle player. His favorite radio station was WAMU, one of the two NPR outlets in Washington. His favorite deejay was Gary Henderson, well known in the bluegrass world. So Senator Byrd said, "NPR? That's WAMU. Sure, let's let 'em do the broadcast." He got his rules committee to go along, and soon the remote equipment was being set up.

Gary Henderson's full-time job was senior engineer at NPR. He got the important assignments, and so he was sitting in the Senate chamber booth one day with Linda when—during a delay—Senator Byrd rose to speak:

> *I hope I am not exceeding the bounds of propriety in stating that the National Public Radio is doing an exceedingly fine job of reporting these debates to the listening audience throughout the country. Not only does the public radio broadcast give to the people the blow-by-blow account of what is going on during the debates, but there is an excellent wrap-up in the evening on the highlights and significant happenings of the day. Linda Wertheimer is doing an excellent job in that respect, and I note that she is assisted today by Gary Henderson, who by the way, emcees an excellent bluegrass program on the FM dial at 88.5 on Tuesday evenings and Thursday evenings . . . and on Saturday mornings.*

The senator went on to thank Gary for his willingness to take listeners' phone calls, "Even though I like the tune, 'Pig in a Pen,' and I do not like to be a hog about making requests, I do exercise my privilege . . . now and then."

**LEFT** Linda Wertheimer covers the political scene in 1983 (NPR photo).

## TRANSCRIPT EXCERPT
# *ALL THINGS CONSIDERED*

**SHOW DATE:**
*1978-02-22*
**CAT. TITLE:**
*Panama Debate
and Vietnam
Experience*

*Author David McCullough speaks with Robert Siegel.*

**McCULLOUGH:** It's as though the specter of Vietnam is in the room all the time in the Senate and in the hearing rooms before the debates began. And people don't have to even use the word, and it's there. And the truth, of course, is that we lost a war in Vietnam, a very costly war, in more ways than just money, obviously.

**SIEGEL:** To a country so small that no one thought it was possible.

**McCULLOUGH:** That's right. And in the jungle and in a place where France went first, just as in Panama. And it's interesting how nations respond to defeat and humiliation. When France was destroyed so overwhelmingly, so quickly in the Franco-Prussian War, for example, their response was to—we will go to Panama, and we will win a great victory against nature. We will show the world that the grandeur of France still exists.

**SIEGEL:** We will build a canal.

**McCULLOUGH:** We will build a canal for all the world to see and use and benefit by. And of course then they failed again. So for us to talk about giving up something that's such a model of American success, which was really such a grand American success story, has very real psychological, emotional effects. It doesn't matter which side of the argument you're on.

And then, of course, we're very gun-shy about consequences for misjudgment. I think it's the kind of judgment that got us into Vietnam that we're concerned about, much more than, say, are we going to literally have to go and fight a Vietnam-like war in Panama.

The Suez Canal has been a battleground for a long time. It's been the cause of the location for bloody wars. The Panama Canal has never been. If there was such a thing as Pax Brittania at one time, we've had Pax Americana in Panama.

So for those people who are reluctant to see us withdraw from Panama or to change the status quo in Panama, to set up a new kind of relationship there, there is the sense that, "Why should we do that when everything has been really so comparatively tranquil there, compared to, say, Suez, the other great crossroads of ocean traffic?"

The arguments are contradictory, just as the history is contradictory, just as people are contradictory. I think also, if I may try and use an analogy that works, I think that it's really unrealistic to accuse those who talk of possible future troubles in Panama of a violent nature, to accuse them of caving in to intimidation. Because these people who talk or think about such consequences aren't being realistic. It would be a little bit, it seems to me, like arguing that if you were in a ship and there was a weak spot in the hull and on suggesting to others on the ship that maybe it would be a good idea to correct that situation, that someone might say, "No, you're being intimidated by the ocean." ■

# REPORTING FROM THE WHITE HOUSE

## SUSAN STAMBERG
*Special correspondent*

In 1979, NPR broadcast a live, national call-in show from the Oval Office at the White House. As anchor/moderator, I introduced the various callers, posed follow-up questions to President Carter, and got off the air on time. A crew of us went to the White House the night before the broadcast to get set up. I have a snapshot of myself sitting at the president's desk, chin in hand, waiting while NPR engineers unwound cables. It was a huge enterprise for our fairly young broadcast organization. The only other such call-in had been on CBS radio almost three years earlier. Walter Cronkite ran that one, so I phoned him for advice.

"You won't have any trouble," Cronkite said. "My only problem was I had a hard time interrupting the president."

So did I! Jimmy Carter's two-hour-long appearance on NPR was the lead story in all the major newspapers the next day. ∎

**RIGHT** President Jimmy Carter sits in his chair beside the fireplace in the library of the White House living quarters on Wednesday, February 2, 1977, in Washington just prior to air time of his nationally televised fireside chat (AP photo).

TRANSCRIPT EXCERPT
## *ALL THINGS CONSIDERED*

**SHOW DATE:**
*1979-10-13*
**CAT. TITLE:**
*Susan Stamberg*
*Interviews*
*President Carter*

**STAMBERG:** Thank you, Shanie, for your question. Our next caller, Mr. President, is in Springville, Alabama. It's Lou Windham. Mr. Windham, go ahead, please.

**WINDHAM:** Mr. President?

**CARTER:** Good morning, Lou.

**WINDHAM:** We're in the petroleum business here in an area of the country that I'm sure you're familiar with. We own two LP gas companies and supply these rural people with propane for heating. At the same time, we're in the oil jobbing business. We find it tough to explain to our customers why every time they buy a petroleum product, it is higher. Now, we cannot see any evidence that the Department of Energy is doing anything. Now, I feel that the majority of the people in this country need a very good explanation as to what the Department of Energy is doing to put the lid on these producing companies.

**CARTER:** Well, that's not an easy question to answer, Lou, because there's very little the Department of Energy or a president can do to prevent foreign countries from raising their price of oil. And the basic thrust that we are pursuing is to cut down on that imported oil. As you know, this past month the rate of increase of energy was more than 100 percent per year on an annual basis. And as I said earlier, about 4 percent of our inflation rate is derived directly from energy costs. This is a very serious matter, and I think you've noticed if you've listened to this call-in show, how many people have raised this same question.

**WINDHAM:** Yes.

**CARTER:** I can't give you any easy answer. There's no reason for me to sit here in the Oval Office and try to mislead the American people. There are only three ways that we can deal with this question. One is to use as little energy as possible through conservation, savings. Second, to use more of the energy that we produce in our own country than we have been doing in the past. And, third, provide federal and other assistance for the low-income families to make sure that they do have enough fuel to heat their homes, and to cook with, and so forth, and also so they can have enough money to pay those bills.

But there's no way that I can mislead you. The prices are high now. They're going to get higher in the future than they are already. And unless our nation unites itself and deals with this very serious threat, we're going to be worse off in the future than we have been in the past.

I inherited this problem. I'm not complaining about it. But it has been an extremely difficult thing to get the Congress to pass any legislation on this issue because it's so controversial. We have still not passed a single line of legislation in the Congress dealing with oil. This year we have a very good prospect of finally getting those laws on the books, which will help you and help me and all your customers and people like them throughout the country. It's been slow in coming, but we're now making some progress.

**WINDHAM:** Mr. President, I would like to congratulate you and the Congress on the move that you have put forth to help these needy people in this crisis we're in, because I feel that that is one answer, and you're to be congratulated on that move.

**CARTER:** Thank you. This will amount, by the way, I think to between $100 and $200 per family to help them with the fuel bills this winter. So if they combine that help, if they're a poor family, with saving as much energy as possible, I think we can get people through the winter.

**WINDHAM:** Thank you.

**CARTER:** Good luck, Lou, and thank you.

**STAMBERG:** Thank you, Mr. Windham. ■

# MORNING COMPETITION

*All Things Considered* was always thought of as a late-afternoon program. Bill Siemering had liked the idea of being out in front of the TV evening news. He wanted *All Things Considered* to be the "earliest electronic record of the day's happenings." And besides, when *All Things Considered* started, many of the stations weren't even on in the morning.

But NPR was FAR stronger by the late '70s. More stations had signed on. And wouldn't a morning program sound great on NPR's new satellite distribution system?

Pilot programs were produced over the summer. Stations heard them and thought they were too commercial-sounding; there was nothing authentic, they felt gimmicky.

The hosts departed (Pete Williams and Mary Tillotson went on to honorable careers in television), and new producers started over. Jay Kernis, put in charge of the daily show, said, "Can we borrow Bob?" Bob Edwards, Susan Stamberg's cohost on *All Things Considered*, agreed, and *Morning Edition* was born. Edwards would do the show with Barbara Hoctor, who would remain with NPR only a matter of weeks. Edwards became a solo *Morning Edition* host; in theory, it was temporary.

Bob's reassuring voice presided over a shaky beginning. What would be termed the Iranian Hostage Crisis began the day before *Morning Edition*'s first broadcast. Sixty-six Americans had been seized. But the debut program's only mention of the hostages came in a short news spot.

*All Things Considered*'s first broadcast in 1971 came on a significant news day—antiwar protests, tear gas, and thousands of arrests in the nation's capital. The demonstration coverage was memorable and extensive, but *All Things Considered* still stubbornly also ran a planned story about an Iowa barber who had started shaving women's legs—married women only.

"

**What would be termed the Iranian Hostage Crisis began the day before *Morning Edition*'s first broadcast. Sixty-six Americans had been seized. But the debut program's only mention of the hostages came in a short news spot.**

**BELOW** Bob Edwards in the studio (NPR photo).

TO:     Joanne Wallace                    DATE:   August 13, 1979

FROM:   Larry Lichty                      CC:

SUBJECT:   A Name for the Morning Program/Service?

    Please poll all station staff, volunteers, and others and send your responses to me:

    If you find it quicker just distribute these ballots and send them back to me for tabulation. Or report the number of votes for each as a first choice and others you find acceptable.

    If you have other ideas just write them at the bottom.

-75 Morning Air or Gas !          -200 Morning Magazine

-5 Daybreak                       -193 Starting Line

)0 First Things First             -340 American Morning

-33 The Morning Show              -66.6 First Thing in the Morning

-10,000 FYI                       +.25 At First Glance

-33.3 At This Hour                -11,000 This Morning

-7 For Your Information           2 Earth Rise

-66 First Edition

The Morning After, Wake up to the World, The Edge of Night , The Edge of Morni
Breakfast at 1600 Pennsylvania Ave. Oh say can You See, By the Dawns Early Ligh
What So Proudly We Hailed, Good Night China, Morning Fix, The Love Boat,
The Red Eye Special, Sunny Side Up, The Npr General, Gazzete, Voice of America A
It's Anybody's Guess. Gross National Product, The Organic Hour, The GAP, or
News for The Great American Public, New Morning with Your Host Bob Dill-un,
SLeepers Awake, The Trumpet Shall Sound, AND We Shall Be Saved.
Morning Obits,  Still Alive, Staying Alive, Phaeton's Charriot, The Appollonic
 Vision, Easy Does It, The DAWN Dissertation, Sunrise Semester, Emotionally Your
 The Laid Back and Loose Natio nal Morning news and Information Presentation and
 Easy going and Inoffenisve Entertainment Show, As the World Turns, Desolation
.Dawn Detonations an  Explosion of News , Information, and Entertainment from
IPR, THE NATIONAL NECROMANCER, The Cosmic Consciousness News Service Show, The
 Plop Plop fizz fizz Comedy and News show, The Survival Hour giving you the News

**memorandum**

**National Public Radio**     2025 M Street, N.W.     Washington, D.C. 20036     202-785-5400

TO:  All Stations                              DATE: November 1, 1979

FROM: Rick Lewis                               CC:

SUBJECT: Morning Edition

    Morning Edition is a news program and more, serving as a reliable and complete source of important information for the listener. Our judgments of "importance" and "significance" are careful and informed.

    As in other NPR programs, we exhibit respect for the listener, and for the listener's intelligence. We remember that intelligent programming need not be dull.

    We provide a perspective beyond the bare facts of the story, through analysis, interpretation, commentary, satire. We resist being purely reactive to events.

    We recognize the importance of "human affairs" and the arts. We also provide information that people can put to use: from consumer and "coping" pieces to weather and time checks.

    We produce the kind of good radio that enhances communication. We use the immediacy of effective sound and primary sources, creative production, and pacing that recognizes the habits of the morning listener.

    We try to mirror ALL of the country--perhaps the hardest thing of all. And we need the help of our member stations.

    Much of this could also describe All Things Considered. In fact, we are providing a service, more than a new artistic concept. The difference will come in personality, pacing, and time of day: we and ATC will often be on different sides of a story, one previewing and the other reviewing. While some will say we are duplicating ATC, I for one don't think it's possible. If we are able to provide as important a service as ATC, we will have had a good beginning.

# FRANK MANKIEWICZ

*President of NPR, 1977–1983*

**When Henry Loomis died** in 2008 at age eighty-nine, after a distinguished career in and out of government, the *New York Times* in its obituary said Mr. Loomis had been appointed by President Richard Nixon in 1972 to be president of the Corporation for Public Broadcasting (CPB), the organization created by Congress "to be responsible for channeling money to public television stations." True enough, except that the CPB was also responsible for channeling money to public *radio*, a fact largely ignored by the media and often by the CPB itself.

But, in addition to being a Nixon guy, Loomis was also— and more importantly in my mind as I became president of National Public Radio—a radio guy. He had earlier served with distinction as the director of the Voice of America, whose independence as a news source led him to resign from the position in a battle with President Lyndon Johnson, who didn't like its reporting on Vietnam. And in those days, NPR was almost entirely dependent on government— i.e., CPB—funding, and my main job seemed to be fighting with public television for that funding, almost always a losing battle. NPR, to public broadcasting's nabobs, was at best an afterthought, if indeed a thought at all.

But there was a quirk in the law that created the CPB— almost alone among U.S. government agencies, it got all of its funding on the first day of the fiscal year, instead of month-by-month as it was spent. This meant that the CPB would have a sizeable pot of earned interest accrued by the end of each year, and the battle between PBS and NPR for shares of that pot became an annual event—which NPR almost always lost, usually being given something less than 5 percent, despite my best and most urgent efforts.

But after two losing battles for the leftover funds, I received a phone call in 1978 from Loomis, with whom I had forged an unlikely friendship and with whom I had shared some lively radio lore. "Frank," he began, "we've got close to $15 million in the pot this year, and I'm thinking of giving it all to radio. What would you do with the extra money?" I didn't hesitate; at NPR we'd been talking about a morning news program to match the success of *All Things Considered* in afternoon drive time, thus almost guaranteeing a local station's call button on listeners' cars in every NPR city. "Why, Henry, " I answered, barely able to conceal the excitement in my voice ($15 million!),

"we'd start a morning news program." "A great idea," he answered, "but what would you do to pay for the second year?" I thought only briefly before answering, "Blackmail, Henry. I'll go to your board and ask, 'Do you folks want to kill one of only two serious news programs on the air?'" He laughed and told me the check was in the mail.

Thus began a frenzied rush by me and Barbara Cochran, who I had just persuaded to leave the job of managing editor of the *Evening Star* to become our news director, to plan and staff what we had finally decided to call *Morning Edition*. An early and emphatic rejection by member stations of the two proposed anchors after a closed-circuit presentation left us something less than a week to come up with a substitute. After assuring him that he would have to do it for only a month at the most, we prevailed on Bob Edwards, one of the anchors of *All Things Considered*, to take on the job while we found a replacement. He lasted for only twenty-five years, until his sudden removal in 2004. Carl Kasell, who voiced the very first newscast, left his newscaster job in 2009.

That first day of *Morning Edition*, I was in Chicago, in an early morning cab on the way to O'Hare, and there on the radio were Carl and Bob. I told the driver I liked the program, and he replied, "Oh, that's *Morning Edition* on NPR. I listen every day."

I sincerely hope that when NPR dedicates its new building, one studio, or at least an editing booth, can have on it a plaque with the name of Henry Loomis. ∎

> "
> **My main job seemed to be fighting with public television for CPB funding, almost always a losing battle. NPR, to public broadcasting's nabobs, was at best an after-thought, if indeed a thought at all.**

**ABOVE** Carl Kasell
in 1977, the year
he joined NPR
(NPR photo).

# BRASS AND CLASS

In 1979, Frank Mankiewicz approached Jay Kernis with a demand: "I want the *Morning Edition* theme to sound manly. Nothing electronic, real instruments, but not violins." B. J. Leiderman was the winner. He composed the manly *Morning Edition* theme, "I wrote the thing on my mother's Acrosonic upright, the tune just came into my head."

He'd been told to open with a classical sound to match the music many of the stations would be playing earlier. So eight bars of faux Baroque, then the melody statement, the *Morning Edition* signature. (Leiderman gets upset when he hears local announcers come in over that part: "They murder it—do not talk over that music.")

He says he made maybe $5,000, but the true payoff is the credit: Jay Kernis told him his name would be mentioned every week, and NPR has kept that promise.

I asked B.J. if he had any celebrity status. "I walk into a room, and women say 'Are you *the* B.J. Leiderman? I love your music.' This has happened 958 times, and I would *marry* the girl who did not then proceed to sing the music from *All Things Considered*. That's the only one I *didn't* write."

# DAVIA NELSON AND NIKKI SILVA

*Producers of the duPont-Columbia University Award–winning, NPR series,* Hidden Kitchens

**1979.** There we were in Santa Cruz. The Kitchen Sisters, two local girls doing a live weekly show on the local community radio station, KUSP-FM, sandwiched between the *Poetry Hour* and Captain McVouty's *Jazz Parade*. We were obsessed with doing the oral history of everyone in our region—cowgirls, fishermen, ancient Italian midwives, politicians. If you moved and had a story to tell we wanted you on the show.

That's when we met "The Road Ranger"—gray jumpsuit, tall shiny boots, shades, and a large black cowboy hat. His Ford Ranchero with the words "The Bloodhound of Breakdown" and "The Champion of the Stranded Traveler" emblazoned on its sides and 700 pounds of vehicle-saving devices strapped in the back. Allan Little, a Vietnam vet, had come back from the war and transformed himself into The Road Ranger, a "costumed crusader" who patrolled a dangerous, windy stretch of California highway, rescuing stranded travelers in their over-heated, broken-down vehicles. When he invited us to go out on patrol and record, we accepted.

We aired the Road Ranger's ride on our Tuesday show. The phone rang off the hook. One listener called in and said, "You should send that in to NPR, they might air it. But you'll have to shorten it." NPR was a rumor to us at that time, something we'd heard about, but never heard. Our station had a killer reggae show but no *All Things Considered*. No *Morning Edition* either. And we had no experience in the "shortening up" department. That meant learning to edit. This was back in the reel-to-reel days. We holed up in the production studio at KUSP and taught ourselves how to cut tape and mix. The tape was rugged, in part because The Road Ranger had run over our 20-foot mic cord as we recorded him changing fuel pumps on the side of the highway.

We mailed the mix to NPR at 2025 M Street in Washington, DC, and waited.

About three weeks later, the phone rang. "This is Alex Chadwick." Who? "Alex Chadwick. From NPR's *Weekend All Things Considered*. Who are you guys?" He liked the spirit, and he liked our approach. Alex said our sound was a bit ragged, but he wanted to air the story on his show. What did we think? We just about fell down.

We began sending in stories—"The Legend of Ernest Morgan: The World Champion One-Handed Pool Player," "Tupperware." Alex and others at NPR urged us to get some training. We were part of the first NPR Training Project at Western Public Radio, and we applied for an internship at NPR in Washington. We spent a month as production assistants and working on our own story, "War and Separation: Life on the Home Front During WWII." It was told mostly through home-recorded letters that people sent back and forth during the war years and was probably the inspiration for the *Lost & Found Sound* collaboration we did with Jay Allison and NPR some twenty years later.

Interning at NPR in Washington was the turning point for us, working with Gary Covino, Flawn Williams, Skip Pizzi, meeting Susan Stamberg, Noah Adams, Neenah Ellis. We were in the final throes of mixing our piece. Something was missing. Just not quite right. Judith Franco, another engineer said, "You should talk to my mom. She has an incredible World War II story." She was exactly right. We dropped everything, rushed over to interview her, and wove her story throughout. It was such a collaborative, exciting time at NPR, with brilliant producers, engineers, and journalists working on something so new and groundbreaking.

We came home inspired and never stopped. ■

**LEFT** The Kitchen Sisters circa 1979 auctioning items for KUSP-FM in Santa Cruz (photo by the Kitchen Sisters).

# THE EIGHTEEN-HOUR REPORTER'S SHIFT

Cokie Roberts, one of the many young, first-rate reporters to join NPR in the early years, complained about the startup of a new program. She and her colleagues were told they wouldn't have to file stories for *Morning Edition* in addition to their reporting duties for *All Thing Considered.* "I told them we'd be working twice as hard for the same amount of money and guess what, that was true." In March of 1979 Cokie had been sent to cover Three Mile Island, the partial meltdown of a nuclear plant in Pennsylvania. She drove north against the traffic fleeing south. She was by herself, no producer or engineer. She'd open up a telephone handset and connect alligator clips to feed sound from her tape recorder. She filed stories for *All Things Considered* and *Morning Edition*, plus spots for the NPR Newscasts.

Cokie stayed with the TMI assignment for several days. *The New York Times* wanted to send Steve Roberts, her husband, to Three Mile Island as well. He declined; he was looking after their two children.

After *Morning Edition* started up, it indeed became clear that Roberts and Linda Wertheimer would be expected to report from Capitol Hill for both of the flagship programs. Cokie remembers, "Steve and I wouldn't get home until late and maybe have dinner around nine o'clock. My kids revealed later that they'd often had dinner at someone else's house—at six."

**Steve and I wouldn't get home until late and maybe have dinner around nine o'clock. My kids revealed later that they'd often had dinner at someone else's house—at six.**

*Cokie Roberts on the long reporter's hours that kept her from home*

TRANSCRIPT EXCERPT
## *ALL THINGS CONSIDERED*

**SHOW DATE:**
*1979-04-08*
**CAT. TITLE:**
*Harrisburg Aftermath*

*Noah Adams talks with Cokie Roberts after her return to Washington from Three Mile Island.*

**MAN:** I wish they would have told somebody. I mean, this worst release started Friday morning, about quarter of seven, and when it was over about ten o'clock, then they told us. And my wife and kids were here. I mean, that's not right! I wish they would have told me then so I could have got them away. But no. They—I don't know. It's just a credibility gap there.

**ADAMS:** The classic credibility gap. We heard a lot about that through the week and in the news reports that followed. Why was that? Didn't anyone know what was going on?

**ROBERTS:** Apparently not. And people felt that they were getting contradictory information. They were hearing one thing from the utility company, they were hearing another thing from the governor's office, they were hearing another thing from the Nuclear Regulatory Commission. And they also worried that they weren't being told the whole truth, that people were holding things back, worrying about panicking them. On Friday, for instance, the people within ten miles of the plant were told to go inside and close their doors and windows, but they knew that glass wasn't going to keep the radiation out.

**ADAMS:** Why were they advised to go inside and shut everything down?

**ROBERTS:** Probably because the health officials worried about people inhaling the radioactive gases. On Saturday, we found out for the first time that people in the control room at Three Mile Island had been wearing gas masks, which means that the air must have been full of the radioactive stuff. And since then, I've been talking to radiologists who say that inhaling radiation is far, far more damaging than absorbing it through our skin.

**ADAMS:** Well, were the people there ever warned about the dangers of inhaling radiation?

**ROBERTS:** No, they were just told to go inside, close their doors and windows.

**ADAMS:** Why didn't they all just leave, just get out of the vicinity immediately?

**ROBERTS:** Many of them did, of course. And the governor eventually recommended that pregnant women and preschool children leave. In fact, they're still out. But of course that was worrisome, too. In a normal disaster, the disaster affects everybody the same way. When flood waters rise, they take away the house and everybody in it.

But this was something different! This mysterious, invisible danger doesn't work that way. And I had many mothers of grade school children come up to me and ask, "What's the difference between my four-year-old, my preschooler, and my first-grader? How is it going to affect them differently?" Of course, many of those mothers did take their children and did leave. And the kids in the schoolyard in Hummelstown, which is just a few miles from the plant, did go back to school on Tuesday, and they talked of nothing but the evacuation.

**KID:** An evacuation is, um, when you go away, when there's something really bad where you live.

**SECOND KID:** My friend went because they said on the radio and TV that pregnant women and preschool children might be scared of it.

**THIRD KID:** We didn't know what was happening because all—the radio ones said we should evacuate and some said we shouldn't.

**FOURTH KID:** Evacuation is like something that—you leave your home until it's done. And then you come back and it's like—and you just like forget about it.

**ADAMS:** You know, when you listen to that tape, you can hear the natural confidence of youth, but you can also hear a little bit of fear, too, in that.

**ROBERTS:** Well, that's right. And the parents are frightened about the long-term effects on the children. They're worried about whether this incident will have any scarring psychological damage. After all, the government is talking about coming in and monitoring these people for years, the children maybe for the rest of their lives. ∎

"

**In a normal disaster, the disaster affects everybody the same way. When flood waters rise, they take away the house and everybody in it. But this was something different! This mysterious, invisible danger doesn't work that way.**

*Cokie Roberts, reporting on the fallout at Three Mile Island*

# THE NEWS VERSUS THE MUSE

At the end of NPR's first decade, Jim Russell, one of the first hosts of *All Things Considered*, as well as the producer and news director, decided to leave. He surprised me, thirty-one years later, when I called to ask about that choice.

"I didn't regret leaving NPR; I had done everything I could imagine doing and I was still in my young thirties. But the main reason was Frank Mankiewicz. I didn't share his vision. His definition of alternative was 'alternative can mean just better.' He saw an NPR that was entirely journalistic and not very lyrical. He talked about a stream of all news radio, 'the best stream in the world.'"

Russell returned to public radio, creating *Marketplace*, the highly successful business show. And indeed, NPR went on to decades of respect as a straight-ahead news gathering organization with worldwide reach. And Jim Russell now says of the Mankiewicz plan, "Who's to say that wasn't a wonderful thing? That could have been one of the world's great strategies."

And I agree. It's wonderful working for an organization that takes the news very seriously and often does that work better than anyone. But it's also great to work with people who treasure the founding vision of Bill Siemering; the sparkling humanity of Susan Stamberg; Jim Russell's off-beat approach.

To me, "Celebrate the human experience" (circa 1967) is simple: Tell the story; tell it with speed and accuracy. Tell it all and tell it with sincerity.

**ABOVE** Ralph Woods's face temporarily replaces the clock on the switching console, a.k.a. Bullwinkle (photo by Ched Hudson).

|  | J | F | M | A | M | J | J | A | S | O | N | D |
|---|---|---|---|---|---|---|---|---|---|---|---|---|
| 1980 | | | | | | | | | | | | |
| 1981 | | | | | | | | | | | | |
| 1982 | | | | | | | | | | | | |
| 1983 | | | | | | | | | | | | |
| 1984 | | | | | | | | | | | | |
| 1985 | | | | | | | | | | | | |
| 1986 | | | | | | | | | | | | |
| 1987 | | | | | | | | | | | | |
| 1988 | | | | | | | | | | | | |
| 1989 | | | | | | | | | | | | |

**MAY 1980**
Mount. St. Helen's errupts.

**MAY 1980**
*A Prairie Home Companion* goes national—but not on NPR.

**DEC 1980**
John Lennon is fatally shot outside his NYC apartment.

**JAN 1981**
Ronald Reagan is sworn in as president.

**MAR 1981**
John Hinckley Jr. fails to assassinate President Reagan.

**JUN 1981**
The first case of AIDS is reported to the U.S. Centers for Disease Control.

**JUL 1981**
Sandra Day O'Connor becomes the first woman on the Supreme Court.

**JUL 1982**
NPR begins overseas coverage of the seige of Beirut.

**MAY 1983**
Amidst NPR's first financial crisis Frank Mankiewicz steps down as president of NPR.

**JUL 1983**
NPR comes close to shutting down.

**OCT 1983**
Doug Bennet becomes the new president of NPR.

**NOV 1985**
*Weekend Edition* is launched.

**JAN 1986**
The *Challenger* space shuttle explodes after liftoff.

**OCT 1986**
Susan Stamberg leaves *All Things Considered* and soon becomes host of *Weekend Sunday*.

**JUN 1989**
The Tiananmen Square protests end in bloodshed when the Chinese government intervenes.

**NOV 1989**
The Berlin Wall falls, bringing the Iron Curtain down with it.

# RECORD GROWTH AND A CLOSE BRUSH WITH DEATH

As NPR entered the 1980s, its new morning show, *Morning Edition*, was still trying to find firm footing. Meanwhile, its accomplished elder, *All Things Considered*, harbored some older sibling rivalry and resentment. But with Frank Mankiewicz driving the network from alternative to mainstream, it would be a decade of tremendous growth and the emergence of NPR as a major news organization. Along the way, though, the dream would almost die.

For me, the '80s began two months early in the cab of a U-Haul truck headed to Washington. It was November of 1979. Barreling down the interstate, I had my fingers crossed, praying I could land a job at NPR. I needed a job! My pregnant wife, Mary Jo, was seated next to me. By May, there'd be another mouth to feed.

Until a week before, I had been reporter and producer for Minnesota Public Radio (MPR), following the up-and-down fortunes of farmers, covering Indian issues—like the trial of Leonard Peltier—and, along the way, interviewing local poets and painting sound portraits of small town life. I was based at the MPR station in Moorhead, Minnesota, across the Red River from Fargo, North Dakota. And in a twist of fate, Bill Siemering, the father of *All Things Considered*, was the station manager.

On the rebound from his firing by NPR, Siemering had agreed to set up the Moorhead station for Bill Kling, the empire-building president of Minnesota Public Radio. Siemering's presence there turned out to be a life-changing event for me. I was a student at Concordia College, where the new station was located. Like every college student, I had one big question on my mind, "What should I do with my life?" Growing up along the Canadian border on the vast North Dakota prairies, radio was my companion; but not just the great rock 'n' roll booming in from stations in Chicago and Oklahoma City. My young wife and I had discovered the CBC program *As It Happens*, the call-out interview show that "brings you the world." It had been a template for *All Things Considered*, which I was now listening to. The engaging women who anchored each program, Barbara Frum on *As It Happens* and Susan Stamberg on *All Things Considered*, might have been sisters. Their curious, open-minded, somewhat irreverent approach to the world resonated with me.

Siemering gave me a job as an intern, flipping the switch for the local broadcast of the college's daily chapel service; a concession Concordia had insisted on when it handed over the license for the station to Bill Kling. After I graduated, Siemering gave me a real job. He asked me to do a project called *Our Home Town*. With a microphone, a cassette recorder, and a map of North Dakota, I traveled to five small towns: a German-Russian community, an Indian Reservation, a Norwegian farming town, and a couple of cowboy towns in western North Dakota trying to cope with massive energy development. I spent the summer documenting the

**ABOVE** *Morning Edition* staff celebrates the award-winning news program's third anniversary in 1982 (NPR photo).

**ABOVE** It takes a lot of people and a lot of energy to put *All Things Considered* on the air every day. These are the hosts, producers, directors, editors, and engineers celebrating its tenth anniversary in 1981 (NPR photo).

lives and capturing the unique voices of regular folks. Siemering stayed longer than he had intended; long enough for me to soak up the values he espoused of respecting the individual, celebrating the diversity of the human experience, and appreciating the emotive power of the human voice.

But after five years, I was looking for new challenges. At the end of a long day of work at MPR's St. Paul studios, I recruited Garrison Keillor to give me some advice. Keillor was in the process of honing a new weekly variety program called *A Prairie Home Companion*. He had actually named it after the Prairie Home Cemetery in Moorhead, across the street from the radio station. After a couple of beers at a nearby pub, I told Garrison I was ready to strike out to seek my fortune but couldn't decide between Washington, DC, and Seattle, Washington. He pursed his lips the way he does when he's pondering weighty developments in Lake Woebegone and asked, "Well, what to do you want to do?" I said, "I want to be a journalist." He looked at me as if I were a little dim and said, "Well, then, of course, you'll move to Washington, DC."

That's where we were headed now, with a portable radio propped on the dashboard (the U-Haul didn't have one), listening to NPR, particularly coverage of the Iranian hostage crisis. It was like a homing beacon. A few weeks after I arrived, John McChesney hired me to be the Midwest regional editor for the new Acquisitions Unit, the precursor to NPR's National Desk. I was elated.

In those first days, I remember attending an *All Things Considered* morning meeting. There was Susan Stamberg, the voice I'd followed to Washington, and there was Robert Krulwich, one of the most gifted and creative radio journalists ever. The discussion turned to an agricultural issue, an area where I had developed some expertise as a reporter and as a young farmhand; four of my uncles were farmers. I made a suggestion, and an amazing thing happened. Though this was my first day in the meeting—the first time these people had ever seen me—I was taken seriously. I think the idea even got on the air. It's a feature of NPR, and *All Things Considered* in particular, that remains. The daily meeting is an open affair. If an intern proposes a story idea, it will be considered as seriously as one from a host. That's one of the things that has kept NPR's approach open and fresh.

FIGURE 2

# NPR MEMBER STATIONS THEN AND NOW

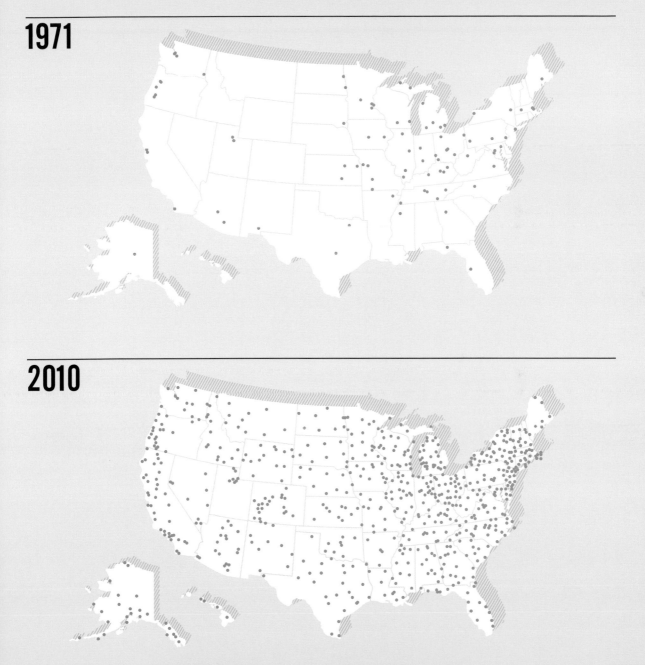

**1971**

**2010**

**SOURCE:** *National Public Broadcasting Archives, Papers of Susan Stamberg*

# DAVID SEDARIS

*David Sedaris is the author of six books, including* When You Are Engulfed in Flames.

**In what was either 1979 or 1980**, Susan Stamberg, the then cohost of *All Things Considered*, announced that she was taking a sabbatical, time off, she said, to work on a book. I was on a ladder that afternoon, painting the ceiling in my living room, and I remember setting down my roller and crying. That's how into public radio I was. Sure, Susan Stamberg would be returning in a year or so, but what was I supposed to do in the meantime? How was I expected to adjust to her replacement? Then Kim Williams—she of the stews with thorns and dirt clods in them—died of cancer, and I was inconsolable. Daniel Pinkwater, Freda Garmaise, the members of the Duck's Breath Mystery Theater: I didn't know these people, but I sure felt like I did.

It never occurred to me that I myself might one day be on the radio. That was all Ira Glass's doing. He heard me read in Chicago one night, and a few years later, after I had moved to New York and taken a job with a cleaning company, he called and asked if I had anything Christmassy that might work for a local show he'd been working on. I recorded parts of the diary I'd kept while working as an elf at Macy's Santaland, and after airing it on *The Wild Room*, he put it on *Morning Edition*, and my life changed overnight.

When people ask what Ira is like, I describe what probably sounds like a fairy, this industrious creature that flies around and makes people's dreams come true. "Only tall," I say. "And instead of a wand, he waves a microphone."

What threw me with *Morning Edition* were the many restrictions on content. "Wait a minute," I said to Ira. "You mean to say we can't talk about feces?" Take away cursing

and bodily functions, and material wise, I'm down to nothing. I don't know how we managed all those essays, but again, I credit Ira, and Manoli Wetherell, the New York studio engineer who kindly acted as our test audience.

As for *Morning Edition*, I've only recently become a regular listener. If having a decent income means eating out whenever you like, having a decent life means being asleep at 6 A.M. I like to be asleep at 7, and 9, and 10 A.M. as well. That's what's good about the Internet—you can tune in to stuff whenever you like. Living in Europe, I feel I should listen to French and British radio as well. BBC 4 is fantastic, I hear, and I plan to become a regular listener. As soon as *All Things Considered* is over. ■

**When people ask what Ira is like, I describe what probably sounds like a fairy, this industrious creature that flies around and makes people's dreams come true. 'Only tall,' I say. 'And instead of a wand, he waves a microphone.'**
*David Sedaris on Ira Glass*

**OPPOSITE** Jacki Lyden (far upper right) and the Chicago bureau staff on the roof of the Carbide & Carbon building (photo by Kevin Horan).

## 1980: CHICAGO BUREAU

### JACKI LYDEN
*Contributing host/correspondent*

**I was already working** in commercial radio in Chicago. Then someone told me to listen to *All Things Considered*, and there was Scott Simon, asking a newly laid off, miserably unhappy steel worker: "If you could make just as much money making pink plastic flamingoes as you do making steel, would you be just as happy to make pink plastic flamingoes?"

"I don't know what you mean, buddy," the guy gruffly said. "I make steel, not flamingoes."

I danced over to NPR's new Chicago bureau. I was the first freelancer to walk through the door. The spirit of camaraderie for the "Chicago group," which includes Ina Jaffe and engineer Richard Rarey, has gone on ever since and is, I think, captured in this old picture, taken on the roof of the Carbide & Carbon building on Michigan Avenue in Chicago. ∎

# PAINFUL
# GROWTH

**ABOVE** Carl Kasell, Bob Edwards, and Jay Kernis in 1980 (NPR photo).

**BELOW** Noah Adams and Leslie Breeding (NPR photo).

I was hired as part of NPR's effort to quickly add more resources to respond to the demands of two growing daily news programs. But the transition was rough. Staff for both *All Things Considered* and *Morning Edition* were feeling the strain, and it caused tensions to rise. Susan Stamberg remembers feeling that her program was being "violated." "It's a strong word to use," she says, "but remember, they took my cohost Edwards and a number of talented staff."

And *Morning Edition* was struggling, too. Management had told reporters that they wouldn't have to file for the new program, just hand over their taped interviews. *Morning Edition* producers would package them into stories for the show. So *Morning Edition* producer Jay Kernis would go to *All Things Considered* after the show was over each evening and ask for things they hadn't put on the air, and he and his staff would craft them into the next morning's show. As Kernis, remembers it, the "first year the show was ghastly."

Ultimately, reporters and their editors began to direct more material to *Morning Edition*, realizing the importance of building a solid show for the big morning radio audience. But it meant extra work, especially for Washington reporters who covered Congress and the White House. Almost daily, they were told to "roll-over" the same story for *Morning Edition* that they'd done for *All Things Considered*.

To this day, *Morning Edition* and *All Things Considered* are like two competitive siblings; each is convinced that the other is getting more of the family's love and resources.

While there were growing pains, the early '80s was also an intoxicating time at NPR, filled with promise. Meanwhile, however, Washington and the rest of the United States were in a funk. The mightiest country in the world could not get the hostages out of Iran. President Jimmy Carter was modeling sweaters in the White House and telling Americans to turn down their thermostats because there was an energy crisis. Inflation was going through the roof, and the nation was suffering through a double-dip recession. It was the worst slump since the Great Depression.

The Democrats were in power, but as the '80s dawned, trouble was brewing for them—and his name was Ronald Reagan.

## 1980: LIVE "TEASE"

# MAURY SCHLESINGER

*Director,* All Things Considered, *1980–1982*

**Living life dangerously.** We usually prerecord the opening "billboard" of the program, which combines the hosts, music, and a "tease" tape. It was April 17, 1980, and it was Independence Day for Rhodesia (now Zimbabwe). The reins of government were to be handed over from the British at exactly midnight there—5:00 P.M. Eastern Time—our start time. We had a live line to the BBC's coverage. And we wanted a "live" tease. This was a crapshoot. We didn't know what would be happening at the exact time. We rolled the theme music, opened the host's mic. Off the air, we listened to the BBC feed. The hosts introduced the "tease" ... Should we use the live feed or a back piece of tape? Time for a snap judgment ... "Take the live feed," I said ... just as twenty-one guns blasted forth announcing the creation of a new nation. Yes, real live radio! ∎

## 1980: MASTER CONTROL

# CHED HUDSON

*Operations architect*

**For the first ten years** at 2025 M Street, Master Control was the technical nerve center of the organization. Technicians on duty monitored NPR programs being delivered to stations on the AT&T landline network, played back prerecorded programs, and coordinated audio routing between NPR studios and numerous remote locations. I'd worked in Master Control for about six months when *Broadcasting Magazine* did an update on NPR following the launch of *Morning Edition*. A photo of Master Control headlined the article, which appeared in the March 17, 1980, issue. The shot captured the gargantuan executive chair, the switching console, the racks of satellite and audio equipment, and, on the near counter, the typewriter for the daily log, the tapes awaiting playback ... and between them the pumpkin pie which my wife had sent in that morning for the guys I worked with. ∎

# THE REAGAN REVOLUTION

"

**The candidate is silhouetted against the sun as it sets over the Rocky Mountains in Grand Junction, Colorado. He waves his cowboy hat to the adoring crowd as he walks off stage with the easy gait of a cowboy hero from the movies . . . which, of course, he was.**

*Linda Wertheimer on Ronald Reagan*

NPR's political correspondent Linda Wertheimer remembers this signature moment in the campaign: The candidate is silhouetted against the sun as it sets over the Rocky Mountains in Grand Junction, Colorado. He waves his cowboy hat to the adoring crowd as he walks off stage with the easy gait of a cowboy hero from the movies . . . which, of course, he was. When he wasn't exiting into the sunset, Reagan was telling voters it was "morning in America," giving them hope for better times.

Reagan's election was one of the most consequential campaigns of the twentieth century. He launched a decade-long era of Republican domination in Washington and a period of free-market ascendancy across the country and the world.

The political story played to NPR's strength. On Capitol Hill, NPR had one of the highest profile reporting teams of any broadcast network in Cokie Roberts and Linda Wertheimer. They, along with Nina Totenberg at the Supreme Court, anchored a group of young and energetic journalists reporting the Reagan Revolution. Barbara Cohen, who had learned Washington's political topography as an editor at the *Washington Star*, was the network's news director. And setting the agenda was NPR's charismatic president Frank Mankiewicz, determined to make NPR a leader in broadcast news and public affairs.

**ABOVE** Cokie
Roberts and Linda
Wertheimer in
1980 (NPR photo).

# JOHN LENNON SHOT IN NEW YORK

Before Reagan could officially take office as the fortieth president of the United States, a fresh tragedy rocked the nation. On December 8, 1980, Mark David Chapman shot John Lennon, the former Beatle, at the entrance of the Dakota apartment building where Lennon lived. NPR covered the death of the controversial cultural icon extensively, along with the rest of the media. But nothing we did was more moving than Verta Mae Grosvenor's essay broadcast on *All Things Considered* on December 15, 1980, when many in New York City and around the world stopped to honor Lennon.

*I believe in magic, and yesterday in an upper West Side bistro, I saw it happen. Because my '60s was sit-ins, not love-ins; because it was not Monkees and Beatles, but Panthers and Young Lords for me; because my song was "We Shall Overcome," not "I Want to Hold Your Hand"; I felt it would be a bit hypocritical for me to go to Central Park and light a candle for John Lennon.*

*But because I believe that John Lennon was a righteous brother, I wanted to do something. So I met with several of my friends for brunch about 1:30. Nobody announced 2 o'clock, but when it came, we knew. A remarkable thing happened: the cafe became absolutely silent. The cafe became magic, and magic was the cafe. For ten minutes. The magic transcended generations and color and culture and politics. Former flower children, ex black militants, old long-haired Marxists, young short-haired ad execs, shallow barflies, deep intellectuals—all came together, in grief, and fell silent. I swear I heard Aretha singing, "Peace, Be Still." Some folks actually prayed out loud; most had their heads bowed. A few had tears; none were embarrassed. I had the feeling that people prayed for John Lennon's soul and their own. I know I did. In these troubled times, when a pair of shoes costs as much as a month's rent, the cost of a Christmas tree equals a week's groceries, the Klan is on the rise, children are disappearing, men's hearts are being cut out, I prayed for John and me and you. I prayed for change.*

> **I still remember how the lights from Shea Stadium lit up the night sky when The Beatles played there in 1965. I still remember wishing I was there. I never did see John Lennon live, but his music had been my life's soundtrack.**
>
> *Bob Boilen on John Lennon*

## 1980: DEATH OF JOHN LENNON

## BOB BOILEN

*Host and senior producer,* NPR Music

**I should have cared more,** but I didn't. I should have cried, but I didn't.

He meant so much to me.

But the day John Lennon died, my life and his music were never more distant.

On the night of December 8, 1980, I was soldering circuit boards in my apartment above a bar in downtown Washington, DC, when I heard the news. I was building a synthesizer; I was in a psychedelic new wave dance band called Tiny Desk Unit.

I grew up with The Beatles. Their arrival in the United States happened when I was eleven. I heard Beatlemania unfold on my transistor radio and black-and-white TV. I still remember how the lights from Shea Stadium lit up the night sky when The Beatles played there in 1965. I still remember wishing I was there. I never did see John Lennon live, but his music had been my life's soundtrack.

I was inspired by The Beatles to pick up the guitar and play, as were so many kids of the day. I think the words of the guitar teacher to my mom were something like, "He's got no musical ability; don't waste your money." It took fourteen years for me to get over that, and one day I quit my record store job and decided to be an electronic musician, a decision that would eventually lead to my work at NPR.

And yet, on the day John was murdered, I recall feeling how he'd lived a pretty amazing life, and we should all be so fortunate. I was twenty-seven at the time. I remember thinking that at least he didn't die young. Now I see how young forty is, how short his life was, how profoundly sad his death was. He was still coming to terms with his own life.

John Lennon's songs and poetry still inspire, I still hear his influence not just on his generation, but on every generation since. I only wish he was around to know that—maybe in his old age he would have cared. ∎

**OPPOSITE** John Lennon is seen here in December 1980. This image was taken just a few days before his assassination (AP photo).

TRANSCRIPT EXCERPT
## *ALL THINGS CONSIDERED*

**SHOW DATE:**
*1980-12-09*

**CAT. TITLE:**
*Interview with Greil Marcus after Lennon Shooting*

**LINDA WERTHEIMER:** I heard the news today, this morning early on the radio. For some, there it was on the newspaper's front page. A few didn't read the paper or watch television, but noticed—noticed something—the way people looked on the way to work. A young girl at a coffee shop reading a paper over someone's shoulder said, "Oh, is that just New York?" What she really wanted to know: Did they mean to kill John Lennon?

We don't know where he'll be in history. Some have said that the classical music of future centuries will be today's rock and roll. But we do know the John Lennon of our times and the songs that are in our minds.

In the literature, he's listed as John Ono Lennon, formerly John Winston Lennon, born in Liverpool, England, in 1940. His first musical group, the Quarrymen, 1955. There were some other now forgotten groups, then the Beatles, 1960, and soon the Beatles changed the world.

**MARCUS:** I, you know, went down from my college dorm to the commons room, where there's a television to watch. I was mainly curious because I didn't even know they had rock and roll in England. And I figured when I got down there that there would be the usual argument with whoever was there over what to watch. And I walked into this room, and there were four hundred people waiting to see the Beatles. And I didn't understand it. I didn't know where they'd all come from, why suddenly this crowd had formed. And so they performed, and it was this bizarre religious experience. Everybody left the room chattering and excited, and I was chattering and excited, too, but I couldn't understand where all this had come from. It was like the world was starting over again. It was just amazing.

**SANFORD UNGAR:** Writer Greil Marcus remembers that everyone had a favorite Beatle. The original litany went like this: Paul, the cute one; George, the quiet one; Ringo, the funny one; and John, the smart one. Smart and complex.

**MARCUS:** In a context of lightness, celebration, joyfulness, pleasure, which, John, you know, certainly communicated, John put an edge of struggle, of doubt, brooding, questioning, nervousness, all the sorts of qualities that one wasn't used to hearing in pop music, one wasn't used to hearing coming over the radio.

And it was really clear right from the beginning, and by the beginning I think I mean like two days after the *Ed Sullivan Show*, that there was someone in this group who was smart, who was self-conscious, who was nervy, who had an astonishingly mocking and sarcastic sense of humor, who was in one way just kidding and in another way not kidding at all.

People consciously and not consciously began to take the Beatles as a kind of metaphor for their own lives, not just their own personal lives, but the common lives they shared with other people, whether it was socially, politically, sexually, whatever.

And that became a very natural way to live one's life with this point of focus, which was the Beatles, and it was really a marvelously lucky thing to be able to play your life off against a symbol that was at the same time four real people who had a great sense of humor, who continually surprised you with their music. And *surprise* may be the crucial word, that for, I suppose, five or six years one lived in a culture of surprise, and that opened you up to any number of new possibilities that you might not have responded to otherwise.

**WERTHEIMER:** And around the country today, people remembered how they responded to the Beatles and John Lennon.

**MAN:** He first of all was an artist. He felt very strongly and very toughly about the condition of the world. But he always found a positive way to express what he had to say.

**WOMAN:** The fact that he had actively taken the role as a house husband, and proclaimed himself as such, kind of was an example to both men and women in this country.

**SECOND WOMAN:** I feel like a friend of mine has died.

**SECOND MAN:** He was everything that anybody was when I was a kid.

**SECOND WOMAN:** Just makes you think what kind of a world do we live in.

**THIRD WOMAN:** He was more than just, you know, a rock and roll star. To my knowledge, he's never told a lie, and he always speaks the truth. ∎

# FIRST WOMAN SUPREME COURT JUSTICE

A month after Lennon's murder, the country's mood changed to relief and joy when Iran released the fifty-three American hostages it had held for 444 days. The release came minutes after Ronald Reagan was sworn in as president of the United States.

But just two months after the inauguration, Reagan himself was shot while leaving the Washington Hilton Hotel after a speech. John Hinckley, Jr., fired six shots, and a ricochet struck Reagan and punctured his lung. Reagan's press secretary, a DC policeman, and a secret service agent were also shot. All survived. The president was rushed to George Washington University Hospital. Greeting his wife Nancy as she arrived at the emergency room, the ever-composed Reagan, always ready with his lines, said, "Honey, I forgot to duck." He was quoting Jack Dempsey's remark to his wife the night the boxer was beaten by Gene Tunney.

Reagan made history later in the year by appointing Sandra Day O'Connor to the Supreme Court. On September 25, 1981, she was sworn in. NPR's Nina Totenberg described the day in this way on *All Things Considered*.

*. . . O'Connor walked up to the bench where the Chief Justice administered the Constitutional oath of office. The chief deputy clerk brought her her robe and helped her on with it over her rose-colored dress. Then Sandra Day O'Connor took her seat on the far left side of the bench. She looked out at the courtroom, and there were those who remembered what she'd said at a recent Senate luncheon in her honor. "Thomas Jefferson and John Adams," she said, "would probably turn over in their graves if they knew a woman had been appointed to the Supreme Court. But Abigail Adams would have liked it." I'm Nina Totenberg, at the Supreme Court.*

# REPORTING THE REAGAN YEARS

**ABOVE** Then Supreme Court nominee
Sandra Day O'Connor speaks while
appearing before the Senate Judiciary
Committee, September 9, 1981, during
her confirmation hearings (AP photo/
Ron Edmonds).

## 1981: SANDRA DAY O'CONNOR, FIRST WOMAN ON SUPREME COURT

# NINA TOTENBERG
*Correspondent*

**Toward the end of the nineteenth century**, the U. S. Supreme Court denied women the right to practice law. One opinion famously said that "the natural and proper timidity and delicacy which belongs to the female sex" makes women "unfit" to be lawyers. By the 1980s, this view may have been archaic, but the Supreme Court was still an all-male bastion, and there was only a scattering of women on the lower federal courts.

Ronald Reagan campaigned on a pledge to name a woman to the Supreme Court, but when a Court vacancy occurred during his first year in office, there was something of an internal battle over whether he should fulfill that campaign promise. Kenneth Starr, then chief of staff to William French Smith, recalls that staff aides examined Mr. Reagan's campaign words carefully, concluding that Mr. Reagan had not made an iron-clad pledge, and some administration insiders urged the president to name Robert Bork or some other conservative luminary. But as Starr observes, "Reagan was not a word parser, and he felt that he had made a moral commitment to appoint a qualified woman to the Supreme Court, that it was long overdue, and that was what our marching orders were."

But in the early 1980s, the list of qualified women with any conservative credentials at all was a short one. Starr believes that O'Connor's name was first suggested by then Justice William Rehnquist, who had known her since their days at Stanford Law School. O'Connor had served as Republican leader in the Arizona state senate, and later as a state trial and appellate judge. She soon won the nod from President Reagan and was quickly confirmed.

O'Connor acknowledges that her appointment was an "affirmative act," that she was not among the most qualified judges or scholars back then. But over time, she would become, as one writer put it, "the most powerful woman in America." On a Court closely divided between conservatives and liberals, she was often the deciding vote on matters as diverse as race and gender discrimination, affirmative action, abortion, separation of church and state, campaign financing, and federal and state power. In 2004 shortly before her retirement, she wrote the key opinion in the Court's first enemy combatant case, declaring that a state of war is "not a blank check" for the president.

When she was appointed to the Court, O'Connor's main concern was that she not stumble. She knew she would be a role model for women. She persevered, even through a bout with breast cancer, never missing a day on the bench. When she retired, she made no secret of her displeasure at President Bush's appointment of a man to succeed her. But her imprimatur was indelible. She presided over a period in American law when women moved from being anomalies in the courtroom to being the majority of the graduates of many major American law schools, a quarter of the federal judges in the country, and nearly a third of the nation's state supreme court judges. ■

> **Reagan was not a word parser, and he felt that he had made a moral commitment to appoint a qualified woman to the Supreme Court, that it was long overdue, and that was what our marching orders were.**
>
> *Kenneth Starr on Reagan's determination to appoint a woman to the U.S. Supreme Court, in spite of detractors*

# KEN RUDIN

*Political editor, Washington Desk*

**The presidential election of 1980,** as it turned out, was not close; Ronald Reagan won a sweeping majority. But it wasn't until late in the campaign, following his debate with President Jimmy Carter, that the American public decided that it had enough of the Democrat from Georgia and would trust the former California governor and Hollywood actor to succeed him.

In the interests of full disclosure, I had been one of the doubters. A long-time "political junkie" who at the time was publishing a small political newsletter, I had long held the thought that Reagan was the one Republican Democrats were itching to run against: They could paint him as a "right-wing extremist"—as California Governor Pat Brown unsuccessfully tried to do in 1966—and in doing so they could skirt Carter's dismal record in dealing with the economy and the taking of the hostages in Iran.

It wasn't until the Republican National Convention in Detroit, in the summer of 1980, when I watched and listened to Reagan up close, that I came away with the feeling that this guy was no pushover.

But if Reagan beat Carter in a landslide, he didn't have much of a honeymoon with the Democrats in Congress, who still controlled the House. And, in fact, there were almost immediately questions about the marriage. There were widespread concerns that Reagan's calls for huge tax cuts without corresponding spending reductions would only make the inflation rate higher. The head of the Federal Reserve Board made his feelings known, and House Democrats were ready to battle the new president tooth and nail. Organized labor had already promised that the economy would be a key issue for the 1982 midterm elections.

On March 30, 1981, less than two months into his presidency, Reagan went to the Washington Hilton Hotel to address the AFL-CIO Building and Construction Trades Department and try to sell labor on his economic policies.

When it was over, and he was headed toward his limousine, six shots were fired in his direction from a 22-caliber pistol. One of the bullets hit Reagan in the chest. Another hit White House Press Secretary James Brady in the brain. Two other men, a Secret Service agent and a DC policeman, were also wounded.

The gunman, a twenty-five-year-old drifter by the name of John Hinckley Jr., was immediately subdued and arrested.

Initially, no one realized that the president was shot, or hurt. The Secret Service quickly took Reagan to the George Washington University Medical Center, about six blocks from the White House, where doctors removed a bullet from his left lung.

As a baby boomer and a political junkie to boot, the day's horrific events immediately brought me back to where I was when other shots rang out in recent history. It may have been March of 1981—but for a brief moment, it was November of 1963, when I heard the news from my seventh-grade homeroom teacher that President Kennedy had been assassinated; or it was April of 1968, when I was at home in the Bronx, and the TV reported that Martin Luther King was killed; or it was a scant two months later, in June of '68, when I woke up in the middle of the night and turned on the radio to hear what happened in the previous day's California primary, only to learn that Bobby Kennedy was shot. In the blink of an eye, all that tragedy came to the forefront of my thoughts as I heard the news about President Reagan.

A worried American public was relieved to learn that Reagan had sailed through the surgery. Making it easier for them was the president himself, who cracked jokes. When he was wheeled into the surgery room, he allegedly said to his doctors, "Please tell me you're all Republicans." And after the surgery, Reagan, still unable to speak, wrote, "All in all, I'd rather be in Philadelphia," a line taken from the comedian W. C. Fields.

The shooting of Reagan, as expected, gave the president an immediate and huge boost in popularity. Congress quickly passed his economic program that called for the biggest tax cuts in history. House Ways and Means Committee chairman Dan Rostenkowski (D) could only marvel: "From a hospital, Reagan has been able to achieve more than many presidents have done from the White House—[he has shown] that he is in total command of the situation."

Reagan, of course, survived the shooting and went on to serve two full terms as president. There is an irony here. Every president elected in every twenty-year cycle since 1840 has died in office: William Henry Harrison (elected in 1840), Abraham Lincoln (1860), James Garfield (1880), William McKinley (1900), Warren Harding (1920), Franklin D. Roosevelt (1940) and John Kennedy (1960). It took the oldest person ever elected to the office—Ronald Reagan was sixty-nine years old in 1980—to break that jinx. ■

**ABOVE** U.S. President Ronald Reagan is shoved into the president's limousine by secret service agents after being shot outside a Washington hotel on March 30, 1981 (AP photo/Ron Edmonds).

# BUILDING NPR'S NATIONAL DESK

Ronald Reagan initiated a seismic shift in America's political world, but prior to his election, Mount St. Helen's provided a stupendous geological warm-up act. It had been rumbling and restless for months, deep in the forests of southwestern Washington State. On May 18, 1980, the mountain literally blew its top, demolishing its northern side and unleashing a massive avalanche of debris.

Howard Berkes, a talented young reporter 200 miles to the south at member station KLCC in Eugene, Oregon, filed a report for *All Things Considered* that evening. Over the next days and weeks, it became clear that this was the most devastating volcanic explosion in U. S. history, with fifty-seven people killed. Later, Howard got an aerial look at the mountain with pilot Gary Harris. This is what he reported on *Morning Edition*.

*(airplane radio sound)*

**Berkes:** *Right now we're coming over the rim of the crater itself, and we're looking right down in the crater now . . . The steam clouds are rising, at least a thousand feet above us . . .*

**Harris:** *. . . It's amazing, the power of that eruption. The trees are absolutely leveled for such a large area, and there's mud where there once was a beautiful river . . .*

Back across the continent in Washington, DC, NPR was gearing up to do more extensive nationwide coverage. And Berkes's reporting was just the kind it was looking for. Barbara Cohen had just recently hired John McChesney, a bearded, cowboy-boot-wearing freelance journalist, to build a national desk. McChesney, a former English professor and an escapee from academia, set to work identifying the best public radio reporters to help cover a nation and feed the insatiable appetites of two daily news shows. When I arrived in Washington, McChesney hired me to be the Midwest editor.

The big challenge was to find station reporters with the time to do the ambitious reporting NPR wanted. Most public radio stations didn't have newsrooms at all, and those that did now had the task of doing local reporting and getting their local versions of *Morning*

*Edition* on the air. The new program's hourly clock had been specifically designed to offer stations multiple options to break away from the network to air their own material.

But, having just launched *Morning Edition*, a program that required a sizeable staff and increased the number of reporters on its Washington desk, NPR was reluctant to hire more full-time, permanent journalists. As McChesney puts it, "It took an act of Congress to get a new reporter position." That wasn't far from the truth, since NPR's budget was set by the Corporation for Public Broadcasting (CPB) which distributed an annual Congressional appropriation to public radio and television. To overcome the hurdle, McChesney began signing talented local reporters to contracts. "It was a way to add reporters without going through the bureaucracy," he says. Barbara Cohen agreed to the strategy, and Howard Berkes was the first to be signed up. You'll recognize some of the other names, too: Jacki Lyden, still a top contributing host and correspondent for NPR, America Rodriguez, and Ellen O'Leary, who went on to help create and manage Youth Radio.

However, after a couple of years, the contract reporters chafed at their second-class status. They were doing the same work as staff reporters, sometimes sitting next to them in bureaus, but they were making a fraction of the salary with no vacations or sick leave, according to Berkes. NPR refused to negotiate, so the reporters filed a complaint with the National Labor Relations Board for a hearing. But just as the hearing began, NPR capitulated, and most of the contractors were hired to full-time staff positions. While seen as an adversary by the reporters during the dispute, McChesney says he had hoped they'd win their case. "What editor wouldn't be pleased to get more than half a dozen new staff reporters," he says.

With the addition of the new reporters, NPR's National Desk was born. It is now the largest desk in NPR's news department with eighty-five reporters, editors, and producers in eighteen locations around the country.

# ART SILVERMAN

*Senior producer,* All Things Considered

**It's hard now to remember** how difficult it once was to get a remote event onto the air.

A Wednesday afternoon in January 1982 illustrates that.

A severe snowstorm had come up that day. In the midst of it, an Air Florida airliner crashed into a bridge across the Potomac River.

We probably heard about it from a local all-news AM station. I was a producer on the weekend edition of *All Things Considered.* There was no organized plan of what to do about the crash.

Reporter David Molpus decided to go to the bridge, and I offered to go along.

We couldn't find a cab outside because of the storm, so we walked up to K Street. Still no cabs.

We found the Farragut West Metrorail station, but we were told trains weren't running because three people had just been killed onboard. Of course we assumed the plane had somehow crashed into the train line.

This turned out not to be the case. These were Metro's first-ever fatal accidents, and the air crash was nearly simultaneous, but unrelated.

In any case, we walked the whole way from NPR's studios to the bridge in the heavy, wet snow. We walked out onto the windy bridge. Near and distant sirens filled the air. We looked down into the dark water of the Potomac and saw nothing. I recorded as David talked to emergency service people. He voiced a stand up from the bridge. Now the problem was how to get that material on the air.

It was a time before cell phones. NPR did not own the sort of portable microwave transmitting equipment TV stations deployed to news events. It became a matter of taking the analog cassette recorder with me back off the bridge. While David stayed out on the river, I started plodding up city streets hunting for a pay phone.

I found nothing outside. Finally, I begged a guard at the Bureau of Engraving and Printing to allow me to unscrew the earpiece of his phone, attach my alligator clips, and play the Molpus recordings back for our record central to record across town.

Later, we would learn that seventy-eight people had died on the river that afternoon, including four motorists. We realized that NPR was in need of some better way to deal with crises that arose not far from our doors. But there was no immediate remedy—and it would take years before cell phones and wireless filing to FTP sites would come to the rescue. ■

**LEFT** Art Silverman in 1986 (NPR photo).

# TOM BODETT

*Author, former commentator on* All Things Considered, *and panelist on* Wait Wait . . . Don't Tell Me!

**"Ted Clark wants to talk to you!"**

I was standing on the half-done roof of a building on the main street of Homer, Alaska. With a shingle in one hand, hammer in the other, I had watched Ann from local public radio station KBBI powerslide her car to a stop below me. I'd been self-recording some local commentaries for a few months, and thought for sure I'd messed something up at their studio the night before.

"Who's Ted Clark?" I shouted back over the air compressor.

"He's executive producer of *All Things Considered*." She yelled. "They want to use one of your commentaries! TODAY!"

For all I know, that hammer is still lying there.

That was August of 1984. *ATC* aired that first piece—about new board-game sensation Trivial Pursuit—then the other two that were on the 10-inch reel I'd sent down with a wish and prayer. And then they kept doing it, just about every week after that for a good long time. To appreciate the gravitas this experience held for me you'd have to understand that public radio in Alaska in the '80s was practically the only radio we had. In many communities, it was the only media at all. Appearing at that time in that place on NPR's flagship news program has no comparable in today's splintered media landscape. It was a published story in *The New Yorker,* a "Picks and Pans" in *People,* and a guest spot on *Oprah* all rolled into one. If you are, on top of all that, a house builder in Homer when you first hear yourself announced by the Goddess of All Goodness, Susan Stamberg herself, your knees go weak.

The next spring I made a visit to the old M Street mother ship in Washington. I met and snapped pictures of Susan, Noah, Ted, Art Silverman, Ellen Weiss. All the NPR royalty and heirs apparent were there. Producer, commentator wrangler, and good friend Debby Dane showed me my reel boxes on her shelf next to Dan Schorr's and Ian "I gotta go" Schoals's. It had been a heady and disorienting winter—recruited by book publishers, courted by advertisers, pitched by art directors—my building career had one short season to go, and I knew it.

That evening there was some kind of party going on at the Stambergs. I drank too much at a bar next door to the NPR studios and arrived late and half in the tank on the back of Tony Brooks's motorcycle. There was no smoking in the house, so I ended up outside in the faded light looking in. Susan appeared at the kitchen window doing something at the sink. I pulled out my instamatic and tried to steal another picture for the folks back home. The Goddess of Goodness looked up, startled by the flash. She could not have seen who was out there but probably deduced it without too much trouble. She smiled warily through her own reflection as I tossed the cigarette, killed the beer, and went back inside. ■

> **"Public radio in Alaska in the '80s was practically the only radio we had. In many communities, it was the only media at all. Appearing at that time in that place on NPR's flagship news program has no comparable in today's splintered media landscape.**

# COWBOY BOOTS

The culture of NPR in the '80s was polyglot. There were New York intellectuals like Robert Siegel; droll Southerners like Noah Adams and David Molpus; earnest Midwesterners like myself; military vets like John McChesney, Alex Chadwick, and Bob Edwards; and veterans of the activist counterculture like Margot Alder; with a few preppies thrown in. There were Ivy Leaguers and graduates of state universities. But one piece of Americana tied them all together—cowboy boots.

"

**Reiner may have worn his more often than anyone besides McChesney. Maybe it was so they could go eye-to-eye, toe-to-toe, mano-a-mano, in those editorial fights over who got to assign Scott Simon's next story.**

My daughter Alexandra, who was born in 1980 and attended many NPR parties and gatherings as she grew up, says that what she remembers most about those gatherings was the boots.

As a toddler, she looked more than one pair of Tony Lama's in the eye as she meandered through the party crowds. Linda Wertheimer had a bright red pair . . . maybe a little reminder of the brilliant sunsets of New Mexico where she grew up. White House reporter and Texas native Jim Angle's were black, so he could wear them under the required dark suit. Even senior editor Steve Reiner, a hip New Yorker with a permanent tan, had a pair. In fact, Reiner may have worn his more often than anyone besides McChesney. Maybe it was so they could go eye-to-eye, toe-to-toe, mano-a-mano, in those editorial fights over who got to assign Scott Simon's next story.

Why the cowboy boot fetish? Who knows? Maybe it was a residue of the boot wearing counterculture; maybe it was Ronald Reagan's western influence (not likely); maybe it was taking a stand against Washington's fashion code. Whatever it was, NPR News never stood taller than in the boot wearing days of the '80s.

## VINCE DESTAJO
*NPR operations architect*

**In the late '70s** and through the '80s, NPR Broadcast and Satellite Operations Technicians were commonly seen wearing the (un)official NPR jacket. Several versions were produced, including customized versions with department names. There were a few *Morning Edition* and *All Things Considered* jackets around. But in those early days, nobody cared much for a jacket that said *ME* or *ATC*. For some reason, the most popular were the "Engineering" department jackets. They were so popular that there were several reorders made to fill all the requests. The building at 2025 M Street shared space with the Federal Communications Commission (FCC), and there were about a dozen FCC staffers who bought NPR Engineering jackets. They simply wanted the look and to wear the post-disco era, varsity-style satin jacket with the cool NPR logo. Not too many survive to this day. Most were stowed away deep in closets or storage never again to see the light of day. But several have survived, including these two. I am in my blue "Engineering" jacket on the right. Toby Pirro is in his jacket on the left. ∎

ABOVE Toby Pirro and Vince Destajo model the coveted NPR jackets (photo by Mark Wagner).

# A PRAIRIE HOME COMPANION GOES NATIONAL— BUT NOT ON NPR

In May 1980, *A Prairie Home Companion*, Garrison Keillor's radio variety show, went national. Keillor had developed the program on Minnesota Public Radio during the late '70s. As it does now, it featured live music, humor, and fake sponsors like Powdermilk Biscuits and Bob's Pretty Good Grocery. At the center of the program was Keillor's monologue "The News from Lake Woebegone." Keillor had created the fictional Minnesota town in musings and sketches on his daily morning show on Minnesota Public Radio during the '70s.

For Minnesotans, of which I was one at the time, Garrison's morning show was a blissful way to stir out of sleep on a frigid winter's morning. One of his fictional sponsors, "Raoul's Warm Car Service," advertised that it would come to your bed, pick you up, still in your cozy blankets, and serve you a bowl of warm oatmeal on the way to work. If only Raoul had been real, I might still live in Minnesota.

But when *A Prairie Home Companion* went national, it wasn't distributed by NPR. In a great miscalculation, NPR President Frank Mankiewicz decided the show was too "elitist." He viewed it as a "put-down" of small town life rather than an affectionate parody. Mankiewicz told me recently that he'd worried that if NPR ran the show, "It would cement our status as elitist." Mankiewicz also asserts that it was way too expensive for NPR at the time. He still says he doesn't regret declining to carry it. Mankeiwicz also points out, rather slyly, that it doesn't really matter anyway, because most listeners think *A Prairie Home Companion* is an NPR program.

It's not. After Mankiewicz passed on the show, Minnesota Public Radio President William Kling organized a new entity to distribute the program, called American Public Radio. It later became Public Radio International. Today *A Prairie Home Companion* has one of the largest audiences of any public radio program.

What made it possible for Kling to distribute *A Prairie Home Companion* without NPR was the new public radio satellite system, completed in June 1980—the first system of its kind in the United States. Now it was possible for member stations to distribute programs on their own, or with network entities other than NPR, even though NPR managed the system.

# LAYING THE FOUNDATION FOR NPR'S FOREIGN DESK

**LEFT** Leo del Aguila, audio engineer, and Scott Simon, correspondent, reporting on war-torn El Salvador in 1984 (NPR photo).

It's hard to imagine today, but during the '70s NPR had no staff reporters based overseas. To cover the news, *All Things Considered* foreign editor Marcus Rosenbaum had pieced together a group of freelancers and stringers from around the world. But these reporters mostly filed short pieces—"voicers," as we call them—without audio clips from interviews and certainly without the "on location sound" that became a signature of NPR reporting. But with *Morning Edition*

preparing to launch, NPR decided it needed a bureau in London. It sent Robert Siegel, who had been a top editor in Washington, to set up shop at Bush House, the headquarters of the BBC's World Service. Siegel's job was to file stories using audio funneled to London by BBC reporters around the globe; to edit freelancers' pieces, and to travel in Europe reporting his own stories, as well.

But there were important stories in the western hemisphere that demanded coverage, too, including shooting wars in Central America.

Early in 1982, Scott Simon, who was reporting from NPR's Chicago Bureau, volunteered for the assignment. Simon was no expert on the political intricacies of Central America, but John McChesney, by then NPR's senior editor, believed that Simon's ability to tell a story with rich detail, and through the perspective of everyday people, would give the conflict a human dimension and make it more comprehensible to Americans.

Simon remembers that one of his first stories was from the town of San Vicente, El Salvador. Rebels had briefly taken over a radio station before being chased off by government soldiers. Simon, his engineer Leo del Aguila, and producer Kim

Conroy encountered the government troops on the road leading to the radio transmitter, and Simon was struck that they were as young as the guerillas they were fighting.

**Simon:** *The guerillas are called the muchachos, but the government soldiers seem no older, fifteen, sixteen years of age, maybe, many leaning at rest on their rifles or threading them atop their shoulders the way many American teenagers do with a baseball bat.*

**Soldier:** *The same as we are. They also have uniforms, just like us.*

**Simon:** *They're as old as you are?*

**Soldier:** *There are older people, younger people, even children in their troops.*

**Simon:** *If they're so much like you, do you find it hard to fight them?*

**Soldier:** *Sometimes we even confuse ourselves which are which, but we have to fight against them because [they are] communist.*

Simon was the first NPR staff reporter assigned to a shooting war. But a few months later, in July 1982, McChesney dispatched a team of three to cover the siege of Beirut. Israel had invaded Lebanon in response to attacks by the Palestinian Liberation Organization on Israeli communities near the Lebanese border. Reporter William Drummond, producer Deborah Amos, and audio engineer Marty Kurcias found themselves in a war zone, with frequent machine gun fire in the streets and Israeli Phantom warplanes dropping bombs from overhead. Their hotel was car-bombed, blowing out most of its windows. People were shaken and injured, but no one was killed. On the morning of August 12, 1982, Marty Kurcias wrote this in his journal:

*More fighting beginning early this A.M. with Phantoms bombing. I slept thru about the first hour of it then woke up and stuck a mike out the window. Last night the fighting was very intense over at the museum and the Hippodrome. Several enormous phosphorous bombs exploded (Israeli), rocking the hotel and literally lighting up my room out of the pitch black. The most spectacular explosion I've ever witnessed. F——g scary.*

**LEFT** Robert
Siegel in London
(NPR photo).

Producer Deborah Amos remembers that the NPR crew was based in East Beirut and had to walk to the fighting in the western section of the city. "Luckily," she says, "the Israelis were very regular about their bombardment. It always began just after 4 P.M., so we knew if we walked out before then we could get back to East Beirut in time to get the call from Washington, on the only phone available, and still get on the air."

Despite the great material being produced, McChesney reasoned that NPR could not serve its listeners simply by parachuting reporting teams from Washington into trouble spots. So over the next several years, he began to build a Foreign Desk in the same way he'd built the National Desk—with contract reporters.

In fact, reporter Tom Gjelten left his staff position in Washington covering labor issues and went to Mexico City on a contract to cover Latin Amer-

ica. From there, he traveled across the region, including to Nicaragua, where at one point he was captured by the Nicaraguan Contras.

Next, Deb Amos left her staff position as a producer and became an NPR contract reporter in Jordan. Over the next several years, NPR signed up contract reporters around the globe, including Sylvia Poggioli in Rome and John Matisonn in South Africa. Alan Tomlinson was hired to cover South America and the Caribbean. Anne Cooper was stationed in Moscow, and Alan Berlow left a staff job in Washington for a contract position in the Philippines. Eventually, by the late '80s and early '90s, most would become NPR staff reporters.

These reporters, and editors like McChesney, Paul Allen, John Dinges and Cadi Simon, began to give NPR a global reach and laid the foundation for NPR's unparalleled coverage of the world today.

**ABOVE**
Scott Simon (second from left) interviews Salvadoran President José Napoléon Duarte (second from right) in San Salvador in 1984. Other NPR news team members: Kimberley Conroy (left) and Leo del Aguila (right) (NPR photo).

**TRANSCRIPT EXCERPT**
## *ALL THINGS CONSIDERED*

**SHOW DATE:**
*1982-08-15*
**CAT. TITLE:**
*Beirut Mental
Asylum Bombed*

**BILL DRUMMOND:** The protective gratings are being pulled up on shops around West Beirut as many people who fled are returning to find out what's left of their businesses and homes. Rema al-Kalil is lucky. Her pharmacy was virtually undamaged, but elsewhere in the city, whole neighborhoods were reduced to piles of rubble. Although West Beirut is devastated, to Rema al-Kalil, who is Lebanese, the city is still her home.

**KALIL:** No damage. Everything is all right, but because of the aircrafts which Israel is coming to Lebanon, when the airplane comes it makes *wooooooo* and everything comes down. It's not because of damage. Look, everything is in its place.

**DRUMMOND:** First of all, tell me why you decided to come back into West Beirut.

**KALIL:** Because I can't leave it; it's my country. Wherever I go, it's like the heart of Lebanon. Nothing goes in Lebanon or runs except in this part of Lebanon.

**DRUMMOND:** Rema al-Kalil and many other Lebanese and Palestinians are angry about the Israeli shelling and air raids. The neighbors on the street outside her shop are angry with the United States as well, for not stepping in sooner to stop the bombing.

**MAN:** The west area of Beirut, we can't say completely have been destroyed, but let's say it's 60 percent destroyed. That means this is a catastrophe. It's a humanity catastrophe.

**ANOTHER MAN:** We are living here without no water, no electricity, nothing to eat. You know, I am coming from 6 kilometers to bring bread for my children, for my family. All the world can see in television what is happening here, can see people smashed into pieces. We are human beings here!

**DRUMMOND:** For days, the Israelis shelled and bombed Palestinian refugee camps in the south of the city, claiming that the civilians had abandoned that area and only the PLO strongpoints remained. Actually, thousands of civilians remained in the camps, either because they chose to or because they could not leave.

The patients of the Islamic asylum for the aged and mentally handicapped stayed throughout the bombing. Over the weekend, Nobel laureate Mother Teresa, working with the International Red Cross, evacuated some of the younger patients from the hospital, where one of the few things still working is the chime clock in the reception lobby.

I'm walking down one of the wards of the mental asylum here in Sabra. There are still around five hundred patients left here, even though around thirty or so children were evacuated this morning. The conditions here are very bad because the staff is much reduced. People have just not been able to come here to work. This hospital has been heavily shelled.

**JEAN-JACQUES COEURS [of the International Red Cross]:** Mother Teresa wanted to come in West Beirut on her own, without any advertisement or publicity around it. She asked to see the most dramatic places in West Beirut, one of them being clearly this asylum for aged and mentally handicapped people. During the shelling and bombing, this asylum has been hit several times, so it was the worst of hell right in the middle of another hell. And since the beginning of June, there were eleven dead and twenty-three wounded among the patients in this asylum.

**DRUMMOND:** Is it possible to say how people who are mentally disturbed react to war situations? Does it cause them any special kind of fear or grief?

**COEURS:** I came here in the morning after shelling, the night shelling. And the only thing I can tell you is that normally people can react against their own fear. They can try to master this fear. But these poor people just can't. They are totally victims of their own fear, of their own nightmares. And for normal people the fear or terror lasts for a couple of hours, but to them it can last for days and even months.

**DRUMMOND:** Let me ask you one final question, Mr. Coeurs. Why would anyone want to shell a mental hospital? What purpose would there be in shelling a mental asylum?

**COEURS:** That's exactly the question I am asking myself, and I still haven't found any answer. ∎

**ABOVE** Correspondent Bill Drummond, shown here beside wreckage from bombings, spent nearly two months covering war-torn Lebanon in 1984 (NPR photo).

# TOM GJELTEN
*Correspondent*

**During the four years** I spent covering war in Nicaragua, the only time I encountered any "Contras" was the day in October 1987 when they detained me. I was traveling in northern Nicaragua with Chris Hedges, who was then a reporter for the *Dallas Morning News*. The Sandinista government had just declared a ceasefire in three small but important war zones immediately below the Honduran border, and Chris and I figured it would be a good time to see if we could find some Contras to interview. (Their name derived from *contrarevolucionarios*, counter-revolutionaries, because they were U.S.–supported rebel forces fighting against the Sandinista government. The rebel leaders embraced the *Contra* name with pride.)

We were headed up a muddy mountain road just outside the town of Quilalí when we rounded a bend and suddenly found thirty heavily armed Contra fighters blocking our way, their rifles pointed at us. Their leader ordered us to get out of our jeep and sit by the side of the road. After a brief interrogation, we learned his name was Panchito. He was fifty-four years old, but he was tough and lean, physically conditioned by three years of nearly constant combat. We told him we had come to see how the Contra troops were doing.

"The last two years have been tough," Panchito told us. "They [the Sandinistas] have been using their [helicopter] gunships on us." As we talked, other Contra fighters gathered around. Everyone had a *nom de guerre*. There was Bigote de Oro (Gold Moustache), a thirty-four-year-old former *campesino* farmer. After five years of fighting with the Contras, his face had hardened into an unflinching scowl. Hermanito was a walking death machine, with a grenade launcher and a vest stuffed with M79 grenades. Tomasito, thirteen, wanted to know if we had any bread we could share. They told us they had marched all night to reach this spot, and they all appeared exhausted. Once we had reassured them we were journalists, they agreed to let us take some pictures.

The pleasantries came suddenly to an end, however, when their local commander showed up, furious that his men had spoken to us. He started screaming, saying he had strict orders not to allow any journalists to enter his zone of operations. He immediately confiscated my cassette tapes, except for one I had discretely tucked in a pocket,

and told us he was going to hold us under guard in a nearby farmhouse until he received further instructions from his own superiors. Over the next few hours, we learned he was called Nolan and was just twenty-five years old. Chris and I wondered if he was high on amphetamines. His pupils seemed dilated, and he was agitated. His hands were shaking, and his voice cracked.

Eventually, Nolan's commander radioed him to say we should be released. "I'll let you go this time," Nolan told us, "but if you ever come back, I'll destroy your jeep."

Just as we were preparing to leave, however, another jeep came up the road, this one carrying a delegation from a Nicaraguan "peace commission," including several young U.S. volunteers. Hearing their jeep approach, Nolan ordered his men into ambush position, taking cover behind rocks and trees. The arrival of the peace delegation enraged Nolan all the more, and we were all ordered back into the farmhouse. After another hour or two, we were all allowed to leave.

A few days later, the "Commander General" of the Nicaraguan Contras, Enrique Bermudez, released a communiqué identifying me by name and accusing me of working in league with the Sandinistas. Bermudez said I had been detained for having penetrated his forces' "zone of operations." NPR Foreign Editor John McChesney immediately lodged a protest with Bermudez, pointing out I had nothing to do with either the Sandinista government or the peace delegations in the country. My report on the experience aired on *All Things Considered* on October 15, 1987.* ∎

*There is a postscript to this story. In March 1991, Chris Hedges (by then working for the* New York Times*) was detained in Iraq with another NPR reporter, Neal Conan. Chris and Neal were held for about a week by Iraqi government forces before finally being released. Chris swore he would never travel with an NPR reporter again.*

**ABOVE** Tom Gjelten (right) sits with three of the Contras who detained him: (from left) an unidentified young guerrilla; Tomasito; and holding the rifle, Bigote de Oro (photo by Chris Hedges).

" There was Bigote de Oro (Gold Moustache), a thirty-four-year-old former *campesino* farmer. Hermanito was a walking death machine. . . . Tomasito, thirteen, wanted to know if we had any bread we could share.

# THE NPR FINANCIAL CRISIS . . . A NEAR-DEATH EXPERIENCE

"NPR COLLAPSES"—That came very close to being a newspaper headline in the early '80s, despite the network's swelling audience and the growing popularity of its new morning show. In fact, NPR came within about forty-eight hours of shutting down in July 1983. NPR was unable to pay the rent for the building that housed its studios and headquarters at 2025 M Street NW, and the landlord was threatening to padlock the doors. At the time, Susan Stamberg believed "it might be the end" of everything she and others had worked more than a decade to build.

"

**NPR came within about forty-eight hours of shutting down in July 1983. NPR was unable to pay the rent for the building that housed its studios and headquarters at 2025 M Street NW, and the landlord was threatening to padlock the doors.**

The problem was that Frank Mankiewicz's ambitious spending to build NPR into a leading media organization was racing far ahead of the organization's income. First came a 20 percent budget cut for public broadcasting initiated by President Reagan. Mankiewicz responded by boldly unveiling Project Independence for NPR. He said he would find private funding to replace the federal grant from the Corporation for Public Broadcasting that was the sole support for NPR's national programming, and he would do it by 1986.

Mankiewicz was convinced that NPR could raise more money from foundations and corporations in exchange for on-air credits. He also unveiled a new program service called NPR Plus; it featured a twenty-four-hour classical music service, jazz programming, and more hourly newscasts. Mankiewicz planned to make money by selling the added programming to member stations. In addition, Project Independence launched NPR Ventures. It included schemes to sell surplus satellite space owned by NPR for things like a national paging system.

## 1984: FUND-RAISER

# PENNY HAIN

*Director/associate producer of* Performance Today

**In 1983, NPR experienced** a serious financial problem and 27 percent of the staff had to be laid off. Dozens of celebrities stepped up to help the company by participating in various fund-raising events. One of those events took place in April 1984 in Boca Raton, Florida, in what was described as a Celebrity Croquet Gala. In addition to professional croquet players, celebrities such as Joan Fontaine, June Lockhart, Peter Jennings, Zsa Zsa Gabor, and many others showed up in their best croquet whites. The main event was billed as "The Great East-West Grudge Match." Zsa Zsa sat on the sideline with her mother and dog. The game was well underway when her dog ran out onto the field and grabbed a ball and was off and running, causing major mayhem. The whole incident appeared on ABC's *Good Morning America* the following morning. ■

**ABOVE** Jolie Gabor and Zsa Zsa Gabor at a fund-raiser in Boca Raton, Florida (photo by Penny Hain).

But the gamble fell short. By early 1983, NPR's cash flow couldn't meet expenses. Stamberg remembers bringing paper from home to write scripts because the vendor would no longer deliver paper. Jay Kernis remembers staff being told to take home any personal electronics they owned, like radios or recorders, because if the doors were locked, the bankruptcy firm liquidating NPR's assets would claim them.

By late spring, a deficit estimated at about $7 million loomed. In an interview with Scott Simon, who was covering the story for NPR news, Mankiewicz gave this explanation for the shortfall in revenue:

*Mankiewicz: What happened, of course, is that we underestimated the length and depth of the recession. Not only was there less money available in the private sector for things like NPR, but there were far more claimants for that money, including many, I must say, far more worthy than we.*

*Simon: To some people, the question that arises from all this is, how could someone who not only listens to the two daily news programs that National Public Radio does, but someone who has a hand in them, be surprised by that. I mean, those news shows were reporting the bad picture in the economy, were reporting that the philanthropic community wasn't coming in with the amount of money.*

*Mankiewicz: Well, there I think you have a failure of management, for which I'm not only willing to take the blame but indeed already have. Uh, we simply lacked either the people or the tools to adequately track it.*

In October 2009, Mankiewicz told me that in the midst of the crisis he had lined up bank loans to close the deficit. "They were willing to lend based on our annual CPB appropriation," he said. "But CPB would not guarantee the

loans." Mankiewicz believes this was because of a fight he'd had with then CPB chairwoman, Sharon Percy Rockefeller. She asked him to lobby Congress to have the funding cuts to public broadcasting restored. He refused, saying he couldn't in good conscience "ask for public broadcasting to be made whole when programs like food stamps were being cut."

On May 17, 1983, Mankiewicz stepped down. But the deficit remained.

Among the staff, there was deep disappointment in Mankiewicz, but at the same time a realization that he'd brought NPR to a new level in the national consciousness. As he was leaving, Susan Stamberg offered this farewell to Mankeiwicz on *All Things Considered.*

***Stamberg:*** *I'm Susan Stamberg. This is Frank Mankiewicz's last day at National Public Radio. And it seems appropriate to say a public goodbye to the man who has been president of this network for the past six years. He leaves at the brightest and darkest time in the history of our twelve-year-old organization. His departure comes in the midst of a financial crisis, a deficit of more than $6 million, forcing drastic cuts in programming and a 30 percent reduction in our workforce. More than a hundred men and women have been laid off. If he leaves at our most difficult time, Frank was also the one who led us through our finest hours. In his years here, our budget quadrupled; our audience doubled. Himself a journalist and*

**LEFT** Adam Hochberg (kneeling, in brown jacket and tie) covering John Edwards's announcement of his run for the presidency, January 2, 2004 (photo by Robert Willett—*Raleigh News & Observer*).

*writer, he understood us. More than that, he liked us. And we returned the feelings, and the respect. Before he came, NPR was the best-kept secret in broadcasting. Frank let the secret out, with relish and style, attracting attention to what we were doing and summoning the resources and support we needed to do it better. He gave us new pride in our work.*

Stamberg says, even though she had asked the board not to fire Mankiewicz, she was really "furious with him" for putting NPR at risk. In fact, she says the original farewell she wrote was a much harsher than the one that got on the air. It was going to say something like, "We had a radio broadcast before Frank Mankiewicz came, and we'll have one after he leaves." But *ATC* producer Steve Reiner and News Director Barbara Cohen came to her and asked her to soften it, so she did. After all, she says, "He did a lot for us . . . he loved us . . . and in the end he took the heat."

To replace Mankiewicz, the NPR board appointed Ron Bornstein of the Wisconsin Public Broadcasting system as interim president. Bornstein brought with him a colleague, Jack Mitchell, to be vice president for programming. Mitchell had been the first producer of *All Things Considered*. According to Mitchell, after two months of wrangling and a tense late-night negotiating session with the CPB (which included arm-twisting by Congressman Tim Wirth on the phone from a car outside CPB headquarters), Bornstein managed to get a $7 million loan. The next day, Bornstein deposited a CPB check for $500,000 in NPR's bank account. The rent was paid, salary checks didn't bounce, the doors to NPR studios remained open, and the programs went on the air.

But there were still severe cuts looming. NPR staff took it upon themselves to seek sources for money. Many lobbied for an on-air fund-raiser to save jobs and programming. The majority of stations, the board of directors, and the interim management were against it. Mitchell says that the new management viewed the staff as "out of control." He says some staff members were personally lobbying Congress for more funds. It became "a power struggle within the organization," he says.

Finally, Robert Siegel, who had returned from London to replace Barbara Cohen as news director, organized a meeting in his office. He recalls that Cokie Roberts, Susan Stamberg, Bob Edwards, Jack Mitchell, and Linda Wertheimer were all there. At first, Mitchell was openly opposed to the fund-raiser, but after what Siegel says was "a remarkable piece of persuasion by a number of people," Mitchell left the office in favor, and the "Drive to Survive" was given a green light.

But Siegel recalls that right up to the last minute, there was still controversy over whether the proceeds would "just go back to the stations to reimburse them for the cost of bailing out NPR, or whether some of it would go to saving programming and jobs." Stamberg says that just ten minutes before the fund drive was to begin, she stood in the sound lock to the main studio with Bornstein. "I looked him in the eyes and said I want your word that this money won't just go to paying off old bills; that it will go to programming . . . or I won't go on the air." Bornstein gave his word.

Only a few station managers agreed to air the fund-drive. Most were too angry and embarrassed by the episode to participate. In just a week, the drive raised over $1 million. Still, more than one hundred NPR staffers, almost a third of the workforce, lost their jobs, the

network's cultural programming was all but demolished, and the company's budget was cut more than 25 percent.

The episode strained relations between NPR and its member stations. One thing was clear to Doug Bennet, the new president of the company starting in October 1983; the funding process for NPR needed to change. Jack Mitchell says that the CPB, embarrassed by the crisis, did not want to fund NPR directly, and NPR itself wanted out of the politically fraught relationship. The solution proposed by Bennet and Mitchell, then President of the board of directors, was to have the CPB send all the money for public radio to the stations and have them buy programs from NPR.

The new funding mechanism, along with greater station representation on the board of directors, gave member stations tighter control over NPR in Washington. However, this had a political benefit: When Newt Gingrich led an attempt to dramatically cut public broadcasting funds in the mid-1990s, he could not paint the network as a Washington-centric operation. Instead he had to contend with local member stations from virtually every Congressional district across the country raising their voices to protect funding for their stations. Gingrich's effort was defeated.

Still, the portion of NPR's funding provided by the government has fallen dramatically since the early 1980s when Project Indepen-dence was launched by Mankiewicz. NPR in Washington gets a negligible amount directly from the federal government. For member stations, the percentage varies, but on average, the Corporation for Public Broadcasting provides only around 10 percent of their resources.

Now, years later, Jack Mitchell says that despite Frank Mankiewicz's management failures, he was pivotal in putting NPR on a trajectory to national significance and deserves to be recognized for that. To that end, Mitchell has lobbied the public radio community to give Mankiewicz the Edward R. Murrow award, the top annual award in the industry. So far the idea hasn't gotten much traction, says Mitchell.

**ABOVE** In 1980 Frank Mankiewicz (far right) speaks to the NPR staff about the expansion of the news operation to the second floor of 2025 M Street (photo by Art Silverman).

# NPR DEBUTS *WEEKEND EDITION SATURDAY* WITH SCOTT SIMON

"The day NPR got over the financial crisis," says Robert Siegel, "was the day we launched *Weekend Edition Saturday* with Scott Simon, and people heard a terrific radio program."

It might have been otherwise, says Siegel. As the financial situation stabilized and *Morning Edition*'s audience grew, the member stations thought adding a sixth day of *Morning Edition*, on Saturday morning, would be a great idea. Still in penny-pinching mode, they wanted to recycle stories from the weekday program on the new show.

"That would have been deadly for NPR," says Siegel. "Most of the people who worked here were young and had great ambitions for NPR," he says. "There was the assumption it would get bigger and better." But recycling the previous week's *Morning Edition* pieces would signal that "our best days and our best radio programs were behind us." Siegel says he thought there would have been a big exodus of staff. "I would have left," he says.

Instead, he asked *Morning Edition* producer Jay Kernis and correspondent Scott Simon to come up with a unique program. The two agreed that they wanted to create a program "that came from somewhere and stood for something . . . with a quality of caring and concern . . . and also a sense of joy." The show would have fewer reporter pieces than the weekday shows and make the most of Simon's engaging personality and fearless yet intimate interview style.

The new show was a big hit. "It clicked immediately," says Kernis. Member stations picked it up faster than any show in NPR's history.

> **Most of the people who worked here were young and had great ambitions for NPR. . . . There was the assumption it would get bigger and better.**
>
> *Robert Siegel on NPR in its tenth year*

**LEFT** Noah Adams's farewell party, 1986. From left: Jonathan "Smokey" Baer, Jay Kernis, Scott Simon, and Noah Adams (photo by Art Silverman).

# JAY KERNIS

*Founding producer of NPR's* Morning Edition *and the creator, with Scott Simon, of* Weekend Edition Saturday, *and with Susan Stamberg, of* Weekend Edition Sunday. *He produced at CBS TV News for fourteen years, served as NPR's senior vice president for programming from 2001 to 2007, and is currently managing editor of CNN/US.*

**We launched *Morning Edition*** in November 1979, and within a few years, member stations wanted sixth and seventh days, so there would be a morning news program every day of the week.

Robert Siegel, longtime cohost of *All Things Considered*, was NPR's news director at the time, and he paired Scott Simon and me to create it, under his guidance. Scott began freelancing for NPR in 1976 and was hired a year later to head a new NPR Chicago Bureau. It was evident from his first reports that Scott was an exceptional reporter. In the field, people wanted to reveal themselves to him. He knew how to use sound to bring you into the heart of a story. His writing was full of telling details, and the way he wrote melded perfectly with his distinctive and personal vocal performance.

For a few weeks, we sat at a table near empty staff offices and asked each other a series of questions: What should the show sound like? What do listeners want to hear on a Saturday morning? What stories and interviews would we include and what would we leave to other shows? Could we produce a show that did more than just present the news—a show that stood for something, without being partisan?

I can report that although Scott and I didn't know each other that well—he was in Chicago and I worked in Washington, DC—Siegel had brought together two people who loved public radio, loved telling stories, and frequently viewed the news through two lenses. First, many news events were the result of the decisions of people in power, and those decisions would have an impact on hundreds or millions of people who might have no say in what happened. What was behind the decisions made by those people in authority? What did they believe, and why did they believe it? Second, many news stories resonate with writers, filmmakers, playwrights, and musicians—who would have different perspectives on the news than the experts and pundits who normally were called upon. We would include those artists when appropriate.

It only took a few weeks, but Scott and I imagined a show that still somehow works a quarter of a century later.

*Morning Edition* was designed to be a coproduction with member stations, that would add local and regional news and features, weather, and in some cases, traffic to the basic NPR feed every ten minutes or so. There was less need for that on Saturday mornings, so the longer *Weekend Edition* segments allowed Scott and producers to present longer interviews—we would let them breathe—documentary-style reports, and music performances.

We wanted the show to have a live quality, produced that morning for listeners in their cars, kitchens, and bedrooms. We decided that, unlike other NPR shows, no commentator would read from a script; they could chat with Scott, but not read.

We wanted the show to have a Chicago/Midwest sensibility, rather than feel like it was coming from the East coast or Washington, DC. When we actually suggested we should produce the show from Chicago, Siegel's reaction was something akin to: not on your lives. It was clear that he felt Scott and I needed a certain amount of adult supervision.

Siegel also gave us an enormous gift when he asked us to incorporate veteran newsman Daniel Schorr's reporting and analysis into the broadcast each week. He taught us a lot about making sense of the news, and he certainly had patience with such a young staff.

News is a serious business, but we also wanted the show to be a joyous radio experience. We were serious about the news but wouldn't take ourselves too seriously. We would push the limits of reporting with sound but also honor and reference some classic radio approaches. For example, we asked composer B. J. Leiderman and arranger Jim Pugh to feature the rhythm of the words "Week-end Ed-i-tion" in the main theme, to compose a sports theme that sounded like a marching band had entered the studio, and a letters theme that included a real typewriter.

Scott handpicked that first staff: great producers like Smokey Baer, who's still with *ATC*; Neva Grant, still with *Morning Edition*; Maria Hinojosa, host of NPR's *Latino USA* and senior correspondent for *NOW* on PBS; original director Cindy Carpien, who went on to produce the show for many years; and original editor Ina Jaffe, LA-based national correspondent.

*Weekend Edition* launched in November 1985—and except for a brief hiatus when Scott cohosted NBC's *Today* show on Saturdays—millions of people have tuned in each week to hear his exploration of the week's news. At the time, the Corporation for Public Broadcasting had given NPR only enough funding for Saturdays, so it would be another year before the launch of a Sunday show, with host Susan Stamberg. ∎

# INVESTIGATIVE REPORTING

While Simon was perfecting the art of the interview on *Weekend Edition Saturday*, some of his colleagues were pushing NPR reporting in another direction. Daniel Zwerdling came to NPR in 1980 from a print background of investigative reporting. He quickly adapted to radio, producing reports on the spontaneous combustion of some Zenith televisions that were burning down houses. The story caused the Consumer Product Safety Commission to launch an investigation. Zwerdling also reported that the best-selling pesticide Chlordane was contaminating homes and causing severe neurological damage to the people who lived in them. After the stories, the manufacturer agreed to take the pesticide off the market.

In January 1986, when the space shuttle *Challenger* exploded seventy-three seconds after launch on a cold Florida morning, NPR's ability to muster investigative talent to a breaking news story was put to the test. Zwerdling and Howard Berkes, along with science editor Anne Gudenkauf, teamed up to break one of the biggest stories in NPR history. Working separately in Alabama and Utah, the two reporters pursued engineers from Morton Thiokol, which had

designed and built the shuttle's engines. They uncovered a story of desperate engineers who tried to convince NASA not to launch on that morning because they feared the cold weather would cause crucial O-rings that connected the rocket stages to fail and the result would be catastrophic for *Challenger* and its crew. NASA ignored the warning and launched. The result was disastrous.

The *Challenger*'s sudden explosion in the heavens grabbed the world's attention and Americans mourned the loss of seven crew members, including schoolteacher Christa McAuliffe. But during the decade of the 1980s, a far more deadly tragedy was slowly unfolding in America. It began with the mysterious death of otherwise healthy young gay men. NPR reporter Patricia Neighmond was among the early chroniclers of the effects of this disease—HIV/AIDS—that would later explode into a worldwide epidemic.

# REPORTING AIDS

**It was a lesson to all of us about commitment to finishing what you start, no matter the end; to sharing your feelings, . . . to making a difference with your life, no matter how short.**

*Patricia Neighmond on the death of Archie Harrison from AIDS*

**1988: ARCHIE'S STORY: AIDS**

## PATRICIA NEIGHMOND
*Correspondent, Science Desk*

**REPORTER** *Patti Neighmond*
**EDITOR** *Anne Gudenkauf*
**TECHNICIAN** *Manoli Wetherell*

**I had been covering the frightening development** of a disease that was striking mostly young, gay men in New York City and San Francisco in the early 1980s. Later, it would be learned that the cause was HIV. And even later, effective treatments that promised a nearly normal lifespan would be developed. But that wasn't our world in the early '80s, and it wasn't the world in which Archie Harrison found himself, infected with a virus that was killing him.

Archie was just thirty-one when he was diagnosed and thirty-three when he died. I first met Archie in the midst of reporting on the new treatment, AZT. It was hoped the treatment would reverse the disease process. But that was not to be the case. NPR's science editor, Anne Gudenkauf, suggested we personalize our coverage by profiling an individual coping with AIDS. We decided on Archie. In our first report, he was smart, thoughtful, and willing to push himself and his thinking.

Our first series of reports focused on Archie's efforts to get better. He exercised, changed his diet, and continued working as an actor. In our very first story, Archie and I walked through his neighborhood, the Hell's Kitchen theater district of New York City. We talked about life, theater, commitment, and his disease. We talked about how he intended to "fight it" and emerge healthy once again.

But that is not what happened. Over the months, Archie slowly succumbed to the devastation of the disease. His immune system plummeted, and he suffered a number of debilitating and difficult problems. Through what must have been a sad and terrifying journey for him, Archie maintained his commitment to me, to NPR, and to the series our listeners had come to understand and take very personally. Throughout this period, Archie received dozens of letters from listeners who were touched by his words.

These were the days when *All Things Considered* would air pieces running from eighteen to twenty-four minutes. Individual cuts of Archie talking might be as long as two minutes with perhaps a ten-second pause. Nothing but Archie thinking, feeling. Such was the power of the story that we could, in fact, feel the silence. The silence struck me most one day when Archie, weak and skeletal, depending on a feeding tube inserted into his abdomen for nutrition, sat in a chair, his partner, Drew, balancing on the chair's arm, and, in answer to one of my questions, looked up at Drew, his eyes watery, and said, "The quality just feels gone."

Archie was speaking about his life. Not long after that interview, Archie decided to stop taking nutrition and no longer take medication. He died peacefully one morning with Drew by his side. Our story aired that evening on *All Things Considered,* and it was one of the original "driveway moments." Listeners wrote to say they had pulled over to the side of the road and cried. They were peeling carrots over the sink and their tears fell. They sat in—yes, the driveway—and cried. We had all become very close to Archie, whether we knew him personally or simply knew him over the air. It was a lesson to all of us about commitment to finishing what you start, no matter the end; to sharing your feelings, no matter how hard; to making a difference with your life, no matter how short. Archie did. NPR simply helped. ∎

# DREW TILLOTSON

*Archie's former partner*

**It has now been more than twenty-one years** since Archie died on August 8, 1988. It feels in ways like a whole other lifetime when Archie was diagnosed with AIDS, in 1986, and when I cared for him until his death. The world has changed quite a bit medically, politically, and culturally for both gay folks and HIV-positive patients. At the time of Archie's illness and subsequent death, "cocktail" treatments for HIV patients were but a longed-for dream.

I moved to San Francisco in 1989, not sure where life would take me. I met a wonderful man, John Edmiston. I went to graduate school, graduated with my doctorate in clinical psychology, and started a full-time private practice. I love my work, and along with clinical work in my practice, I teach, supervise, consult, and write. I married the "wonderful man" legally in September 2008 (before California's Prop 8 was voted on that November) and we celebrated nineteen years together this past July. John and I settled into a new house several years ago and are both healthy and thriving, and our careers keep us quite active. We have two great pooches, Olive and Bacci, and enjoy all that California offers.

I miss Archie, and dream about him from time to time. I imagine he would be amazed at how treatment for HIV has progressed, sad that he was not able to avail himself of it, but content that his illness and story touched many on NPR's *All Things Considered*. My life was enriched by knowing him, loving him, and caring for him in his illness. I learned at a young age that life is precious and that anything that is not life-enhancing is a waste of time and energy. I also learned to have the courage and conviction to speak my mind and to remain an activist for change, particularly around same-sex love, marriage, and families. We are out of the Dark Ages I think, but there's still much work ahead. To quote the character Prior Walters at the end of Tony Kushner's *Angels in America*:

"More life. The great work begins." ■

**RIGHT** Archie Harrison (left) and partner, Drew Tillotson, circa 1987 (photo by Cordelia Anderson).

TRANSCRIPT EXCERPT
## *ALL THINGS CONSIDERED*

**SHOW DATE:**
*1988-08-09*
**CAT. TITLE:**
*In Memoriam:
Archie Harrison,
AIDS Patient*

**PATRICIA NEIGHMOND:** Another visit with Archie. Wednesday, last week, Archie sits on his bed, a new water mattress. He's so thin now that the regular mattress is uncomfortable. When he leans back, he props his knees up with a pillow, his back against two cushions. His face is chalk-white. The hollows of his eyes are large and reddened, but they are dramatically different from the eyes I saw one month ago, eyes that were angry and frightened, eyes that seemed to ask a thousand questions. Now Archie's eyes seem to sparkle again. They seem to give a thousand answers, not to be sad or uncomfortable, to know that this is the right decision for Archie, that this is how he wants to die.

Archie's friend Sarah is here. Sarah came to New York ten years ago with Archie. She wants to be a costume designer. Sarah holds on to Archie's hand tightly. She does not let go for the entire evening. And Archie's companion, Drew, sits close, too, listening to every word. He holds Archie's shoulder, strokes his arm, laughs now and then as Archie talks about the night he made the decision to stop taking the medication and the feeding.

**HARRISON:** That night I went to bed, and I slept so well, for the first time in weeks, talked a lot in my sleep. I think I talked to a lot of people because I've been getting a lot of phone calls from people who I haven't talked to in a long time, good friends, loving people who I just haven't seen, and I think we made psychic touch somehow, and they've called and are coming by to see me now.

**NEIGHMOND:** In fact the days have been filled with people coming to say good-bye. It's beautiful, says Drew, to watch. I asked Archie if he has spoken with his parents. He has. His parents listened to what he had decided to do. His mother, he says, was too upset to talk about it. His father finally agreed to support him in whatever decision he made. The next day Archie awoke feeling better, he says, than he had felt in months. Drew says Archie woke up early, saying he wanted to go to the museum. Archie listened as Drew describes their day.

**TILLOTSON:** I got to push him in the wheelchair, and we went to the modern wing of the Metropolitan, and it was like seeing paintings but like seeing every square inch of the paint and really relishing, just relishing, that day. God, that was such a great day. Now that he's feeling this way, it's like I don't want him to go. It's as if, you know, it's like he was never sick. It's like now that he's living again, I don't want him to go.

But the whole lesson for me is the letting go, and realizing that this is what I and several of his friends around him had wanted all this time, for him to reach this level of peace, regardless of whether he stayed in his body or not. We just wanted him to be at peace, and he is, and so I can't tell you the relief that is. Knowing that he will pass at a place like this, and how blessed he is, how blessed we are, that this happened. It is a miracle. It's a real miracle that he reached this point.

**HARRISON:** I still get a little afraid sometimes, but I know this is the right thing. It's time to let my body have a rest now. It just, it worked real hard, and so did I, and my spirit is going to soar. And I, I feel so much love now. I just really do. That's all I want to say. That's it. I can't say any more about it.

**NEIGHMOND:** That was eight days ago. Yesterday at 11:52 in the morning, after two days of semiconsciousness, Archie died. As he wanted to. At home, with Drew and two close friends by his side, holding him. ∎

> **Now that he's feeling this way, it's like I don't want him to go. It's as if, you know, it's like he was never sick. It's like now that he's living again, I don't want him to go.**
>
> *Drew Tillotson, speaking about his partner, Archie Harrison*

# BIG CHANGES AT *ALL THINGS CONSIDERED*

By the fall of 1986, after fourteen years of hosting *All Things Considered*, Susan Stamberg felt "worn out and ground down" by the daily deadlines. In addition, she was ill. "I didn't talk about it at the time," she says, "but I had breast cancer, and I thought a lot of it had to do with stress." Stamberg says her cohost at the time, Noah Adams, suggested she take six months off to get treatment and then return, but she was determined to leave completely and says she has no regrets. It was hard to shake old habits though. "For years," she says, "I found myself clearing my throat a few seconds before 5 P.M. (the start time for *ATC* back then). It took a good three years to wind down from the daily pressure."

**THIS PAGE** Susan Stamberg reviews galleys of her book, *Every Night at Five: Susan Stamberg's All Things Considered Book,* in 1982 (NPR photo).

129

# A TRIBUTE TO SUSAN STAMBERG

" **Many people have contributed to getting NPR on the air and keeping it there. But, I'm convinced that if it hadn't been for Susan, NPR would not be here today, certainly not with an audience in the range of thirty million weekly.**

Let me just say this about Susan Stamberg. Many people have contributed to getting NPR on the air and keeping it there. But I'm convinced that if it hadn't been for Susan, NPR would not be here today, certainly not with an audience in the range of thirty million weekly.

The first time I heard NPR, I was a college student out on the northern prairies. I was longing to feel a part of the wider world. For me, NPR was a rich stream of challenging ideas and new voices; a window to a more diverse outside world. And what hooked me and hooked many other people I know was the force of Susan's personality, intellect, and curiosity, and her infectious laugh and sense of fun. Radio was and remains a personality-based medium. People listen, and, in the case of NPR, give their hard-earned money, because they feel a personal connection to the people who share their mornings, their daily commutes, or their evening meal preparations.

NPR came on the scene at an inauspicious time for radio. Everyone thought it was dying; that it was old technology, inferior to TV. But in the midst of that, Susan beamed her warm and thoughtful self out across the country and became a friend and companion for millions. She gave NPR a foundational audience of loyal and generous listeners to sustain us through the difficult times of the 1980s. Now, in a new century, even as many of our commercial brethren seem intent on burying this audio medium, standing on Susan's shoulders, NPR and public radio are reaching new heights.

Susan's departure set off a round of musical chairs. News director Robert Siegel launched a search for another female host to partner with Adams. But then, says Siegel, "We heard intelligence that Noah had been sighted in the company of Bill Kling," at Minnesota Public Radio.

Indeed, Adams accepted an offer from Kling to go to Minnesota and do a live radio show, to take the place of *A Prairie Home Companion.* (Keillor had recently decided to take a break.) Adams and his wife and producer Neenah Ellis created a variety show called *Good Evening* live from the World Theater in St. Paul. It was a chance for Noah to indulge in one of his great passions—music. He featured artists like Lyle Lovett, Shawn Colvin, and Harry Connick, Jr., "all folks on the way up," he says, "who we could get (to perform) for scale and expenses."

Now Siegel was facing the prospect of a flagship news program with NO hosts. So, he made a command decision and essentially hired himself to be an *All Things Considered* host. "It was the only job at NPR I really wanted," says Siegel. He says he had taken the news director's job during the crisis because, he thought if he hadn't, he would have "been out on the street."

NPR's new president, Doug Bennet, approved the move, and Siegel was back on the air. Adams came back within a couple of years, and the two were later joined by Linda Wertheimer. The trio went on to host *All Things Considered* for more than a decade.

## EARLY 1980s: SIDEWALK MARKS

# SUSAN STAMBERG
*Special correspondent*

**On a balmy evening in 1981** or '82, several of us had worked late, updating a changing story for *All Things Considered,* and left our M Street offices to discover that the pavement in front had been resurfaced—freshly cemented squares blocked off with frail walls of string held in place by small wooden pegs. I leaned out over the string, and with my forefinger traced my initials— S.S.—and the date in the wet cement. Colleagues began adding their initials. We started laughing, feeling giddy, carefree, and slightly sinful, bending there defacing public property. Our boss, the news director showed up, and I called out, "We're playing Grauman's Chinese—come help!" Others added handprints, shoe prints. Eventually we ran out of sidewalk, and people called laughing goodnights to one another and went home. In the morning, all the initials, the dates, everything had been erased. Trowels had smoothed new cement over those squares. We hadn't been able to leave our marks. ■

# WEEKEND EDITION SUNDAY LAUNCHES

It didn't take Stamberg long to find her way back to the host's chair either. Just a year after stepping down from *All Things Considered*, she was teaming up with producer Jay Kernis to create a comfortable Sunday morning retreat for radio listeners. Stamberg had been reporting in the intervening year, and Kernis said he stopped her in the hall one day and told her she shouldn't be in the position of having to "sell" her stories to one of NPR's shows, she should have a show of her own. Conveniently, he'd been assigned to put a Sunday version of *Weekend Edition* on the air. But, Stamberg said she didn't want a hard news show, and she told Kernis, "I don't want to give up my weekends, I have a husband and a son." She hadn't given up the agonies of a daily news show to do that, she said.

What Stamberg agreed to do was what she envisioned as a radio equivalent of the Arts and Leisure section of the *New York Times* Sunday paper. The pilots for the program featured a coffee pot and toaster in the studio to evoke a Sunday kitchen table mood. They didn't last, but the live piano did. Pianist Stef Scaggiari joined Susan live in the studio to play the opening theme and the music between the program's features. The program introduced the rest of the country to *New York Times* puzzle master Will Shortz, who had a weekly mind-challenging puzzle for listeners. *Weekend Edition Sunday* also featured a segment with the *Car Talk* guys, Tom and Ray Magliozzi, helping make a huge hit out of their own hour-long show, which NPR began distributing nationally in 1987.

Kernis granted Stamberg's request to not work the weekend, so the show was recorded Friday afternoon for broadcast Sunday morning. But then, news broke on a Sunday morning . . . Big News. One weekend in June 1989, the Chinese sent tanks into the streets to crush the Tiananmen Square uprising. Hundreds, possibly thousands, died. Stamberg called her producer Bob Malesky to say she would come in, notwithstanding a croaky voice and a high fever. She was sick with the flu. Malesky said no, that he was comfortable dropping in a story from the Sunday duty reporter to inform listeners of the situation.

But, Stamberg says, the stations that carried the show weren't happy. They insisted the show needed to be produced and aired live on Sunday morning. Stamberg wasn't prepared to give up her weekends, so she lobbied for NPR's Liane Hansen to get the job. Hanson took over the Sunday morning host's chair, and the program has been hers since.

**LEFT** NPR was directly across the street from CBS studios, and in 1990 the *Weekend Edition Sunday* staff thought it would be funny to take their picture out front. Back row, from left: Anne Goodwin-Sides, Connie Drummer, Liane Hansen, Bob Malesky, Ned Wharton. Front row, from left: Fred Wasser, Walter Ray Watson (photo by Bob Malesky).

# REPORTING PERESTROIKA

## ALEX CHADWICK
*Managing editor,* Conversation Sound

*Former longtime NPR correspondent and host Alex Chadwick won the Overseas Press Club Award for best foreign reporting in 1989—a year when there was a lot of foreign news—for coverage of the Velvet Revolution, the fall of Communism in Czechoslovakia.*

**I'd held a lot of different jobs at NPR**—producer, reporter, program host, a creator of *Morning Edition*—but I had little experience in foreign reporting, especially covering a big, breaking story. The fall of the Berlin Wall promised to change that.

Even with the slow thaw of events in the summer and fall of 1989—demonstrations in Eastern Europe, Baltic claims of autonomy, the crisis of confidence in Communist leadership—the sudden domino collapse of Communist governments that November surprised us. We rushed Robert Siegel to Berlin. I followed several days later, crossing paths with Robert at a press conference in Paris. He headed back home, and I went on to Berlin . . . where pretty much nothing was happening.

It was like the day after New Year's; the city that had gone on a spectacular news binge now wanted to nurse its hangover in utter quiet. Everyone knew there was more to come in the crash of the Cold War, but where?

I had dinner with Sylvia Poggioli and her husband, Piero Benetazzo, an Italian journalist (and beloved figure within NPR). Both advised me to go to Prague, and quickly; Piero had reported from there a generation earlier when the Czechs had briefly challenged Soviet power.

Crossing into East Berlin the next day felt illicit—but that's where I could get a nearly empty noon train for Prague. I read and studied notes—pre-Google, you still had to carry what you needed. Somewhere along the journey, it occurred to me that I would be arriving alone at night in a city I didn't know, that there would be no customary Foreign Desk local "fixer" waiting, and that I did not speak Czech.

From the Prague train station I took a cab to Charles University, determined to hire the first person there with good English who was willing to work immediately. The nighttime stone lobby at the School of Language and Philosophy was cold and drafty; a passing student went to fetch someone, and that's how I met Natasha Dudinska. She was twenty years old, small, underfed, but with a fierce energy. I didn't realize it then, but Natasha was a leader of the student strike that had shut down the university days earlier and that now posed an almost unthinkable challenge to the government.

We went looking for one of Piero's old dissident contacts; he told us of a clandestine emergency meeting of the government's inner circle; we were in another taxi (and thankfully rolling tape) when a bulletin came on the radio: the government was resigning. No one knew what would happen next.

For the ten days that followed, I reported daily details of what came to be called the Velvet Revolution . . . led by students, joined quickly by an underground opposition of intellectuals, and then thousands, tens of thousands, hundreds of thousands of fellow Czechs rallying in public squares, factories, schools, and meeting halls. They could reimagine their future; the Soviet tanks would not come.

Natasha was at constant meetings of the student strike, but I used her as an interpreter when she had time. And I listened to her stories—a family divided by political events, a young woman of wonderful intelligence but also great doubt. I told NPR editors about seeing the astonishing events of that time in Prague through Natasha, and they allowed me enough extra time to gather more interviews and background notes. I flew home on a Wednesday in early December, and the following Saturday Scott Simon's show put aside twenty minutes for Natasha's story.

The piece struck an immediate response—colleagues called and wrote, as did many listeners; a filmmaker found Natasha; the report was anthologized; it won the Overseas

Press Club Award for best foreign reporting; when NPR later issued a double CD collection of greatest hits over its first twenty years, Natasha was the capstone.

She was an extraordinary young woman in extraordinary times of hope and courage. And NPR allowed a reporter to follow his instincts, and write a piece that was both larger and smaller than its usual news coverage ... a very personal story about great events. My friend Deborah Amos—also in Prague at that time—told me that she was later asked by another colleague about what had happened then: had Natasha and I fallen in love?

"Oh, everyone fell in love with her," Deborah answered, "everyone fell in love with the moment, with the city, with this time that no one thought would ever come again." ■

**ABOVE** Alex Chadwick and Lynn Neary, weekend cohosts of *All Things Considered*, in 1985 (NPR photo).

## 1989: FALL OF THE BERLIN WALL

# DANIEL SCHORR

*Senior news analyst*

**It went up in 1961** on my CBS watch and came down in 1989 on my NPR watch. I'm talking about the Berlin Wall, that ugly stretch of masonry that turned East Berlin into a prison for East Germans yearning to escape.

I can remember as though it were yesterday, East Germans shot as they tried to scale the wall. I can remember American and Soviet tanks confronting each other at Checkpoint Charlie.

I was with President Kennedy in 1963 when he went to Berlin and denounced the wall and all that it stood for. And I was with President Reagan in 1987 when he stood at the wall and challenged, "Mr. Gorbachev, tear down this wall."

The wall was like a centerpiece of my career as a foreign correspondent. It seemed only natural that when Scott Simon inaugurated the *Weekend Edition Saturday* program in November 1985, I would speak to him from Berlin.

When I walked through the Brandenburg Gate into East Berlin, it was the first time in twenty-eight years that I could do that.

On a shelf in my NPR office is a fragment of the Berlin Wall—a Cold War keepsake. ∎

**LEFT** Berliners reunite under the gaze of East German *Vopo* (police) following the official opening of the Berlin Wall on November 9, 1989, symbolizing the end of the Cold War (Sipa via AP Images).

# CHANGES AT THE TOP OF THE NEWS DEPARTMENT

After Robert Siegel traded his manager's chair for the host's chair at *All Things Considered*, NPR President Doug Bennet hired Adam Clayton Powell III to replace him. Powell was the son of the controversial Congressman from Harlem. His roots were mainly in commercial radio, but he had clinched the NPR job with an insightful and detailed critique of NPR news programs. But after several months, there was uneasiness among many on the staff with Powell's news decisions. It was felt they tilted too much toward commercial, mass market sensibilities. Powell's aloof, or shy, interpersonal style frustrated those more inclined to a vigorous discussion of resource allocation. He butted heads with several senior members of his staff, including John McChesney and Marcus Rosenbaum, then the national editor. Powell fired both, though both would ultimately be rehired after Powell left. Powell resigned in 1990, due partly to staff discontent, after a little more than two years on the job.

Again, NPR looked to its London Bureau for a leader. Bill Buzenberg took over as vice president for news in early 1990, just after the decade concluded and as communism was collapsing in the Soviet Union and its satellites. Buzenberg was a hard-charging reporter, and he brought the same passion to his new job. His expansion of the news department in the 1990s would cement NPR's place as one of the nation's top news organizations.

**ABOVE** *ATC* producers' lineup, 1986.
From left: Peter Breslow, Art Silverman, Richard L. Harris, Maury Schlesinger, Christopher Koch, and Neal Conan (photo by Art Silverman).

FIGURE 3
# WHEN PEOPLE LISTEN

| 5–6AM ▶ | 6–7AM ▶ | 7–8AM ▶ | 8–9AM ▶ |
|---|---|---|---|
| 841,800 | 1,822,900 | **2,720,200** | **2,449,800** |

| ◀ 12–1PM | ◀ 11–12PM | ◀ 10–11AM | ◀ 9–10AM |
|---|---|---|---|
| **1,617,500** | **1,614,600** | **1,670,000** | **1,809,700** |

| 1–2PM ▶ | 2–3PM ▶ | 3–4PM ▶ | 4–5PM ▶ |
|---|---|---|---|
| **1,505,400** | **1,511,400** | **1,683,100** | **1,917,700** |

| ◀ 8–9PM | ◀ 7–8PM | ◀ 6–7PM | ◀ 5–6PM |
|---|---|---|---|
| 632,200 | 848,100 | 1,413,000 | **2,048,300** |

| 9–10PM ▶ | 10–11PM ▶ | 11PM–12AM ▶ | 12–1AM ▶ |
|---|---|---|---|
| 538,900 | 451,400 | 348,300 | 241,800 |

**SOURCE:** *Act 1 based on Arbitron Nationwide, Fall 2009, Person's 12+, Monday–Friday.*

The 1990s
**BY RENÉE MONTAGNE**

# 1990

| | J | F | M | A | M | J | J | A | S | O | N | D |
|---|---|---|---|---|---|---|---|---|---|---|---|---|
| 1990 | | | | | | | | | | | | |
| 1991 | | | | | | | | | | | | |
| 1992 | | | | | | | | | | | | |
| 1993 | | | | | | | | | | | | |
| 1994 | | | | | | | | | | | | |
| 1995 | | | | | | | | | | | | |
| 1996 | | | | | | | | | | | | |
| 1997 | | | | | | | | | | | | |
| 1998 | | | | | | | | | | | | |
| 1999 | | | | | | | | | | | | |

**FEB 1990**
Nelson Mandela is released from prison.

**AUG 1990**
The Gulf War begins after Iraq invades Kuwait.

**MAR 1991**
Neal Conan is held for a week by the Iraqi government.

**NOV 1991**
*Talk of the Nation* launches.

**DEC 1991**
The U.S.S.R. officially dissolves, ending the Cold War.

**APR 1992**
The Rodney King riots hit Los Angeles..

**DEC 1992**
David Sedaris makes his first appearance on NPR's *Morning Edition.*

**APR 1994**
The 100-day-long Rwandan Genocide begins, resulting in the deaths of over 500,000 Tutsis and Hutu political moderates.

**OCT 1994**
NPR launches its first Web site.

**APR 1995**
NPR begins streaming audio on-line.

**NOV 1995**
*This American Life* debuts on WBEZ Chicago.

**JAN 1998**
*Wait Wait . . . Don't Tell Me!* debuts and the Monica Lewinsky scandal breaks.

**FEB 1998**
War erupts in Kosovo.

**AUG 1998**
President Clinton finally admits to an improper physical relationship with Lewinsky.

# NPR TAKES YOU THERE

The 1990s dawned in a downpour in Soweto, the day that Nelson Mandela walked free.

It was a blessing, a good omen.

"Rain," one Sowetan told NPR, "causes Africans to rejoice."

On that Sunday in February 1990, the world also rejoiced, as it caught a first glimpse of a man who had become a symbol of freedom, while locked up for twenty-seven years. On *Weekend Edition*, host Liane Hansen summed up the breaking news: "Today is a day that will make history."

In those first days of the decade, the world seemed to be shaking off the totalitarianism and oppression that had held millions in its grip in the latter half of the twentieth-century. When Mandela was released from prison, many were still marveling at the sudden and dramatic fall of the Berlin Wall, just months earlier. The labor movement Solidarity had broken the Communist grip on Poland, and its leader, Lech Walesa, was on his way to being elected Poland's president. Soviet leader Mikhail Gorbachev's political and economic reforms known as *perestroika* were in full swing.

By 1991, the Cold War was over.

The massacre at Tiananmen Square in '89 foreshadowed horrors to come: genocide in the Balkans and Rwanda, new wars in the Gulf and Chechnya, the shock of Black Hawk Down, and the rise of the Taliban. But at the moment of Nelson Mandela's release, the world seemed to be opening up. And NPR was there.

**ABOVE** President Nelson Mandela, wearing a garland, left, greets supporters on his arrival at a pre-election rally held in the Genadendal township, 93 miles east of Cape Town, South Africa, on October 10, 1995 (AP photo/Sasa Kralj).

**OPPOSITE** Renée Montagne, in 2006, is a senior host of *Morning Edition* and broadcasts from NPR West in Culver City (photo by Sandy Huffaker).

# NEVA GRANT

*Senior producer,* Morning Edition

**February is summer in South Africa**, and the summer of 1990 was historic: After twenty-seven years in prison, Nelson Mandela walked free. The day the announcement came, I was in the black township of Soweto with my NPR colleagues, interviewing residents about his expected release—which everyone knew was imminent, but nobody quite believed would come. But that afternoon, the news suddenly crackled over radio and television: The world's most famous political prisoner would walk out of jail the next day.

As producer on the team that traveled from Washington to cover the story, I had prepared for this moment for weeks. I knew Mandela had near-mythic status among black South Africans. He was one of the leaders of the African National Congress, a militant and eloquent opponent of Apartheid. Even behind bars, he was a leader: the father of a country that had not yet been born.

I was prepared to cover that story. But nothing prepared me for next few minutes. As if summoned by hidden music, hundreds of Soweto residents poured out into the street. They broke into song—"Mandela is coming!" and began to dance the Toi-Toi, a step-march of celebration and defiance. My colleague Vince Muse and I were holding microphones and began moving slowly backward, unwitting drum majors to a joyful parade.

Celebrants clustered around us, eager to share this historic moment with listeners in North America. "Our father, our daily bread, is coming" one man shouted, his head thrown back. A woman rushed toward us, laughter interrupting her words. She gestured to her little boy and said "HE will see him in the flesh! He will see the leader that I have never seen!" People cheered and pumped the air with their fists, embraced and wept.

In my years at NPR, I had covered election night victories, award ceremonies, many happy occasions. But I had never seen joy like this. It felt complete and unchoreographed. It was joy that seemed to have been saved up for years, aged to a kind of perfection, then released all at once, in the space of a summer afternoon. ∎

In fact, when it came to overseas reporting, NPR was about to come into its own. "Not that the world knew it," laughs Anne Garrels, who was among the first full-time foreign correspondents to be hired by NPR, leaving network television in 1988 to do the longer, more nuanced stories that were possible at NPR at that time. She remembers the thought that nagged her during her last years in television, "Your mind begins to shrink to the amount of news you are going to get on the air." Garrels went on to set up NPR's first fully functioning overseas bureau, in Moscow in 1991. Up until then, with the exception of the London Bureau, overseas reporters were stringers, or on contracts, and working—as best they could—out of their homes.

Sylvia Poggioli, whose sign-off, "I'm Sylvia Puh-joe-lee," earned her legions of fans in the '80s, had this response when asked how long it took to get a paid staff position at NPR: "Let's put it this way: the restaurant had already been named!" That would be a dining establishment in Salem, Oregon, named for Poggioli by a listener entranced by her low, alluring voice, well before Poggioli actually came on staff in 1993. (As one listener has put it, "You imagine Sylvia Poggioli in a 1940s suit, holding a cigarette, her long dark hair swept under a fedora. And stuck in the hatband, a square of paper reading: PRESS").

For foreign correspondents far from NPR's swelling listenership across the United States, it could be tough getting interviews, especially with the big names. "In those days, no one knew who NPR was," remembers Garrels. "And NPR was fighting ignorance in the rest of the world. I remember trying to get an interview with Boris Yeltsin and trying to convince them NPR was a major player. For one thing, the 'public' in National Public Radio could easily be translated as 'government.'—'No!' you'd say. And inevitably they'd ask, 'Well, where do you get your funding?' And you'd say, 'Actual listeners send in their money.' Trying to describe a model of NPR in Moscow, or most places outside the U.S. . . ." At this, Garrels trails off.

In 1990, NPR was, in fact, on the cusp of being a major player. For the first time, it was able to field teams of reporters for major news events. I was part of the team that went to South Africa, and our on-air voices added up to something of a rainbow: South African John Matisonn, who knew every political player worth knowing; Phyllis Crockett, so smitten by the place that she later returned, took the name *Noluthando*, and stayed; and Richard Gonzales, who was there when Mandela first stepped out of the Western Cape's Victor Verster prison.

Up in Johannesburg, while the anchors of America's evening news networks settled into a four-star hotel downtown, the NPR crew set up shop in a rather shabby suburban hotel that had, until then, mostly sheltered traveling Afrikaans salesmen. Our engineer, Vince Muse, rigged up a small studio in his room using the technology of the time—a "comrex encoder unit." The comrex was bulky, hard to use, and didn't give great results. It did, however, enhance the quality of tape sent over a phone line.

This was a luxury. Most of the time, reporters did not have a comrex. They sent their stories right over the phone, which required a good deal of creative jury-rigging. First, you unscrewed the mouthpiece of the phone, which houses the little microphone in the handset; then attached two alligator clips to the two metal terminals; then plugged the other end of the clips into your cassette recorder; and then you rolled your tape. At our Johannesburg hotel, phone calls were routed through a switchboard downstairs and messages were relayed to you as you walked by.

# You imagine Sylvia Poggioli in a 1940s suit, holding a cigarette, her long dark hair swept under a fedora. And stuck in the hatband, a square of paper reading: PRESS

*Sylvia Poggioli, as imagined by one NPR listener*

**ABOVE** Senior European Correspondent Sylvia Poggioli in 1992. The only light available is from candles and the miner's helmet that Sylvia is wearing (NPR photo).

As might be expected, this process made it hard to set up interviews and go out on the street to report what was happening. International calls could take minutes or hours to get through, and any call that lasted over a few minutes could be breathtakingly expensive.

(Generally for reporters in the field—domestic and overseas—when you wanted to sound really nice on the air, and you weren't in a hurry, you simply shipped your tape to DC. And when it came to recording that script in your noisy hotel room, it helped to sit under a bedspread.)

In South Africa, the promised end of apartheid was so momentous that the foreign coverage, and America's anchors, also ended up on local television from time to time—which was how it came to be that one of the biggest names at ABC News saved me from one of South Africa's infamous hoodlums, known as a *tsotsi*.

It was several weeks after Mandela's release. I was doing a feature on South Africa's "independent homelands," traditional tribal areas that the apartheid government had spun off as supposedly independent "nations." It was a means of keeping the rest of the country in the hands of whites. I had gone to one of these homelands, called Bophuthatswana, to gather tape from what was billed as a small rally organized by the newly legal African National Congress. Instead, I found myself driving into the dust kicked up by thousands of exuberant protesters. They stretched to the horizon, it seemed, peacefully marching into a local township. Then, suddenly, the demonstrators wheeled around and began stampeding past me, gunshots crackling in the air. Bophuthatswana's soldiers had fired on the crowd, killing at least seven, wounding hundreds more, and scattering the remainder into a riot.

That rare thing, a fast-food place in a township—the Chickin'-Lickin'—was the first business to go up in flames. Others followed.

My feature story turned into a breaking story, and I was the only reporter there.

Because dusty township streets had no names (true even in Soweto, with millions of residents), I did what I'd learned to do: offer locals a ride in exchange for directions. Three teenaged ANC "comrades" piled into the car, and for the rest of the day, helped me navigate around the rocks that had been rolled across the streets, offering a raised fist and shouting *Amandla*—power!—the high sign to young rioters as they steered me through the chaos.

I collected tape all day long, but there was no possibility of filing live for NPR, as few in the townships had a phone (for all intents and purposes, cell phones didn't exist yet), and one couldn't make an overseas call from a pay phone. At dusk, as the fires died down and my guides started to lead me out of the township, we came across a scene that made even my tough young companions gasp. Manning a barricade were several large, very threatening and very drunk street *tsotsis*.

One was headed our way.

"Quick," whispered Sipho, who was riding shotgun, "back up, fast." As he spoke, he stuck his fist out the window, and shouted, "ABC . . . ABC . . . journalist!" In the midst of my failing effort to get away, I paused to correct the young man, "NO . . . no . . . NPR . . . NPR!"

Even after hours in the car watching me record, Sipho still didn't get it—or perhaps he figured he was far better off with a journalist from "ABC . . . ABC." Moments later, a scowling face was leaning in the window, a face that slowly broke into a smile, as this particular tsotsi wanted to find out, "Do you know Peter Jennings?"

# AMY DICKINSON

Ask Amy *nationally syndicated advice columnist and panelist on* Wait Wait . . . Don't Tell Me!

**I first started working at NPR** in 1992, after moving to Washington from London. I was a single mother with a young child and very rusty from my previous career in journalism. I was also prone to inexplicable and sudden-onset crying, an unfortunate leftover from my divorce.

I started out working in NPR's headquarters on M Street, filling in for a booker on *All Things Considered*. The place looked like Marconi's hellhole—a rabbit warren of corridors, cables and radio booths—and smelled like Port Authority. Cartons of cigarettes had been stubbed out into the ashcans and gallons of coffee spilled onto the carpet. Most people don't associate smells with radio, but I do, and it's the scent of Larks and three-day-old Pepperidge Farm danish.

It seems that no one had told some staffers that it was time to cut their ponytails; between the hairstyles, Birkenstocks, and bikes parked in the hallways, the place seemed to run on fumes left over from another time. The weirdest thing was being at work and hearing all of these familiar and well-loved NPR voices—only now they were real voices—in the hallways or in the elevator, and having this strong impulse to adjust the volume on my radio. That and seeing Nina Totenberg brush her hair in the bathroom.

I had worked in television network news and was used to a somewhat different professional ethic. My previous experience had been that people at the top of the news chain discussed possible stories and then decided what would go on the air. They then told underlings what to cover and how.

This was a different construct altogether. Every morning the staff of *All Things Considered* would meet—all of us—and discuss what we thought should be on the show. The meetings lasted sometimes for two hours and covered every conceivable (and some inconceivable) topic. There was a lot of laughing and some shouting.

It didn't matter if you were a production assistant or a lowly booker filling in for a few months, if you had an idea and dared to bring it up, your idea would be batted around the table, discussed from every angle, and accepted or rejected on its merits. And I'm not talking about a lofty thing here—sometimes there was room in the show for something exceedingly silly, and that's how I ended up impersonating talk show host Larry King, and changing the words to the National Anthem, and reviewing an R-rated movie in the persona of an eight-year-old girl named Tiffany.

It is not only the most democratic way to put a show together, but the smartest.

It's also the most fun.

I was dying to do stories, but I didn't know how to do radio. I kept pestering Ellen Weiss to train me in radio and to let me do stories, until she told me that I didn't need permission. If I wanted to do a story, I should just do it. And if I wanted to learn how to "do radio," I should just figure it out. And I did.

I worked as a booker, production assistant, and commentaries editor during the '90s. *All Things Considered* was willing to have me work around my parenting schedule. My daughter Emily spent part of her childhood as something of a fixture at NPR's studios. She made her radio debut at age five, contributing her voice to a story—and produced her own piece for *All Things Considered* when she was in high school.

My affiliation with NPR is the longest running, happiest, and most rewarding professional relationship I've ever had. I've had plenty of other jobs during the time I've worked for various NPR programs, but National Public Radio is the only place that has felt like home. ∎

**ABOVE** Panelist Amy Dickinson at the April 29, 2010, taping of *Wait Wait . . . Don't Tell Me!* (photo by Jerry Schulman).

# AIR
# SUPERIORITY

**ABOVE** Deborah Amos in Kuwait City in February 1991 (photo by Neal Conan).

No one could have known at the time, but NPR was on its way to becoming one of the best known broadcasters of world news. The Gulf War would be the turning point. As *Talk of the Nation* host Neal Conan likes to put it, in the late '80s when he was NPR's bureau chief in London, he was the only staff person in the world between Long Island and Oahu. NPR had earned a reputation for excellent coverage of domestic news and political news out of Washington, DC, and while it had done some award-winning reporting in the '80s, circling the globe between those two island points meant stretching the scarcest of resources.

Bill Buzenberg remembers arriving in DC to become NPR's news director in early 1990, having spent three years, himself, working out of the BBC's Bush House as NPR's London Bureau Chief, and thinking, "We need to grow our coverage to be the kind of serious network that the BBC is." NPR's then president, Doug Bennet, and CFO Sid Brown agreed, and NPR's board was supportive. From these conversations and initiatives grew NPR's "Excellence Fund," a way of paying for large, costly news coverage— for example, reporting on the Gulf War, which

**THIS PAGE**
A destroyed Iraqi tank rests near a series of oil well fires in northern Kuwait during the Gulf War (AP photo/David Longstreath, File).

**ABOVE** Scott Simon in Saudi Arabia about twelve hours before the ground war began, February 1991 (photo by Staff Sergeant Michael Hughes of the 82nd Airborne).

began soon after the fund was in place. The Corporation for Public Broadcasting put in a substantial sum for the coverage, recalls Buzenberg, and NPR's member stations did something they'd never done before: They agreed to add a surcharge to their local fund-raising, dedicated to funding NPR's war coverage. That fund-raising brought in hundreds of thousands of dollars more—an effort possibly helped by a new gift for donors: an NPR T-shirt, showing planes dropping microphones, beneath the words *Air Superiority*.

One front-page story that came out of that short-but-costly war featured Conan, along with his colleague Chris Hedges, of the *New York Times*—the two ended up in the hands of Saddam Hussein's Republican Guard.

They'd spent weeks with other journalists, all of them tightly controlled in Kuwait by the U.S. military. When Iraq surrendered, suddenly, as Conan put it, a trip across the border "seemed reasonable to us." He remembers driving past the Vermont National Guard, and then into a group of Iraqi soldiers south of Basra.

"I'm not sure they knew the war was over," says Conan. "Still, they were robbing anyone who came down the road. They had turned brigand!"

The Iraqi soldiers captured Conan and Hedges, and then turned their captives over to the Republican Guard, who drove them to Basra, where, says Conan, "We found the Civil War we came there looking for. We could see the green flags of Iraq's Shia resistance, lots of smoke, and tracer fire coming straight at our jeep."

Back in Washington, NPR staff experienced a very nervous several days before Conan's whereabouts were known—by then he was in Baghdad, put up by the *mukhabarat*, or secret police, at the Hotel Diana, along with dozens of other foreign reporters. When the captives were freed, however, and finally hustled onto a bus headed for Amman, Jordan, Conan jumped out. He flagged down an Iraqi cab in the hopes of getting to Jordan fast enough to get his adventure on Scott Simon's *Weekend Edition*. "$400 to go 150 miles!" he says, and still, "I just missed the deadline, and ended up filing for *Weekend All Things Considered*."

In the end, the Gulf War would bring a million new listeners to NPR News, at the time when its reach was just 7 million. While all the networks saw ratings go up during the conflict, with NPR, that new audience stayed. This kind of surge and growth would become a trend for the next twenty years. Big news, mainly bad news, brought in listeners—and once they'd discovered NPR News, they got hooked.

**ABOVE** Neal Conan (in baseball cap) with radio reporter Lou Garcia, shortly before Conan's departure for Basra, Iraq ,in February 1991 (photo by Donatella Lorch).

**LEFT** Neal Conan, in Jordan, talks with *All Things Considered* host Lynn Neary in March 1991, shortly after he and several other journalists were released by Iraqi soldiers (photo by Jacki Lyden).

# WOMEN COVER THE WAR

Before the '90s, there were a handful of reporters on contract, plus freelancers—some like Deborah Amos. Amos had won awards as an NPR producer, but when she wanted to report on (and in) the Middle East, the only way to do it was to quit her job in DC and freelance.

That was in 1985.

In 1991, Amos joined a list of reporters sent to the Gulf, including Scott Simon and John Burnett, but tilting heavily in favor of women: In addition to Amos, there were Anne Garrels, Deborah Wang, and Jacki Lyden. They were not the first women to do war reporting—early feminist Margaret Fuller was sent to Europe by the *New York Tribune* in the 1840s, where she covered a revolution in Italy; Martha Gellhorn's coverage of World War II is still considered among the finest; and in the Gulf War, CNN's Christiane Amanpour cut a dramatic figure. But, as NPR's then senior foreign editor Cadi Simon put it, "You really never saw a reporting team made up of mostly of women."

Cokie Roberts, who arrived with the first generation of NPR women, has long been fond of saying that NPR attracted and kept so many talented women because the salaries were too low for men.

She wasn't joking. And it was still true in the early '90s. The low wages and a lack of permanent positions offered an opportunity for women to break in. Sylvia Poggioli says that women reporters expanded the reach of NPR's journalism. Looking back on the Bosnian War, she says, "One story where women reporters could play a unique role was on the massive number of women who were raped. [Rape] was being used—in Bosnia, Albania, and elsewhere in the Balkan wars—as a weapon. And men simply could not get that story. Partly, perhaps, because they didn't want to. And if they did, it was not possible for them to talk to these women."

Poggioli won a Peabody Award for her coverage in 1992, at the height of the ethnic cleansing in Bosnia. Looking back, though, she is most proud of being one of the journalists whose stories moved international criminal tribunals to formally declare rape and sexual violence war crimes—and crimes against humanity.

# SYLVIA POGGIOLI

*Senior European correspondent*

**In May 1993**, the Bosnian war was in its second year. And the Serbs, who were besieging the capital Sarajevo, were under international pressure to sign a peace deal.

The self-declared Bosnian Serb Parliament was meeting in an abandoned ski resort. Its name was Paradise Valley. But the mood was tense and sinister. Members of the special elite forces—headbands on their foreheads, long knives dangling from their belts—strutted around. Foreign reporters were treated with extreme suspicion—we were all seen as enemies of the Serbs.

I was in the lobby with producer Taki Telonidis when we heard the melancholy voice of a man singing. Taki picked up a microphone and tape recorder and went looking for the voice. Seconds later, the singing suddenly stopped . . . followed by breaking glass. Taki came back with a glum look—it was clear to me that the man did not want to be recorded. And it got worse: the man, a soldier in full combat gear, stormed in and lurched over to us. He jumped up and down in uncontrolled fury, all the while waving a Kalashnikov and a long sharp knife inches away from our faces. It was an eternity before his commander arrived and calmed him down.

After an all-night "parliament" session, we filed our report and left at dawn. Of all the dangers I faced in Yugoslavia—from besieged Sarajevo to the NATO bombing of Belgrade and the fighting in Kosovo—this encounter with the irrationality of war was the most unsettling episode and the one I remember most vividly. ∎

**LEFT** Sarajevo residents walk up through the old city with water containers on May 17, 1993 (AP photo/ Rikard Lama).

# HEARING IS BELIEVING

NPR's Michael Skoler was also honored with one of journalism's highest—an Alfred I. duPont-Columbia University Award—for his coverage of the genocide in Rwanda at a time when most nations hesitated to call it genocide.

It was in the spring of 1994.

In a season celebrating the historic inauguration of Nelson Mandela as president of South Africa, in the middle of Africa, hundreds of thousands of Tutsis were being massacred by Hutus. The ethnic killing in Rwanda happened in a matter of weeks; it was all done by hand, with machetes and guns and spears; and it was on a scale so massive and gruesome that those in the outside world found it hard to grasp. Or even believe it was happening.

For NPR listeners, one story in particular made it real: Michael Skoler told of traveling through the countryside, of scenes of frightened refugees, and of boys and girls lifting their clothes to show burns and wounds made by spears. And then he came across a small church. It sat among eucalyptus and pine trees, amid the soft buzzing of crickets. Lovely, but for the dozens of bodies lying in the grass. Before he entered the church, Skoler tied a bandana on his nose and mouth. Holding a microphone, he began to relate what he saw as he walked through the door. Listeners heard birds singing overhead, but Skoler's sudden intake of breath spoke to a different sense: the smell, strong now, of death. For the next twenty-one excruciating minutes on *All Things Considered*, listeners entered a hellish world they might not have been able to imagine, but that was too vivid to ignore.

# RICHARD GONZALES
*Correspondent, San Francisco*

**In 1994**, Daniel Schorr, Ray Suarez, and I were in a studio together preparing for a special broadcast. Before going on the air, the engineer prompted us for voice check levels, and Schorr responded by saying, "Hello Bob. Hello Bob. Hello Bob." I was perplexed because I knew that the engineer's name was not Bob. I remember wondering, "OK, Dan's a broadcast legend, but what's he talking about?"

Schorr picked up on my puzzlement and said, "That was the way we would set our levels before going on air with Edward R. Murrow. We sometimes called him Bob."

I almost swallowed my tongue. I understood Schorr to be saying, "Look, boys, there is a line that runs from Murrow, me, and the old CBS News operation through to what we do here every day at NPR." It was one of those studio moments I'll never forget. ■

**RIGHT** Daniel Schorr, 1987 (photo by NPR).

"The blood is on the floor—is so thick it's dried to a kind of muddy brown dust. There are bodies," he tells us in a low voice, "scattered all over the church . . . Some lie on mattresses, some on the floor. By the altar, there are probably thirty . . . clustered around. One . . . is an infant, with parents, it seems, on either side. There's a suitcase open . . . you can see baskets, plastic water cans, combs, brushes, sandals, sneakers, tins of food, a bottle of talcum powder. . . . Above the whole scene is a small wooden statue of Christ with one hand raised."

As he passes through the church, one can hear Skoler finding it harder and harder to breathe.

# REPORTING IRAN

## JACKI LYDEN
*Contributing host/correspondent*

**In 1995**, NPR had not had a correspondent in Iran in years. In the United States, I had made a number of Iranian contacts; including the Shah's former cabinet minister for women. I truly wanted to get Iranian voices into my tape recorder; so imagine how I felt when my first interview told me that "No one here will speak to you on tape." Frankly, I broke out in hives! I could imagine all NPR's money going for naught. But then, I met one of the Ayatollah Khomeini's nephews, who opened a collar of his shirt, showed me a secret sun medallion and said "to get to the true Iranians you must consider the Zoroastrians." He meant the pre-Islamic past; code for "don't just look at the regime." It was a turning point. I met dozens of people who poured out their hopes and dreams to an American reporter: women, clerics, intellectuals, children, teachers, reformers; thirteen hours of tape. One philosopher even said: "The minute I saw Khomeini on TV, I knew we were doomed." Some of the people I met then are involved in the reform movement to this very day. When producer Davar Ardalan and I collaborated on a series after I returned, Iranians here told us they had never heard anything like this from Iran. It was a moment when people had begun to question the revolution of 1979—and they still are. ∎

**LEFT** Iranian women stand in line at the entrance to the polling station in Tehran on May 23, 1997. Urged to vote or answer to God, Iranians chose a new president in an election that marked a significant challenge to the hard-line mullahs who had ruled since the 1979 Islamic Revolution (AP photo/Darko Bandic).

## DESPITE ODDS, WOMEN'S MOVEMENT PERSISTS IN IRAN

# JACKI LYDEN
*Contributing host/correspondent*

# DAVAR IRAN ARDALAN
*Former supervising senior producer, weekend programming*

*Originally aired in February of 2009, this piece documents one of the most remarkable and under-reported stories in Iran—the strength and character of its women's movement. Through politics, literature, religion, and poetry, women's voices have at times been like roars, and, at others, like whispers of dissent. Women continue to be both targets of persecution and agents of change, and for more than a decade, NPR's Davar Ardalan and Jacki Lyden have been tracking those changes. It began in 1995 when Jacki went to Iran at a time when not many female reporters had been there.*

**I remember thinking** that no one would talk to me on tape—that no one would be brave enough to question the revolution of 1979, which so many women and Iranian students had helped bring about. Few of those young women students realized that while they may have disliked the autocracy of the Shah, his pro-Western ways included a view of women as equals. For decades, Iranian women had been unveiled, had divorce and marriage rights, had the right to choose a husband, rather than have one chosen for them, and were very visible in public life. And then, almost overnight, it changed.

### A Pro-Western Shah
Guity Ganji, a beautiful woman in her forties, took me for a hike just above Tehran's Albourz Mountains. We were hiking just past the country's infamous political prison, Evin, which is set incongruously in a beautiful valley. Ganji had been close to the Shah's female minister for women's affairs. How out of place she felt now, she said, with this hike—her moment of freedom.

"I feel sort of alienated from these people," said Ganji. "I think a lot of people feel like I do because of what's happening. [It's] especially harder for women . . . because the way we are treated, the way they behave toward us. It's aggravating. And I look at professional persons—just think if I were professional and working with men and the way they would behave toward you. And they don't look at you at all."

### Return of the Veil
That was a feeling any Western woman could understand, especially one trying to conduct interviews in headscarves with earphones on. What was somewhat harder to understand was how the Islamic Republic had co-opted the revolution so that now women had to live in black scarves and head-to-toe gowns.

In a real sense, the Shah had been forcing traditionalists in Iran into modernity, causing a deep clash of culture. By encouraging women, even his own wife, to go about unveiled at public functions, the Shah was handing the Shia clergy an issue every traditional Muslim elder could defend: Women should be veiled.

When the veil came back, for all those Iranian modern women—and there were legions of them in the professional classes—it wasn't so much about wearing a piece of cloth as it was about the abnegation of self. Perhaps no voice expressed it better than that of Azar Nafisi, an Iranian professor.

### "Whispers of Dissent"
I met her in 1995 in a university classroom in Tehran. Today, Nafisi is an internationally renowned writer, the author of *Reading Lolita in Tehran* and one of Iran's best known women in exile. As a professor, she used Western writers such as Nabokov as a way to challenge autocratic thinking.

Now living in Washington, D.C., Nafisi says women remain for her at the forefront of the cultural struggle within Iran even though her own dissent, and that of thousands like her, was increasingly repressed by the new regime after the revolution.

"It is very unreal, going back thirty years ago to the way these whispers of defense, these whispers of dissent were articulated," said Nafisi. "I was one of the dissenters. I was very, very active in the student movement here. We were demonstrating against the Shah. . . . We were asking for the overthrow of the regime, and among ourselves—those, for example, who were religious, those who were Marxist, those who were nationalists—there was a polarization."

Nafisi devoted much of her twenties in America to political movements dedicated to abolishing the monarchy in Iran, which was seen as a puppet of the United States. She was typical of the young student abroad, and Iran sent many young women abroad. Other young Iranian women were recruited into joining communist and noncommunist guerrilla groups. But a far greater number were uneducated, lower-class women who participated in street demonstrations in 1978 and 1979, answering the call of the Ayatollah Khomeini to demonstrate against tyranny.

By 1979, the pro-Western Shah was sick with cancer and on a plane to Egypt. Of all the groups that had opposed him—women, nationalists, Marxists—no group won hearts and minds like the Islamists.

The new regime under the Ayatollah Khomeini executed thousands of people. Women went from being judges and lawyers to being non-entities, if they were lucky.

## Repeal of the Family Protection Law

One of the women who never went home again after the Revolution is Mahnaz Afkhami, the Shah's former minister for women's affairs. Under the Shah, she'd worked for women's rights and helped push through the Family Protection Law. That made her a post-revolutionary target. To go back to Iran meant death, yet she never gave up working for women's rights in her homeland.

"People, individual women, are feeling that they need to assert themselves as individuals," said Afkhami. "They need to have a role, they need to have a say, both in what they want to be and how they want to lead their lives, and how they want to relate to other members of their family and their society. It's not necessarily the same answer for everyone."

The Family Protection Law was repealed in 1979. That meant women, among other things, had no right to divorce. For a time, women's voices were banned from the radio, and female singers were barred from television. Family planning was abolished and the birthrate soared, straining the economy. But Iranian women never really resigned to this. By 1997, almost twenty years after the revolution, women were demanding change.

## "I Won't Be Silent"

It wasn't just secular female intellectuals who wanted reform. I met Azam Talehgani in 1997. The daughter of a prominent ayatollah, she was fifty-eight and ran a settlement house for poor women. Talehgani had decided to run for president, even though she said she knew the Ruling Council of Guardians would never choose her—a woman.

"Let them be silent. I won't be silent," said Talehgani. "And even if I remain silent, the women won't be silent. I can't tell you how many phone calls I've received in the past few days of people thanking me for speaking out and demanding that woman be considered as presidential candidates. And I tell them that our government officials have been put on notice and our movement will continue."

Another woman who would not be silent was Shahla Lahiji, a publisher who would eventually go to prison for peacefully pushing back. She wrote stories in which she demanded equal rights for women. By the 1990s, the Iranian state had reversed itself—family planning clinics distributed contraception.

"Ten years ago, we couldn't talk about women rights as well as we can talk about this," said Lahiji. "Maybe it is the result of our struggle, which was not with any violence, but it was daily, like bees, like ants."

Women once again rose to become lawyers and investigating judges—women like Mehrangiz Kar. But she, too, would spend time in prison.

"Before, it used to be said the laws on the books were like revelations from God and therefore not subject to » change," said Kar. "But in the last year, there has been more dialogue in every aspect of the society about a need for change. We are hopeful that this will be a good sign toward more moderation."

### "Those Who Wish Them Cloistered"
But of those who tried to bring awareness to the plight of women trying to create a civil space for themselves in a theocracy, no one attracted as much attention as Shirin Ebadi.

Ebadi, a human rights lawyer, received the Nobel Peace Prize in 2003. At the ceremony in Oslo, Norway, she talked not just about women's rights, but about Iran's ancient tradition of human rights.

"I am an Iranian, a descendant of Cyrus the Great, the very emperor who proclaimed at the pinnacle of power 2,500 years ago that he would not reign over the people if they did not wish it," said Ebadi, "and promised not to force any person to change his religion or faith and guaranteed freedom for all."

In 2006, she published a book in English called *Iran Awakening*.

"It is not religion that binds women, but the selective dictates of those who wish them cloistered," she wrote. "That belief, along with the belief that change in Iran must come peacefully and from within, has underpinned my work."

Ebadi, whom I had met during my 1995 trip to Iran, advocates moderation and the use of Islamic law to reform Iran's system. She believes in peaceful, nonviolent change from within. She had an increasingly educated class of young people to draw on—by the time her book came out, more than half of all university students in Iran were women. In applied physics at Azad University, 70 percent were female. The post-revolutionary young woman was an educated young woman.

This belief in peaceful resistance was underscored by the "One Million Signatures Campaign." The idea was that women and men from all walks of life would collect a million signatures to educate women about their rights and to demand changes to laws that discriminated against them. When they demonstrated in Iran in June 2006, some seventy were arrested.

Perhaps because Ebadi had become such a powerful symbol, it was almost inevitable the government would crack down on her. Ebadi has experienced intensified harassment. In December, her office dedicated to the defense of human rights was shut down and her computers seized.

Human Rights Watch says it fears for her life. With the ascendancy of the conservatives, especially since the election of President Mahmoud Ahmadinejad in 2005, where is the Iranian women's movement today? To Azar Nafisi, it is simply a force that cannot be defeated, no matter who is in power in Iran.

"You see what no regime can do is take away from their people the past, the memory of what they had achieved," said Nafisi. "What the Iranian women had achieved became a weapon to fight for the rights that were taken away from them. And that is why so many women go back to the past.

"They talk about the women's organization that was created. They talk about writing books. These new women who are now participating in these regressive laws in Iran are also writing about women senators at that time. They are talking about the minister for women's affairs at that time. They're interviewing her on their Web sites. You know, I think the past is creating the way to the future, and that is why the women are so much at the forefront."

I have no doubt that Iranian women will keep singing, keep shaping the future, simply staying alive and resisting. Always resisting. ∎

**ABOVE** Long-time
collaborators
Davar Ardalan
(left) and Jacki
Lyden in 2002
(photo by Bill
O'Leary).

# LOOKING WEST

Throughout the '90s, NPR's foreign coverage grew as it attracted grants from, among others, the Carnegie Corporation, the MacArthur Foundation, the Ford Foundation, and the German Marshall Fund of the United States. As Cadi Simon put it, "We expanded because we could."

It was also in the '90s that NPR began to cast its gaze west.

NPR had long had reporters based in the West, individually and in bureaus in Los Angeles,

San Francisco, and Seattle. But many of the stories coming out of this side of the country were regional features. Then suddenly, in the early part of the decade, there was news—big news: the police beating of Rodney King, then the trial, and the riots that followed; the trial of the rioters who, on live national television, dragged trucker Reginald Denny from his rig and beat him nearly to death with a brick; the million-dollar wildfires that burned through the hills of Oakland, Laguna Beach, and Malibu (commentator Patt Morrison would later quote Shirley MacLaine, who, evacuating her seaside home amid one disaster, quipped, "The area code for Malibu should be changed to 911"). Then, there was the earthquake in Los Angeles and the low-speed chase and murder trial of O.J. Simpson. Much of the news was sensational, and introduced the world to California's four seasons: fire, flood, earthquake, and drought. Disasters—human-made and natural—arrived in quick succession.

So, too, did political issues that would spread across the nation in years to come. Probably the most prescient: California voters passed a proposition restricting services to illegal immigrants, amid growing resentment as their numbers increased. By the early '90s, Los Angeles was well on its way to becoming a Latino city, with Spanish a first language for many residents.

In late 1993, reporter Mandalit del Barco was hired away from member station WNYC in New York to NPR's LA Bureau, fresh from covering the first attack on the World Trade Center. "The National Desk editor said he wanted someone who could speak Spanish," she remembers. "Barely a month later, I was in my apartment, still surrounded by unopened moving boxes, when I was shaken awake—along with the rest of LA—at about 4:30 A.M. The walls seemed to turn to liquid. I jumped out of bed, ran to a doorway, phoned the news desk, and went on the air live, describing the little I knew of the 6.7 earthquake." That was January 1994, when reporters would find themselves working for the next few weeks behind yellow plastic banners, indicating the damaged building containing the LA Bureau was off limits—to everyone else.

**RIGHT** Mandalit del Barco in the field, 1993 (photo by C.M. Hardt).

For del Barco, it never let up. A year later, she was covering a devastating mudslide along the Pacific Coast Highway. Transportation officials directed her to park her car and then ride with rescue workers to where she could interview victims. When she got back, she was interviewing a supervisor when she glanced toward where she'd parked her car and "discovered, to my horror, that my car was waist deep in mud. Mud that had carried it far down the road. My tape recorder was still rolling when I gasped, 'Oh my GOD!'—a response that made it on the air the next morning." At some point, a photojournalist snapped a shot, "and by the end of the week, my little hatchback had become the 'poster car'

for the mudslides. It was featured in *Newsweek* and the *New York Times* and on the cover of the *LA Weekly*." Since the hatchback belonged to del Barco, she was on the hook for the damage, but, she remembers, "NPR sent me flowers."

In the early '90s, NPR bought a building for its headquarters in Washington, DC (and it managed to move its entire news operation in a single day, coming on air at 6 A.M. with *Morning Edition* without missing a deadline). By the end of the decade, NPR management would launch a search for a building in greater Los Angeles, to create an "NPR West." NPR had come to realize that the West was rich in stories, listeners, and funders.

## 1992: ETERNITY

# BARRY GORDEMER

*Senior producer,* Morning Edition

**It was the first night of rioting** after a jury acquitted four Los Angeles Police officers of the beating of motorist Rodney King, which had been caught on videotape. NPR's Ina Jaffe was on the streets of LA recording sounds, voices, and church services. Around three in the morning, she began feeding snippets of audio back to Washington for her report on *Morning Edition*. I, along with three other producers, scrambled to assemble her piece in time for the lead segment at 6:10 A.M.

In those days, we put pieces together using reel-to-reel tape decks. Each reel was about the size of a medium cheese pizza. Ina Jaffe's voice would be on one reel, another would contain interview clips, another, street ambience, a fourth would contain music. A studio engineer would blend or "mix" the four reels together to create the final piece. Normally this is done ahead of time. This piece would have to be mixed live.

Each of us worked on a different section of the story. With about two minutes to go before airtime, three of us sprinted into the studio. The fourth producer would not have his section ready until after the piece began.

At 6:10 A.M., *Morning Edition* host Bob Edwards began reading the introduction to Ina's story. "Standby on one," I

said, meaning get ready to fire off the first tape deck. When Bob said "Ina Jaffe reports" I shouted, "Hit it!" Another producer in the room told the engineer to fade up the street sounds on tape deck two when the first clip of tape ended. He stood behind the engineer, knees bent with his right arm extended in front of him, his palm facing the floor. "Ready to sweep up the sound," he said. "Aaannd bring it up!" On the word "up" his knees straightened and his palm turned toward the ceiling as his arm rose quickly, yet gracefully, over his head.

Just then, the fourth producer burst into the studio with his portion of the piece, but he dropped the reel on the floor. It rolled on its edge, unspooling the tape like a ball of yarn. Somehow the engineer wound it back on the reel just as part one of the piece was ending. "Hit it," I shouted. But the tape deck hesitated. Every eye in the room met every other eye in the room. I couldn't breathe. A beat later, it started to play.

When the show was over, I listened to the recording of the broadcast. There was only about a second of dead air before the tape deck kicked in. But in the studio, time had stood still.

I still replay that moment, that second, that eternity over and over in my mind. I've had lots of other eternities since then. But that one lasted the longest and the shortest. ■

## TRANSCRIPT EXCERPT
### *ALL THINGS CONSIDERED*

**SHOW DATE:**
*1994-10-28*
**CAT. TITLE:**
Bell Curve *Book*
*Assertions Disputed*

*Barack Obama, then a prominent civil rights lawyer in Chicago, comments on Charles Murray's controversial book,* The Bell Curve*, with Noah Adams.*

**BARACK OBAMA, Commentator:** Charles Murray is inviting America down a dangerous path.

**NOAH ADAMS, Host:** Civil rights lawyer, Barack Obama.

**OBAMA:** The idea that inferior genes account for the problems of the poor in general, and blacks in particular, isn't new, of course. Racial supremacists have been using IQ tests to support their theories since the turn of the century. The arguments against such dubious science aren't new either. Scientists have repeatedly told us that genes don't vary much from one race to another, and psychologists have pointed out the role that language and other cultural barriers can play in depressing minority test scores, and no one disputes that children whose mothers smoke crack when they're pregnant are going to have developmental problems.

Now, it shouldn't take a genius to figure out that with early intervention such problems can be prevented. But Mr. Murray isn't interested in prevention. He's interested in pushing a very particular policy agenda, specifically, the elimination of affirmative action and welfare programs aimed at the poor. With one finger out to the political wind, Mr. Murray has apparently decided that white America is ready for a return to good old-fashioned racism so long as it's artfully packaged and can admit for exceptions like Colin Powell. It's easy to see the basis for Mr. Murray's calculations. After watching their income stagnate or decline over the past decade, the majority of Americans are in an ugly mood and deeply resent any advantages, real or perceived, that minorities may enjoy.

I happen to think Mr. Murray's wrong, not just in his estimation of black people, but in his estimation of the broader American public. But I do think Mr. Murray's right about the growing distance between the races. The violence and despair of the inner city are real. So's the problem of street crime. The longer we allow these problems to fester, the easier it becomes for white America to see all blacks as menacing and for black America to see all whites as racist. To close that gap, we're going to have to do more than denounce Mr. Murray's book. We're going to have to take concrete and deliberate action. For blacks, that means taking greater responsibility for the state of our own communities. Too many of us use white racism as an excuse for self-defeating behavior. Too many of our young people think education is a white thing and that the values of hard work and discipline and self-respect are somehow outdated.

That being said, it's time for all of us, and now I'm talking about the larger American community, to acknowledge that we've never even come close to providing equal opportunity to the majority of black children. Real opportunity would mean quality prenatal care for all women and well-funded and innovative public schools for all children. Real opportunity would mean a job at a living wage for everyone who was willing to work, jobs that can return some structure and dignity to people's lives and give inner-city children something more than a basketball rim to shoot for. In the short run, such ladders of opportunity are going to cost more, not less, than either welfare or affirmative action. But, in the long run, our investment should pay off handsomely. That we fail to make this investment is just plain stupid. It's not the result of an intellectual deficit. It's the result of a moral deficit.

**ADAMS:** Barack Obama is a civil rights lawyer and writer. He lives in Chicago. ∎

**LEFT** President Barack Obama at the NPR 2007 presidential debate (photo by David Lieneman/NPR).

# ZEROING
# OUT
# PUBLIC

Even as NPR's reach extended to every corner of the United States, and listeners—in polls—identified themselves almost equally as liberal and conservative, public radio's early reputation as a bastion of liberalism came back to haunt it.

In the '80s, conservatives dubbed it "Radio Sandinista." And in 1994, the "Republican Revolution" took aim at NPR, and PBS, by pushing to defund the Corporation for Public Broadcasting. Newt Gingrich led the charge. He had just been elected Speaker of the House for a Congress with both houses controlled by Republicans for the first time in forty years. In early 1995, he had this to say in a luncheon speech on Capitol Hill, as reported by the *Washington Post*, "I don't understand why they call it public broadcasting. As far as I'm concerned there's nothing public about it. It's an elitist enterprise. Rush Limbaugh

is public broadcasting!" In brief, he intended to "zero out" funding for the CPB.

There was talk of dismantling public broadcasting by selling off its valuable spots on the dial, and on the television spectrum, to private broadcast companies. However, even as Speaker Gingrich was promising to prevent any new money from being appropriated to the CPB, NPR was receiving a tiny fraction of its funding directly from that source. A substantial percentage of the budget came from dues paid by hundreds of member stations, and many member stations depended on grants from the CPB. So NPR was fighting for them, too.

Slashing those funds would be devastating for the smaller stations—many of which brought public radio to rural areas and areas not served by big city newspapers. NPR's president, Del Lewis, along with the presidents of the CPB,

**ABOVE** Linda Wertheimer and Mara Liasson interview President Clinton at the White House on December 22, 1993 (photo courtesy of the William J. Clinton Presidential Library).

PBS, and other public radio groups were quick to respond, making the case on Capitol Hill. To a great extent, listeners and viewers made their own case: Public broadcasting had finally become, for them, an invaluable service. Many testimonials, letters, and op-ed pieces later—the effort to defund the CPB failed.

Years later, Newt Gingrich himself said that he had become a contributor to NPR. "On my way to work I listen to NPR and appreciate" it, he said in a 2003 speech, adding, "NPR is a lot less to the left . . . or I've mellowed. Or some combination of the two." (If Gingrich was listening to NPR on his morning commute, he would've been hearing *Morning Edition,* making him one of the many new listeners, who discovered NPR's morning magazine, along with *All Things Considered,* as NPR approached its fortieth anniversary.)

"

## I don't understand why they call it public broadcasting. As far as I'm concerned, there's nothing public about it.

*Newt Gingrich, in a 1995 speech*

# PUTTING FUN ON THE RADIO— OR NOT

"

**It had already won a Peabody! And still they wouldn't say 'Yes' to the show! They don't have to raise money. They don't have to get stations. I had the highest honor in broadcasting. What else could I do?**

*Ira Glass on NPR's decision to pass on* This American Life

Every decade, NPR has bungled something big. In the '90s, that turned out to be Ira Glass and *This American Life*. Ira Glass's radio show is, of course, one of the great successes of public radio. The stories he assembles are profound and witty, winsome and ironic, conversational and subtle, sometimes all at once. And they are *not* brought to you by National Public Radio.

Not that Ira didn't try.

"I started working for NPR when I was eighteen, in 1978. So by 1995, I'd done everything." Glass had been a producer on *All Things Considered*. He'd hosted the weekend version of *All Things Considered* and *Talk of the Nation*. Plus, he'd produced several episodic series, spending entire years in Chicago public schools, where he fashioned story lines and characters based on real students and teachers. His mingling of straight journalism with the quirky, sometimes funny, sometimes sad, and always unexpected side moments—not necessarily on-point interactions usually left out of a story—was widely regarded as bringing something entirely original to storytelling on the radio. This was all done for NPR, by someone who had "been there since I was a kid." Then, in 1995, Ira Glass came to his longtime

public radio home and offered them not a series but an entire show. He'd created it for WBEZ in Chicago, and he called it *This American Life*.

Looking back on this years later, Ira Glass was still shaking his head. NPR passed on the chance to distribute *This American Life*, even though, right then in the mid-1990s, the network had created something called the programming board. At the very moment Glass approached NPR, the programming board was looking to create and distribute new shows, especially on the weekends, where listenership was weak.

And it was hoping to attract a younger audience.

Glass had already successfully placed *This American Life* on 110 stations, including 7 in the top ten markets. The show was fully funded, and it had been honored in its first year with a Peabody Award. As Ira emphasizes, "It had already won a Peabody!" He continues, "And still they wouldn't say 'Yes' to the show! They don't have to raise money. They don't have to get stations. I had the highest honor in broadcasting. What else could I do?"

Turns out, there was an answer to that. A crazy one, really. Here is what the programming board decided: *This American Life* would be a really great show, if only Ira wasn't the host. "To them, and I'd know them all since I came to NPR, I was just a kid. Part of what was happening was that—because I'd been a teenager there—it was hard to take me seriously."

It was just the sort of social dynamic Ira Glass would go on to mine in many of his episodes. All of them distributed by, as Ira puts it, "NPR's archrival" PRI—Public Radio International.

TRANSCRIPT EXCERPT
## *MORNING EDITION*

**SHOW DATE:**
*1992-12-23*
**CAT. TITLE:**
*Elf at 34th St. Macy's
Reads from Diary*

**RENÉE MONTAGNE, HOST:** This is *Morning Edition*. I'm Renée Montagne.

In addition to whatever goes on at the North Pole, there is a Santa Claus industry in thousands of stores and malls across America. David Sedaris needed a job and went to work in the Santa business as an elf in Macy's Department Store of 34th Street in New York. These are excerpts from his diaries. His elf name was Crumpet.

**DAVID SEDARIS (MACY'S DEPARTMENT STORE'S ELF):** I wear green velvet knickers, a forest-green velvet smock and a perky little hat decorated with spangles. This is my work uniform. I have spent the last several days sitting in a crowded, windowless Macy's classroom undergoing the first phases of elf training. You can be an entrance elf, a watercooler elf, a bridge elf, train elf, maze elf, island elf, magic-window elf, usher elf, cash register elf, or exit elf. We were given a demonstration of various positions in action acted out by returning elves who were so on-stage and goofy that it made me a little sick to my stomach. I don't know that I could look anyone in the eye and exclaim, "Oh,

my goodness, I think I see Santa," or, "Can you close your eyes and make a very special Christmas wish?" Everything these elves say seems to have an exclamation point on the end of it. It makes one's mouth hurt to speak with such forced merriment. It embarrasses me to hear people talk this way. I think I'll be a low-key sort of elf.

Twenty-two thousand people came to see Santa today, and not all of them were well-behaved. Today I witnessed fistfights and vomiting and magnificent tantrums. The back hallway was jammed with people. There was a line for Santa and a line for the women's bathroom. And one woman, after asking me a thousand questions already, asked, "Which is the line for the women's bathroom?" And I shouted that I thought it was the line with all the women in it. And she said, "I'm going to have you fired." I had two people say that to me today. "I'm going to have you fired." "Go ahead; be my guest." I'm wearing a green velvet costume; it doesn't get any worse than this. Who do these people think they are? "I'm going to have you fired." And I want to lean over and say, "I'm going to have you killed."

The overall cutest elf is a fella from Queens named Richie. His elf name is Snowball, and he tends to ham it up with the children, sometimes tumbling down the path to Santa's house. I generally gag when elves get that cute, but Snowball is hands-down adorable. You want to put him in your pocket. Yesterday Snowball and I worked as Santa elves, and I got excited when he started saying things like, "I'd follow you to Santa's house any day Crumpet." It made me dizzy, this flirtation. By mid-afternoon I was running into walls. By late afternoon, Snowball had cooled down. By the end of our shift, we were in the bathroom changing our clothes and all of a sudden we were surrounded by five Santas and three other elves. All of them were guys that Snowball had been flirting with. Snowball just leads elves on—elves and Santas.

Today a child told Santa that he wanted his dead father back and a complete set of Teenage Mutant Ninja Turtles. Everyone loves those turtles. A child came to Santa this morning, and his mother said, "All right, Jason, all right, tell Santa what you want. Tell him what you want." Jason said, "I want Proctin & Gamble to stop animal testing." The mother said, "Procter, Jason, that's Procter & Gamble. And what do they do to animals? Do they torture animals

Jason? Is that what they do?" Jason said, "Yes, they torture." He was maybe six years old.

This morning I worked as an exit elf telling people in a loud voice, "This way out of Santaland." A woman was standing at one of the cash registers paying for her pictures while her son lay beneath her, kicking and heaving, having a tantrum. The woman said, "Riley, if you don't start behaving yourself, Santa's not going to bring you any of those toys you asked for." The child said: "He is, too, going to bring me toys, liar. He already told me." The woman grabbed my arm and said, "You there, elf, tell Riley here that if he doesn't start behaving immediately, then Santa's going to change his mind and bring him coal for Christmas." I said that Santa changed his policy and no longer traffics in coal. Instead, if you're bad he comes to your house and steals things. I told Riley that if he didn't behave himself, Santa was going to take away his TV and all of his electrical appliances and leave him in the dark. "All your appliances, Riley, including the refrigerator. Your food is going to spoil and smell bad. You're going to wish you never even heard the name *Santa*." The woman got a worried look on her face and said, "All right, that's enough." I said, "He's going to take your car and your furniture and all of your towels and blankets and leave you with nothing." The mother said, "No, that's enough, really."

This afternoon I was stuck being photo elf with Santa Santa. During most days, there's a slow period when you sit around the house and talk to Santa, and most of them were nice guys, and we sit around and laugh. But Santa Santa takes himself a bit too seriously. I asked him where he lives, Brooklyn or Manhattan, and he said, "Why I live at the North Pole with Mrs. Claus." I asked what he does the rest of the year and he said, "I make toys for all the children." He actually recited "The Night Before Christmas," and it was just the two of us in the house. No children, just us. He says, "Oh, little elf, little elf, straighten up those mantle toys for Santa." I reminded him that I have a name, Crumpet, and then I straightened up the stuffed animals.

Santa Santa has an elaborate little act for the children. He'll talk to them and give a hearty chuckle and ring his bells, and then he asked them to name their favorite Christmas carol. Santa then asked if they'll sing it for him. The children are shy and don't want to sing out loud, so Santa says, "Oh, little elf, little elf, help young Brenda here sing that favorite carol of hers. Late in the afternoon, a child said she didn't know what her favorite Christmas carol was. Santa Santa suggested "Away in a Manger." The girl agreed to it, but didn't want to sing because she didn't know the words. Santa Santa said, "Oh, little elf, little elf, come sing 'Away in the Manger' for us. It didn't seem fair that I should have to solo, so I sang it the way Billie Holiday might have sang if she'd put out a Christmas album.

[Singing] "Away in a manger, no crib for bed, the little Lord Jesus lay down his sweet head." Santa Santa did not allow me to finish.

This evening I was sent to be a photo elf. Once a child starts crying, it's all over. The parents had planned to send these pictures as cards or store them away until the child is grown and can lie, claiming to remember the experience. Tonight I saw a woman slap and shake her crying child. She yelled, "Rachel, get on that man's lap and smile, or I'll give you something to cry about." And then she sat Rachel on Santa's lap, and I took the picture, which supposedly means, on paper, that everything is exactly the way it's supposed to be, that everything is snowy and wonderful. It's not about the child or Santa or Christmas or anything, but the parent's idea of a world they cannot make work for them.

**MONTAGNE:** David Sedaris worked as an elf in Macy's last year and the year before. He now cleans apartments in New York. His *Santaland Diaries* were produced by Ira Glass. It's eleven minutes before the hour. ∎

**LEFT** David Sedaris in 1982.

# DOUG BERMAN

*Esteemed executive producer,* Car Talk *and* Wait Wait . . . Don't Tell Me!

**It probably won't surprise you** to learn that *Car Talk* began by accident.

Back in the mid-1970s, the programming at WBUR in Boston was described as "eclectic." This was an understatement. My memory is unclear, but I think an average afternoon consisted of "The Welder Show," "The Vegan Show," "The Taxidermist Show," and the "Vegan Welder Taxidermist Show." It was that kind of place.

In the fall of 1977, Victor Wheatman, the program director at Boston's WBUR Radio, decided to spend an hour talking about car repair. He somehow reached Tom and Ray Magliozzi at their little-known, funky garage in Cambridge and asked them to join a panel of seven expert mechanics. Tom agreed, figuring it would be good for business. Ray demurred, not wanting to miss his transcendental meditation class.

When Tom showed up at the appointed time, he discovered he was in fact a panel of one. But he gamely answered the questions that were phoned in as best he could, and when the hour was over, the host said, "Gee, that was great. Want to come back next week?" And Tom said, "Sure, but can I bring my brother?"

As the legend has been handed down, the brothers arrived the following week to find that Wheatman had been fired during the intervening seven days. And in place of the kind of adult supervision you'd expect at a major metropolitan broadcast powerhouse was a scribbled little note that said "Have fun, and try to watch your language."

The guys tried to take it seriously, but eventually, their natural instincts won over, and they figured, "if we're not getting paid, we might as well goof around!"

Oddly, the resulting decade of benign neglect was, I believe, what allowed Tom and Ray to become entirely comfortable on the air, and completely and utterly themselves. Since no one had ever come down on them for saying exactly what they thought, in the exact language in which they thought it, that's what "being on the radio" was to them. They never learned how to do "stuffy public radio announcer."

So when I joined up with them as producer ten years later, all it took were a few minor tweaks to get the show ready for its NPR debut (make the calls shorter than forty-five minutes; teach the guys to insert the phrase "I don't know, but I wouldn't be surprised if" in front of their most libelous allegations; and occasionally translate words like "khakis" into "car keys" for those outside of Boston). ∎

Postscript by Tom Magliozzi: *Dougie's being modest about his role. I mean, don't get me wrong; he didn't do much! But he did more than that.*

**LEFT** Scott Simon gets a driving lesson from the *Car Talk* guys, Ray and Tom Magliozzi (NPR photo).

## IAN CHILLAG

*Former producer for* Fresh Air

**Not long after I started at *Fresh Air*,** there was a party honoring executive producer Danny Miller's 25th anniversary with the show. I was a kid. I'd just turned 25, and I joked it was possible I was born the day he started, that maybe my mom was listening to the first show he ever produced and it was so terrible it drove her into labor. The joke didn't land with everybody, and, at the end of the party, I realized somebody had misunderstood me and thought Danny was in fact my father.

My first memory of the show is my actual father picking me up from school and driving me home with it on. We pulled into our garage, and it wasn't over yet. He wanted to sit there and listen. I couldn't even tell you who Terry was talking to, but I had just learned about carbon monoxide poisoning, and I remember thinking this radio show was going to kill us both.

This is all to say: the show had long been a functioning and special thing by the time I got there, and I came in as the youngest producer by a few years. The machines on which the producers were cutting tape were, if memory serves, steam powered, and I didn't know how to use them. And upstairs there was an archive of tapes with more amazing 55-minute interviews than I had memories in my head.

**RIGHT** Terry Gross, host of *Fresh Air*, and Ray Suarez, host of *Talk of the Nation*, in June 1996 (photo by Jennifer Bishop).

But even if you are the youngster at *Fresh Air*, it's hard to feel like the wide-eyed and youthful one when you work around Terry. She's like a kid—a mature kid with a weirdly comprehensive knowledge of jazz and the *Great American Songbook*, sure. But she's kidlike, in the way she's eager to wake up and see how much she can learn that day. And in the way she doesn't care if it's a smart, Peabody-Award-winning-Terry-Gross-kind-of-a-question, or a dumb one; she just wants you to tell her the answer. Even if you were born the day Danny and Terry started their show, there's something about them that makes you wish you could get to be as young as they are, someday. ∎

# CREATING SHOWS THAT STICK

NPR had better luck creating a couple of new shows of its own in the '90s. When talk shows took off in commercial radio, NPR decided it needed to put one on the air. Still, *Talk of the Nation* came into being rather organically. As it happened, science correspondent Ira Flatow wanted to start a science roundup—say, two hours, at the end of the week.

Then news director Bill Buzenberg remembers making a deal with Flatow: "If you can raise the money for 'Science Friday,' I'll find funding for the other four days." Not a bad bet, because, like foreign coverage, science reporting at NPR was

always able to find generous support. When the funding came through, the network held a contest to give the new talk show a name. Producer John Ogulnik won the grand prize—lunch, on NPR—for coming up with a name based on *The New Yorker*'s "Talk of the Town." *Talk of the Nation*, or *TOTN*, as it was known in the building, premiered with John Hockenberry as host. He left soon after, and the respected Chicago journalist Ray Suarez took over the host chair in 1993 and held it through the rest of the decade.

It was also during this time that NPR was finally able to tap the creative, theatrical spirit of

**ABOVE**
Ira Flatow interviews penguins in Antarctica in 1979 (photo by Katherine Bouton).

Chicago, with a show called *Wait Wait . . . Don't Tell Me!* The key may have been that its executive producer worked entirely outside of DC. Doug Berman created *Wait Wait . . .* from Boston, where he produced NPR's other beloved, and slightly lunatic, production—*Car Talk*. Host Peter Sagal likes to think of Berman as "the pastry chef on the public radio menu."

But Berman did have quite a challenge, says Sagal, "It was a news quiz that offered no real prize, and a comedy show produced by a company not known, shall we say, for hilarity." Berman also had to make some tough decisions

soon after *Wait Wait . . .* got off to a rough start, beginning with signing up a new host. This is how Peter Sagal, a self-described "obscure playwright and screenwriter living in Brooklyn," packed his car and moved to Chicago.

From here Sagal picks up the story:

*"One of the first things we did was to have an existential crisis, in the form of a meeting. All of us—myself, senior producer David Greene, and producers Diantha Parker and Leslie Fuller, with Doug Berman joining us by phone from Boston—sat around a table at the offices of*

WBEZ and considered the question: What did we want to be? Should we remake the show into more of a serious news quiz, with tough questions and real prizes, so that listeners could find ways to feel smug—or, I guess, smugger, this being public radio—or . . . should we just use the whole news quiz concept as a flimsy excuse to make rude jokes, take cheap shots, and just generally enjoy ourselves until somebody stopped us?

I won't tell you what we decided. Have to maintain some mystery.

Having solved our existential crisis, we had to actually figure out how to make the show better. Some elements of the show would remain the same.

We would have our panel—in studio at that time—and listeners on the phone answer ques-

tions. At one point, our panelists would present three news stories, only one of which was true.

And of course, there would be Carl Kasell, who had always been a part of the show, and we all knew, always would be. But how best to use him? To that point, Carl had been a kind of master of ceremonies, intoning lots of hopefully funny bits of narration to move the show along. But it occurred to us that as funny as Carl was, he was at his funniest when he wasn't trying to be funny . . . such as, for instance, when he was trying to imitate various newsmakers. And thus was born "Who's Carl This Time?"

Most talk shows have celebrity guests, and we figured we'd better follow along, but we didn't want to ask our celebrity guests the usual kinds of questions, and second, we couldn't think of a

# PAULA POUNDSTONE

*Standup comedian, author, and panelist on*
Wait Wait . . . Don't Tell Me!

**My first NPR performing experience** was on Garrison Keillor's show. He was recording at a theater in New York. I arrived early and sat in the empty theater to watch the rehearsal. I didn't feel nearly educated enough to be on an NPR show, but it didn't seem I had enough time to earn a quick college degree before he saw me sitting there.

Even Garrison's rehearsals are brilliant. He was working on a scene with two or three other cast members. That great band of his oompahed and clanged behind him. He had written a fake commercial for a nonexistent smash Broadway play named *Squash* that sponsored the show, and he had given his foley artist, Tom Keith, the task of finding a signature sound to identify *Squash*. Tom worked stage left making a mouth sound into a microphone. It was a squishy sound, with spit, lip, and cheek vibration. It was the kind of sound I was repeatedly sent to the hall for perfecting during class in the second grade. Tom "plff"ed and "phlpp"ed out across the theater.

Garrison appeared to be deeply involved in the scene he was rehearsing, but he stopped every few minutes, after a *Squash* noise ("pwalsh"), and said, "Almost."

I was hooked. Who wouldn't be?

In 2001, I was lucky enough to become a panelist on *Wait Wait . . . Don't Tell Me!*, NPR's weekly news quiz show.

Our listeners tend to make a hobby of statistics, and many have made note that I don't win a lot. They'll proudly tell me that they were listening on the night that I won, as if they're in possession of a rare coin or an early edition of a Darwin book with a misprint where he accidentally claims we descended from apps. It's true; I don't win a

lot, but let me just say the other panelists were born into the world knowing more about current events than I was. If that's not cheating, I don't know what is.

On the tenth anniversary of *Wait Wait . . .*, we had a wonderful dinner in Chicago. Since the show has only three panelists at a time, we had never been together all at once. We sat at round tables nibbling our appetizers while the producers read us some factoids they'd assembled about the show and its progress—how many stations it started out on, how many stations it's on now, etc.

Then, they mentioned how many times someone had gotten zero correct answers during the "Lightening Round." They said there'd only been one. I laughed with the others and looked around the table for the poor soul who had such an off night. It turns out it was me. It had only been about two weeks before, too, and I had totally forgotten. It's a good thing they didn't ask me about it during the lightening round. ∎

**ABOVE** *Wait Wait . . . Don't Tell Me!* panelists Adam Felber, Paula Poundstone, and Roy Blount, Jr. (photo by Don Hall).

**FIGURE 4**

# WAIT WAIT . . . THAT'S NOT MY JOB!

"Not My Job" is a game on *Wait Wait . . . Don't Tell Me!* where a celebrity guest takes a three-question multiple-choice quiz on a topic unrelated to the celebrity's field of expertise. Top stories include:

**1 BRIAN WILLIAMS**
**YOU ARE THE WORST ACT EVER TO PLAY THIS STAGE** The NBC news anchor and Florence Foster Jenkins, a famously bad singer.

**2 LUCY LAWLESS**
**WE DIDN'T HAVE THE CHANCE TO SAY THANKS** The actress and great American innovators who died recently.

**3 THEY MIGHT BE GIANTS**
**YOU MIGHT BE GIANTS, BUT HE REALLY WAS A GIANT** The musicians and Andre Rene Roussimoff, a.k.a. Andre the Giant.

**4 ASHLEY JUDD**
**THAT PRIZE WAS RIGHTFULLY MINE! MINE!** The actress and the history of Nobel Prizes.

**5 MARK HALPERIN**
**YOU'RE THE ONE AND ONLY—AND WE DO MEAN ONLY—PRINCE OF SEBORGA** The author and a man who spent his life trying to convince the world that Seborga, his little Italian village, was an independent kingdom.

**6 JASON SCHWARTZMAN**
**TURNS OUT, MR. PRESIDENT, THE CHINESE DO HAVE A PHRASE FOR IT, BUT YOU WOULDN'T HAVE WANTED TO SAY IT** The actor and Asian idioms that President Obama might find useful in his next trip to Asia.

**7 STEVEN CHU**
**YOU ARE THE LOSING-EST BUNCH OF LOSERS IN THE HISTORY OF LOSING** The Nobel Prize–winning physicist and The Washington Generals, one of the biggest losers in all of sports.

**8 KELLY SLATER**
**SURFING'S GREAT, BUT ARE THERE NACHOS?** The surfer and the world's second-coolest sport, bowling.

**9 JOSEPH SIMMONS**
**WALK-DMC** Run, from the group Run-DMC, and competitive race walking.

**10 NEIL SEDAKA**
**OOPS. . .WE CAN GLUE THAT BACK TOGETHER, RIGHT?** The musician and the museum visitor who tripped and put her hand through a priceless masterpiece by Picasso.

**SOURCE**: *Omniture; top "Not My Job" stories from NPR.org from 1/1/2009 through 5/31/2010*

celebrity who'd actually agree to appear. So, for celebrities, we invited various public radio stars, and—to be different—we'd ask them about something they didn't know anything about. Susan Stamberg, who among her other fine qualities is always willing to try anything that's not illegal, was our first guest, and her topic was three really hard questions about bestsellers in the news. Pretty quickly, we figured we should make the questions multiple choice, so as not to embarrass or threaten people who were less patient with us than Susan, and thus "Not My Job" was born.

The rest of the show came together in a similar, improvisational way over that first year. It took us years of experimentation to figure out just how to start the show . . . we tried asking the panelists to come up with a "headline they wished they had seen that week," we tried having the panelists introduce themselves to the first listener by asking a question. In the end, we realized we should just get on with it and let the panelists make themselves known . . . and they always did."

In just a few years, *Wait Wait . . . Don't Tell Me!* would be so well known, the likes of Tom Hanks would call in to play "Not My Job." Movie stars, sports legends, musicians, and presidential spokesmen and women would chance humiliating themselves for the fun of winning a news quiz.

## LISA SIMEONE
*Host,* World of Opera

**About ten years ago**, I was hosting *Performance Today* and had a live phone interview with grand old bandleader Frederick Fennell on his 85th birthday. In the middle of the interview, I started hearing strange murmurings in a woman's voice, while Fennell was talking. Then beeps and squeaks and strange sounds. Suddenly, Fennell yelled, "Elizabeth, get off the phone!"

Apparently his wife, Elizabeth, was on the extension.

I kept it together and went on with the interview. But the female interruptions continued, until finally Fennell screamed, and I do mean screamed, "Shut up, Elizabeth!!"

Remember, this was live.

I was dying to laugh. I didn't dare look at the control room, where the engineer, director, and various producers were watching. Out of the corner of my eye, I saw two of them drop from sight, presumably on the floor in hysterics. I swallowed and continued the interview—you can hear me saying solicitously, "Mr. Fennell? Mr. Fennell?"

By noon, the whole building knew about it. Alas, NPR cleaned it up before the refeed, so much of the country heard just a standard, ordinary (boring, in my book) interview. ∎

**"**

**Pretty quickly, we figured we should make the questions multiple choice, so as not to embarrass or threaten people who were less patient with us than Susan Stamberg.**

*Peter Sagal on the birth of "Not My Job"*

# PRELUDE TO
# A CRISIS

As it turned out, the biggest news story NPR covered at the end of the '90s sounded, to many at first, like something out of a novel—a political potboiler perhaps: the accusation that President Clinton had a liaison with White House intern Monica Lewinsky. NPR's Mara Liasson calls it "the single most dramatic moment in my eight years of covering the White House."

By a fluke of scheduling, Liasson and *All Things Considered* host Robert Siegel were preparing to interview President Clinton just hours after the news broke of his possible dalliance with Lewinsky. It was NPR's rare sit-down with the president, and in the days leading up to it, Liasson remembers, "I was so excited because I had my own little scoop—a source told me something he was going to say in his State of the Union address, about social security." Instead, this interview, set up by the White House as part of "their drumroll for the State of the Union," was transformed in the wake of a political crisis of historic importance. Liasson and Siegel had no details of the scandal other than the few they had read in the *Washington Post* and had to come up with new questions in just hours. At heart, this was about a cover-up of an affair, not the alleged affair itself. Still, says Liasson, "We looked at each other and said 'Well, we have to ask him about this thing . . . but what do we ask him?!' It's really strange asking a president of the United States about an affair."

In the end, Robert Siegel put the question directly to President Clinton, who denied an affair, saying he was cooperating with authorities. "I don't know any more about it than I've told you," the president added, "and any more about it, really, than you do."

"

## We looked at each other and said 'Well, we have to ask him about this thing . . . but what do we ask him?!' It's really strange asking a president of the United States about an affair.

*Mara Liasson on interviewing President Clinton
the day the news of his affair with Monica
Lewinsky broke*

# REPORTING ONLINE

## RICHARD DEAN
*Former producer, new media services*

**In 1993, hardly anyone was online**. It was like a secret club. And there was one Web browser. No, not Firefox, not Explorer . . . this was back in the days of Mosaic.

At the time, I was an associate producer and director on *Weekend All Things Considered,* tasked with producing a weekly cooking segment. After the show, it fell to me to send recipes to everyone who sent in a self-addressed, stamped envelope. Sometimes there were thousands.

I had also discovered (courtesy of *Weekend Edition Sunday* producer Ned Wharton) CompuServe and America Online, where NPR fans filled the chat rooms, discussing everything from Will Shortz's quiz to our weekly recipes.

Having spent some time in NPR's Audience Services answering listener phone calls, I knew we'd stumbled on something much larger: how to better engage with devoted and curious NPR listeners using Internet technologies.

But back then, most of NPR's staff still used typewriters. Reporters and producers loathed the amber mainframe terminals perched on each desk. Reel-to-reel tape hung in edit booths. We were a decidedly analog organization.

Undeterred and with the quiet approval of my show's producer, I put up a rudimentary *Weekend All Things Considered* Web site, hosted by Ellicott City's Clark.Net. NPR Online was born in December 1993 in the cradle of my apartment. Back then we weren't NPR.org —we had the unwieldy address: www.clark.net/pub/watc. *Weekend Edition Sunday* went online, too, a couple of months later.

By mid-1994 it became clear to a few of us that the Internet was the future. "This is the future of reaching our audience," I boldly told Public Information VP Mary Morgan, "Can I be in charge?" She said "Yes." My new title was producer, new media services.

A few weeks later I met KBSU's Jim Paluzzi in an elevator at NPR. I felt like I'd found another human on Mars. We bonded over our shared vision for digital media and radio. Soon afterward, Jim flew me out to Boise, and together we created NPR's first official Web site (and NPR's Gopher, remember those?).

That spring, we launched NPR.org , and our old Clark.net addresses were abandoned.

To say that NPR resisted the move into the online world would be a bit of an understatement. Many employees refused to have e-mail addresses. Hosts objected to their pictures being on the Web site. Committees were formed to approve each and every Web site change. Editors wouldn't allow Web addresses on the air, fearing we'd alienate the unwired masses.

By 1995, underwriting exec Lenore Tuttle and I pushed that comfort level even further. We put up the first banner ads, modeled on *Wired* magazine's then very controversial efforts to bring in cash. Silicon Graphics had donated three Web servers to NPR in exchange for on-air and online credit.

These boxes needed names befitting our dazzling new online efforts. *Weekly Edition*'s Rebecca Martin (now at Youth Radio) named our servers Majorca, Minorca, and Ibiza after the Spanish islands.

In February, 1995, Jim Paluzzi and I were approached by Real Networks who could magically stream audio over a 14.4Kbps dialup modem. Whoa. At long last, the Web was about to get audible.

We kept everyone except NPR's executives in the dark until launch day, April 10, 1995. That day we fielded dozens of angry calls from member stations fearful of NPR reaching listeners directly. We fielded dozens of angry internal e-mails about the abysmal quality of the audio, which did sound like 1940s AM radio.

We also received thousands of thrilled e-mails from listeners. ∎

**Many employees refused to have e-mail addresses. Hosts objected to their pictures being on the Web site. Committees were formed to approve each and every Web site change . . .**

**LEFT** Screenshot of NPR's Web site in 1995 (image from Richard Dean).

TRANSCRIPT EXCERPT
## *ALL THINGS CONSIDERED*

**SHOW DATE:**
*1998-01-30*
**CAT. TITLE:**
*Web News
Popular After
Clinton Scandal*

**LINDA WERTHEIMER:** The White House crisis, as it's been called, has inaugurated a new era for Internet-based news services. Broadcasters and print journalists are online receiving and disseminating information faster than traditional media ever could.

NPR's Brooke Gladstone reports.

**BROOKE GLADSTONE:** Some rejoice that Internet news has come of age.

**SCOTT CHARON, INTERNET MEDIA ANALYST, *FORRESTER RESEARCH:*** The Web news sites have really been put on the map with this story.

**GLADSTONE:** Scott Charon analyzes the online news industry for Forrester Research.

**CHARON:** The Internet has the capability to offer a lot more depth and a lot more cheap and easy access to viewers.

*Begin audio clip, news broadcast on Internet*

**ANNOUNCER:** Stay tuned for the latest news on MSNBC on the Internet and MSNBC on cable. Remember, MSNBC News, when you really want to know.

**GLADSTONE:** Jack Schaefer, the deputy editor of Microsoft's online magazine *Slate,* says the story about President Clinton has moved Web news out of the category of a niche service into the mainstream.

**JACK SCHAEFER, DEPUTY EDITOR, *SLATE* ONLINE MAGAZINE:** Web sites like MSNBC noticed a tripling of their traffic. Likewise, the *New York Times* recorded a 30 to 40 percent increase in viewership. Fox News doubled its average 1.1 million unique viewers.

**GLADSTONE:** Schaefer says there was finally a reason for people to go to the Web and avail themselves of the technology that had been gathering dust in the living room.

**SCHAEFER:** Sex, power, scandal, lies, coverups—soap opera writers can't imagine anything this fantastic.

**LESLIE WALKER, WEB SITE EDITOR, THE *WASHINGTON POST*:** It's a chance for newspapers to enter the real-time news business and compete directly with TV and radio in ways they haven't done before.

**GLADSTONE:** Leslie Walker edits the *Washington Post*'s Web site. The *Post* was the first mainstream news operation with a scoop on the allegations, because they put it on the Web site at midnight before it appeared in the paper. She says the Internet site offers more depth than a daily paper can provide, because it can store documents, old stories, provide context at the click of a mouse.

**WALKER:** People came in on this Clinton story, and then they branched off and they read our background briefings on Whitewater, on Paula Jones, on campaign finance—because they want to know: How do all these pieces of this very complicated story fit together?

**GLADSTONE:** But mistakes happen when the news cycle is hurried. The *Dallas Morning News* put a story about a White House witness on its Web site, and withdrew it before it hit print.

**JAMES LEDBETTER, MEDIA CRITIC, THE *VILLAGE VOICE*:** Within the length of a *Nightline* broadcast, the thing was up, publicized, and gone.

**GLADSTONE:** Gone, but not before it was carried by many other news services. James Ledbetter is the media critic for the *Village Voice*. He says that the velocity of the news cycle has been accelerated.

**LEDBETTER:** That doesn't necessarily mean that the facts emerge any faster.

**GLADSTONE:** Ledbetter says that readers may rely on the editorial judgment of news organizations they already know, like the *Times* or NBC, but news groups or one-man services like The Drudge Report, which started the ball rolling on President Clinton, don't undergo the same editorial scrutiny.

**LEDBETTER:** We know that the World Wide Web has been used to manipulate the sale of stocks by planting tips and rumors. And there's really no guarantee that what you're getting is accurate, or even if it is accurate, what the motivation of people is for putting it out.

So that, just for example, and I'm not saying this as an accusation, but how would anyone know if Matt Drudge was or was not on the payroll of Paula Jones's lawyers? You don't know.

**GLADSTONE:** It's that element of doubt that casts a shadow on the Internet. But Web news is no longer a fad, it's a fact. And users will need more than computer skills to interpret it.

Brooke Gladstone, NPR News, New York. ∎

TRANSCRIPT EXCERPT
## *ALL THINGS CONSIDERED*

**SHOW DATE:**
*1999-07-19*
**CAT. TITLE:**
*Kosovo Mass
Graves Uncovered
and Identified*

"

## Serbian soldiers marched about five-hundred people from the villages just north of town into the valley and separated them. Women, children, and older men were sent away to camps; the younger men were never seen again . . .

*Scott Simon, reporting from Lukare*

**ROBERT SIEGEL:** This is NPR's *All Things Considered.* I'm Robert Siegel.

**LINDA WERTHEIMER:** And I'm Linda Wertheimer.

The war in Kosovo is over, but death remains part of daily life there. Almost every day bodies are uncovered. It's estimated that 10,000 Kosovo Albanians were killed during the war, but not in acts of war. As NPR's Scott Simon tells us, many were slaughtered and left in mass graves. This report is quite graphic.

**SCOTT SIMON:** Ever since British forces rolled into Lukare, northeast of the capital, villagers have told the soldiers that bodies are buried under a field of overgrown grass along a roadway. Last April 19th, as some remember it, Serbian soldiers marched about five hundred people from the villages just north of town into the valley and separated them. Women, children, and older men were sent away to camps; the younger men were never seen again, until perhaps on Saturday.

*SOUND BITE OF PEOPLE*

**SIMON:** A group of soldiers from Britain's Irish Guards and villagers began to dig. They turned up the ground with small garden shovels so they would not scratch or crack human bones. The bodies were not deeply buried. The men who'd put them in the ground had apparently been working quickly. When the British soldiers came upon the thin, reedy bones of fingers or hit the hard dark block of a skull, they put down their shovels and reached down with their hands. Carefully, even gently, they would sweep soil off a shattered skeleton of a face and run their hands down through the dirt, feeling for arms, legs and shoulders. Then five soldiers, wearing surgical masks to strain out the stench of death, would crouch down to lift the body out of the dirt and lower it onto a black plastic sheet and look.

**UNIDENTIFIED MAN #1:** When you've seen the body there will be a member of the International War Crimes Tribunal we'd like to speak to. It's very important that we get all the details.

**UNIDENTIFIED MAN #2:** Yes, sir.

**UNIDENTIFIED WOMAN #1:** (Foreign language spoken)

**SIMON:** The soldiers and villagers found six bodies in the ground on Saturday, all of them men. The youngest was a boy of 19; the oldest 48. They were all wearing field boots. Major Ian Sariff of the Guard said many of the bodies uncovered in Lukare were buried with personal belongings that helped identify them—a driver's license or jewelry.

**UNIDENTIFIED MAN #3:** One of the bodies that was exhumed so far had a cell phone. The sister, in fact, of the deceased recognized the cell phone and, indeed, I wasn't aware of whether or not it was in working order; I assumed it wasn't, but she recognized it as a personal item of his. So that was a contributing factor, but the identification papers and the general appearance and clothing were sufficient for her to identify the body anyway.

**SIMON:** But on Saturday, two bodies could not be at first identified. A British officer came down to where families stood along the road and asked family members to step up in twos.

**UNIDENTIFIED MAN #4:** As we call you forward to look at the bodies, the only way you'll be able to identify the bodies is by their clothes and one or two possessions. I would appreciate if you could do it as we instruct you to maintain the dignity of those who have died.

*SOUND BITE OF FAMILIES*

**SIMON:** Soldiers carried out the first body and laid it on the ground. The sad fact is shoes and shirts last longer than flesh. All that remained of the man was bone and mud and flies. The soldiers placed a delicate pile of possessions on his collapsed chest—a black wallet, a plastic watch, a half-crushed pack of Serbian cigarettes. A dark-haired woman in a red shirt came forward and asked the soldiers to bring the man's black coat around his shoulders. When they did, she said she could see it was her husband. She did not begin to cry until she was speaking with war crimes investigators. Her face began to stiffen as if she wanted to scream, and then she sobbed.

The next body was brought out. His skull was smashed and the British officer placed a rubber glove over the dent for dignity. Two men in light blue jackets squinted as they looked down at the body, as if beginning to recognize an old friend at a reunion. Within a moment, they began to shiver. The body was the brother of one of the men and the other man's father.

By the end of the weekend, fifteen bodies were dug up in Lukare; twelve were identified. British officers estimate that thirty more bodies may be buried in two sites nearby. They will pull bodies out of the ground all week. Forensic scientists will then begin to determine how the men were killed and who killed them. The slaughter in and around Lukare will hardly be the largest uncovered in Kosovo, and that may be almost what seems most sinister. Massacres have been sown into the ground. ■

**OPPOSITE**
A gentleman
surveys a
bombed out
Kosovo in 1999
(photo by Peter
Breslow).

**ABOVE**
Scott Simon
interviews locals
in Kosovo in 1999
(photo by Peter
Breslow).

# END OF A DECADE— TURN OF A CENTURY

NPR's News Division entered the '90s covering stories of promising beginnings: a democracy movement abroad, and, at home, a young president bringing a new generation to power.

The decade ended with some hopes realized and others dashed.

For NPR, though, the decade was an era of astonishing expansion. The good economic times meant more generous gifts from donors; the creation of the NPR Foundation; and the seeds of an endowment that NPR hoped would underwrite the network for decades to come.

Even the darkest news, like foreign conflicts and domestic political storms, benefitted NPR. When big news broke, people tuned into NPR. The decade saw listenership jump from just over 8 million in 1990 to 14.6 million at the close of 1999. The number of stations carrying NPR programming grew to nearly seven hundred.

For the first time, one could travel virtually anywhere in the United States and still hear NPR. As it turned out, those who discovered NPR in the 1990s stayed on as part of the public radio community. And that allowed NPR to enter the twenty-first-century stronger than ever before—with a large, vibrant, and growing audience.

**The decade saw listenership jump from just over 8 million in 1990 to 14.6 million at the close of 1999. The number of stations carrying NPR programming grew to nearly seven hundred.**

FIGURE 5

# NPR EXPENSE BREAKDOWN
# FOR FISCAL YEAR 2009

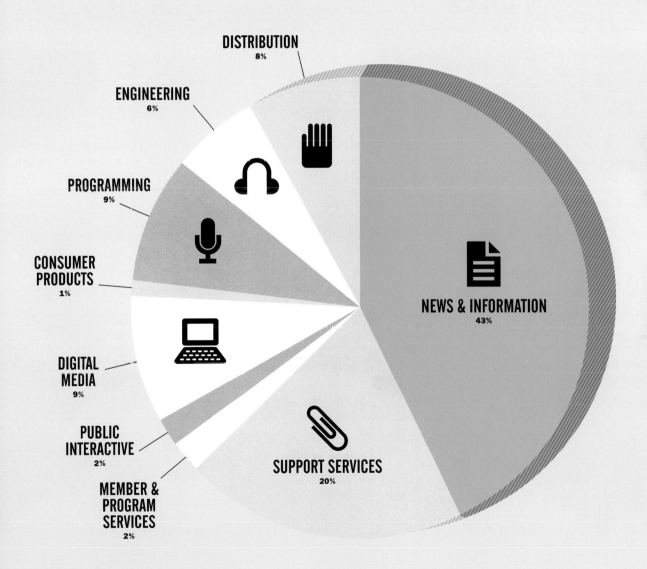

**DISTRIBUTION**
8%

**ENGINEERING**
6%

**PROGRAMMING**
9%

**CONSUMER PRODUCTS**
1%

**DIGITAL MEDIA**
9%

**PUBLIC INTERACTIVE**
2%

**MEMBER & PROGRAM SERVICES**
2%

**NEWS & INFORMATION**
43%

**SUPPORT SERVICES**
20%

**SOURCE:** *NPR FY2009 Audited Financial Statements (Parent Company Only), FY2009 ended September 20, 2009*

# 2000

|  | J | F | M | A | M | J | J | A | S | O | N | D |
|---|---|---|---|---|---|---|---|---|---|---|---|---|
| 2000 |  |  |  |  |  |  |  |  |  |  |  |  |
| 2001 |  |  |  |  |  |  |  |  |  |  |  |  |
| 2002 |  |  |  |  |  |  |  |  |  |  |  |  |
| 2003 |  |  |  |  |  |  |  |  |  |  |  |  |
| 2004 |  |  |  |  |  |  |  |  |  |  |  |  |
| 2005 |  |  |  |  |  |  |  |  |  |  |  |  |
| 2006 |  |  |  |  |  |  |  |  |  |  |  |  |
| 2007 |  |  |  |  |  |  |  |  |  |  |  |  |
| 2008 |  |  |  |  |  |  |  |  |  |  |  |  |
| 2009 |  |  |  |  |  |  |  |  |  |  |  |  |

**JAN 2000**
Y2K, the millennium begins.

**JAN 2000**
*All Songs Considered* debuts online.

**SEP 2001**
Terrorists attack the U.S.

**NOV 2001**
The U.S. begins the hunt for Osama Bin Laden.

**FEB 2003**
War erupts in Darfur.

**MAR 2003**
The U.S. launches military action in Iraq.

**OCT 2003**
*StoryCorps* debuts.

**DEC 2004**
Renée Montagne and Steve Inskeep become the new hosts of *Morning Edition*.

**AUG 2005**
Hurricane Katrina hits the Gulf.

**APR 2008**
The *Tiny Desk Concert* is born.

**MAY 2008**
A massive quake hits Chengdu, China.

**AUG 2008**
Hurricane Gustav hits Haiti.

**AUG 2008**
*Planet Money* blog debuts.

**DEC 2008**
The Greased Cheetahs become the NPR relay race champions.

**JAN 2009**
Barack Obama is sworn in as America's first African-American president.

**JUN 2009**
Bernie Madoff is sentenced to a 150-year prison term for securities fraud.

# THE MOST EXTRAORDINARY STORY

NPR entered the twenty-first century covering the closest presidential election in modern American history. When the fight between George W. Bush and Al Gore ascended to the Supreme Court, *All Things Considered* supervising senior producer Chris Turpin (now the show's executive producer) remarked to a colleague, "This may be the most extraordinary story any of us will ever cover."

That was a decade ago.

Over the next ten years, NPR would go on to cover the terrorist attacks of 9/11; wars in Iraq and Afghanistan; a hurricane that nearly drowned New Orleans; a catastrophic earthquake in China where NPR journalists were the only western media on the scene; and a global economic collapse bigger than any since the Great Depression.

As audiences for other news organizations shrank, NPR's listenership grew more than 60 percent in a decade. While other news companies closed overseas bureaus, NPR opened ten foreign bureaus in ten years. The network completed the shift it had begun years earlier from an alternative news source to a primary source, where listeners could find breaking news, investigative stories, and original enterprise reporting.

In the first decade of the new millennium, NPR created daily news programs faster than ever before in its history. *Day to Day*, *The Tavis Smiley Show* (later rechristened *News & Notes*), *Tell Me More*, and *The Bryant Park Project* all emerged within five years of each other. Only *Tell Me More* would survive the decade.

And for the first time, NPR developed programming for media other than radio—original podcasts, blogs, photography, and video.

## OPENING WORDS

## SCOTT SIMON
*Host*, Weekend Edition Saturday

**I've been blessed** to bring a lot of news to people. But few words I've uttered affected me more than the opening to our show on January 1, 2000:

"The world had a party last night. People danced around the totem heads of Easter Island. Big Ben struck twelve, and the night skies of London cascaded with light. The Eiffel Tower erupted with fanfare and fireworks. Two million people watched the thousand-pound crystal ball touch down in Times Square. Hollywood poured three million watts of light over the hills. Five million people cheered on the beaches of Rio.

"Four numbers turned on the calendar. That won't happen for another thousand years.

"The toll of time should remind us to cherish the time we have. So let us be among the first to tell you that today is Saturday, January 1, 2000." ∎

**OPPOSIRE**
Ari Shapiro, correspondent, in 2006 (NPR photo).

# WE COULDN'T
# GO BACK

In September of 2001, I was an editorial assistant on the overnight shift for *Morning Edition*. I ran scripts to the show's host, compiled a summary of the day's program for local stations, and generally did whatever was necessary to help the show get on the air. As the host, Bob Edwards, told me years later, "It was a shit job, but you did it. That's why I liked you."

It didn't seem like a shit job to me. An NPR junkie from early childhood, I still pinched myself that I was actually working with people whose voices I'd been listening to for years. I also pinched myself to stay awake.

My work day started at 1 A.M. I had finished an internship with Nina Totenberg a few months earlier, and I wasn't used to the schedule.

On the night of September 10, I could barely keep my eyes open. I decided that if it was an uneventful morning, I would go home early. Around 8 A.M., I walked upstairs to drop off a note on a colleague's desk. When I came back to the second floor to get my bags, everyone was gathered around the television. There was smoke coming out of the World Trade Center.

I spent the next hour calling people in and around the World Trade Center. I remember reaching a secretary at a financial firm on one of the top floors. I asked her if she would go on the air live to describe what she was seeing. She said she couldn't, because the building was being evacuated. That was not long before the towers collapsed.

9/11 changed the world, and no less so NPR.

Jay Kernis was NPR's senior vice president for programming at the time. He remembers standing in the *Morning Edition* production area that morning and saying, for the first time in NPR's history, "We're about to go into 24-hour coverage."

*Morning Edition* provided constant live reports until 1 P.M. Neal Conan and *Talk of the Nation* then took over until *All Things Considered* went on the air at 4 P.M. Scott Simon and the weekend team anchored coverage from late at night until *Morning Edition* went back on the air at 5 A.M.

"Everyone in the world was saying, 'What can we do? What can we do?'" remembers Edwards. "Well, we in broadcasting knew what we could do. We had

**LEFT** Smoke billows from the twin towers of the World Trade Center in New York after planes crashed into each tower on September 11, 2001 (AP photo/ Gene Boyars).

> "
>
> ## That morning, everyone in the public radio system realized NPR needed to be more responsive to breaking news.

a job to do. Just do our jobs the best we could, and that was important. That was what we could do positively as part of this horrible tragedy."

For the next few weeks, everyone at NPR worked grueling hours. Each morning, Barbara Bradley Hagerty (then Barbara Bradley) would arrive to report the latest on the investigation for *Morning Edition.* Just before she went on the air at 5 A.M., she would do calisthenics to wake up. I watched her run laps from *Morning Edition* to *All Things Considered* and back until she was alert enough to sound coherent on the air.

People at NPR joke that our unofficial motto used to be, "Report it a day late and call it analysis." 9/11 was the turning point away from that mindset. Immediately after the planes hit, when every TV news station was carrying live coverage of the disaster, *Morning Edition* was still playing its taped broadcast for the day. For the crucial first moments after the planes hit,

NPR listeners had no information about what was happening.

That morning, everyone in the public radio system realized NPR needed to be more responsive to breaking news. "I think we recognized we really couldn't go back," says Ellen Weiss. 9/11 was her first day as supervising senior editor of NPR's national desk after twelve years running *All Things Considered.* She is now NPR's senior vice president for news.

"There was always a fear that we would become CNN, a fear that we'd lose who we were and why people listen to us," remembers Weiss. 9/11 "was a moment where I began to recognize that somehow we had to figure out how to be where we needed to be when we needed to be there, and that we could come up with our own formula. And gradually we began to develop a much clearer set of principles about how to deal with breaking news."

# REPORTING 9/11

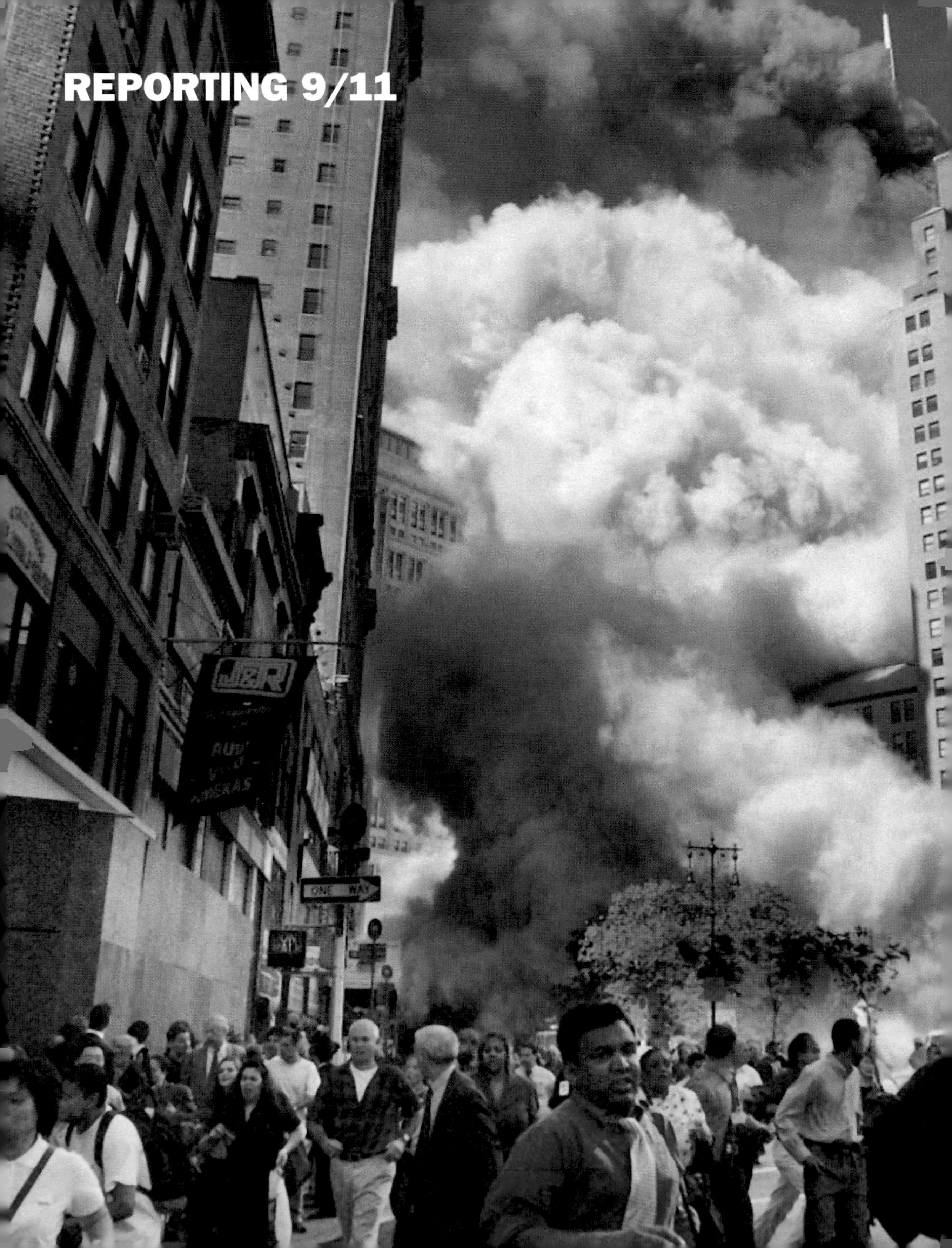

## 2001: SEPTEMBER 11

# MARY LOUISE KELLY
*Former correspondent*

**The morning of the 9/11 attacks** started like any other at *All Things Considered*. Senior producer Chris Turpin and I were sifting through newspapers, checking in with editors, getting ready to lead the show's morning meeting. I remember taking a call from Rob Gifford, then NPR's Beijing correspondent, to discuss a story idea. I didn't bother to mention the live footage we were watching of the first twin tower. We all thought it was an accident, at best worth a short report for that afternoon's show. But when the second plane hit a few minutes later, I told Rob, "I gotta go—now." We started calling everyone we knew in New York, trying to find eyewitnesses for *Morning Edition*. Then our correspondent Tom Gjelten called to tell us that the Pentagon had been hit. Suddenly all our phones lit up at once; they didn't stop ringing for days. ■

> I rode into the center of the ash at the World Trade Center, past police barricades, until I couldn't take the heat anymore. But anyone who'd survived had gone.

## 2001: SEPTEMBER 11

# JACKI LYDEN
*Contributing host/correspondent*

**I began that morning early,** working at my desk at about 8 A.M. in Prospect Heights, Brooklyn. My windows faced southeast. A phone call at about 8:48 from my brother in Wisconsin. I looked out my window and saw smoke rising over the treeline—got on the phone, and was immediately our first reporter on the air with Bob Edwards. I remained on the phone and sometimes on air for two hours, while the entire drama unfolded, listening to sirens race all around me. I had no way of knowing if I would ever be able to talk to the staff in DC again that day, so I told Bob Edwards, live, "I'm riding my bicycle into Manhattan." And I did—pushing through a huge throng of people coming East over the Manhattan bridge—they hid me. I rode into the center of the ash at the World Trade Center, past police barricades, until I couldn't take the heat anymore. But anyone who'd survived had gone. I kept vigil, and reported live from Ground Zero, for the next six mornings. ■

**LEFT** Pedestrians on Park Row flee the area of the World Trade Center as the center's south tower collapses (AP photo/Amy Sancetta, FILE).

## TRANSCRIPT EXCERPT
# TALK OF
# THE NATION

**SHOW DATE:**
*2001-09-11*
**CAT. TITLE:**
*Terrorism Coverage
Visual and Emotional
Reaction to World Trade
Center Destruction*

**NEAL CONAN:** Let us now get in touch with Craig Childs. This is a man who was on Fifth Avenue this morning and witnessed the crowd reaction to the planes crashing into the World Trade Center towers.

Thank you so much for joining us.

**CRAIG CHILDS (*Morning Edition* Commentator):** Certainly.

**CONAN:** Can you describe what you saw?

**CHILDS:** Well, I can give a visual and emotional sense of what it was like there because I arrived just moments after the plane struck the towers from about a mile or so away. I came around the corner and could see flames just crawling up the sides of the buildings and a robe of gray smoke heading off to the southeast. And people standing around at that moment were just voiceless. People were coming out of the subway onto the street and just standing there transfixed, staring at this thing. People every once in a while would point and shout and say that there were people jumping out of the towers. But, of course, from where we were, you really couldn't tell. You know, a person that high up is indistinguishable from a falling desk or a file cabinet. And that's when people started looking around at the buildings above us, and I heard a sigh rise up, just thousands of people gasping at once. And I looked up and saw that the south tower was collapsing. And I don't even know if the word *collapse* is correct here. It just disappeared. The lines that defined the building dissolved, and the building just vanished.

**CONAN:** It must be difficult for a New Yorker to even conceive of that happening.

**CHILDS:** Well, I imagine it would be. I'm coming from rural Colorado. I'm only here for a few days. And so this is a pretty striking event for me to [technical difficulties] New Yorkers respond to this and to watch myself respond to it. Walking around hearing people—one man came up to me, and he was just shouting. He said that we should be bombing people right now; that he wants to kill somebody. And I didn't know how to respond to him. You know, this is a very fragile time. We could go any number of directions here. You could feel the fragility on the street. Just people not sure whether to head for anger or head for tears.

**CONAN:** And maybe as an outsider, you might have been able to appreciate that; have a little bit of perspective on it, but nevertheless, a participant as well, as you watched it.

**CHILDS:** Yeah. Well, not knowing this city very well but starting to learn how people move here, you can see right now that pedestrians are owning the streets; that it's a very different sense of movement. People are making eye contact now. People are looking for some kind of emotional outlet. They're looking for some kind of—they're looking for something, somebody to talk to.

**CONAN:** As we look, and it will be days before we have a clearer idea, perhaps, of what the meaning of this is and who was responsible and how all of this went about, but, Craig, as you look for some meaning today, right now, do you find any?

**CHILDS:** It's difficult to find meaning in something like this, especially so swiftly. What really struck me is that when the south tower came down, just so many hands went up in the air and it looked as if people were trying to stop it, they were trying to reach up and grab the building. Just thousands of hands just shooting up into the air all around me. People were just horrified. And I guess what I'm seeing now is that the city has been turned from a machine into something organic. It's just filled with emotion, not necessarily the panic that you might imagine; just sheer emotion everywhere.

**CONAN:** And like so many other phone calls we've had today, yours is being drowned out by the sound of emergency vehicles.

**CHILDS:** Yes.

**CONAN:** Craig Childs, thank you so much for speaking with us.

**CHILDS:** Certainly.

**CONAN:** Craig Childs is a commentator on NPR's *Morning Edition*. He comes to us normally via station KVNS in Colorado. He was on Fifth Avenue this morning as he watched the collapse of the towers of the World Trade Center. ∎

# REPORTING AFGHANISTAN

**ABOVE** Guy Raz (with microphone), host of *Weekend All Things Considered*, in the town of Khost, Afghanistan, interviewing a shopkeeper in May 2002 (NPR photo).

# PETER BRESLOW

*Senior producer*

*Kabul February 6, 2002*

**First the bad news:** As I sit and write there is no water, no electricity, and no heat. Our generator is broken. Our toilet is broken. Our satellite phone is broken. And our pieces aren't getting on the air, because, we are told, the shows' appetite for things Afghan is declining precipitously. The weather in Kabul has switched from crisp Colorado sunshine to biting cold and snow, and I'm wearing as much fleece and Capeline as my skeletal structure can support, but still, the end of my nose is as chilly and drippy as a Labrador's.

Now the good news: We have a great staff who are doing their best to try and make life comfortable. Zalmai is our translator. He graduated second in his class in engineering but has the heart of a poet. Andar is the can-do guy who runs the show. He is the former chess champion of Afghanistan. Shaffi is the cook who is also a kickboxing champ. (I'm sure a better kick boxer than chef . . . although with our instructions he's using less lard and more olive oil. We eat a lot of lamb and chicken, overcooked vegetables and the occasional plate of pasta for which al dente is but a faint dream.)

These guys all suffered under the Taliban and the Mujahadeen. Shaffi, who is certainly the sweetest person in central Asia, was hired to train some Talib bodyguards. When he did his job too well and slightly roughed up one of his sparring partners, they cracked his head open with a rifle butt. Today he wears the scar above his left eyebrow. Zalmai has survived bullets, grenades, and rocket launchers. He's got a brown spot in one of his eyes where some shrapnel burned him during an attack that occurred as he was filling sandbags in his end of town . . . ordered to do so by one of the warring factions. He had to flee to Pakistan when the Taliban heard that he was assisting women in a hospital. While in Pakistan, he was drugged and robbed. The fighting has prevented him from furthering his education at home and taking advantage of an international scholarship he was awarded.

We've given everyone NPR caps so now it looks like a very minor league baseball team is piling out of the car when we show up.

Kabul is surrounded by unwelcoming peaks, which have become snowcapped in recent days. Parts of the city look like an archaeological dig. The south end of town has been shelled to Hiroshima proportions. With the adobe quality of the construction, the ruins truly appear to be something from Masada or Mesa Verde. Other areas, like ours, are in good shape. NPR is renting a three-bedroom house that, when the electricity and water are functioning (before 8 A.M. and after 6 P.M.), is always chilly but comfortable enough for a quasi-war zone. There are shops with goods . . . we bought Oreos (double-cream filled), Ritz Crackers, Rice Krispies, and tuna fish the other day. But we paid through the nose.

Wherever you go there are women, children, and ragged old men begging for a ten-thousand Afghani note (less than 30¢). If you start giving out money, you are immediately surrounded by a quickly expanding crowd of grabbing hands that pursue you into the car. We are all bundled up against the stinging cold, while these people wear the thinnest of wraps and no socks.

Women are still clad in their baby blue burkas, still unsure whether someone might throw acid in their faces if they bare them. I tried on a burka the other day. It is totally claustrophobic, and eliminates peripheral vision and the ability to see where you are stepping. I don't understand how these women aren't falling on their noses half the time. Still, they make the Afghan gals intriguing, as beneath every veil could linger Isabella Rossalini.

We've been sharing the house with Sonia Pace, the *Voice of America* correspondent, and Guy Chasen of the *Wall Street Journal*. (We've been using *VOA*'s sat. phone when ours doesn't work.) Guy has now left . . . ordered out of the region by his editors for safely reasons after the kidnapping of his colleague Dan Pearl. Guy's translator helped the *Journal* procure the computer hard drives with the al Queda materials on them that the *Journal* turned over to the **»** government some weeks ago. Some people think the hard drives are the reason for the Pearl kidnapping. Now, people are after the translator. He came over the other night scared out of his wits, people hunting for him. His wife is due with their baby this week, he's had to sleep in a different place every night and now has fled to Pakistan, where he is hoping the United States will grant him a visa and asylum.

Yesterday, we made our first foray out of Kabul, about 2½ hours south to the town of Gardez. Last week, two opposing factions there opened fire, killing sixty-one people. We were on hand for a prisoner exchange, which came off without incident. The ride to Gardez involved a climb over an icy mountain pass, and we were all relieved to find that our driver was not a hotdog and really took his time. It was a bone-chilling scene waiting for the exchange to take place. We stood on a hillside, the snow and wind swirling, surrounded by men armed to the teeth with Kalyshnikovs, rocket propelled grenade launchers and anti-aircraft artillery. Some guys customized their guns with fluorescent tape; others wore a half dozen grenades around their waists. (Try not to trip, Buddy.)

But Afghans are very friendly to guests and one of the warlords invited us out of the cold and into his wood heated hut for some tea. We gave him an Oreo. When it came time for the prisoner exchange, the group we were with asked for a piece of paper to write down the names of the men they were handing over. Scott supplied them with a sheet from his reporter's notebook, which just happens to be emblazoned with the logo of the National Lesbian and Gay Journalists Association. So little did these fearsome warriors know that they carried a slip of paper bearing the imprint of a group that proclaims, "We're here. We're queer. We're on deadline."

Right now we're waiting to receive from Islamabad a new charger for the satellite phone to replace the one that got fried from all the fluctuations in electricity. After it arrives, we'll head out of town to Bamiyan, where the Taliban destroyed the giant Buddhas last year. ∎

**ABOVE** Scott Simon and Peter Breslow in Afghanistan with a local (photo by Peter Breslow).

" 
**The journey there is a grueling, rattling eight-hour struggle over narrow, washboard dirt roads clinging to icy mountain-sides, plunging into dust-choked valleys and up and over the desolate Shebar Pass. . . . When a car comes the other direction, you scramble for a nook in which to pull over.**

# PETER BRESLOW

*Senior producer*

*Kabul February 11, 2002*

**Today I paid my first bribe ever** for electricity. If it works it will be well worth it. For the past three weeks life has revolved around an endless tangle of extension cords, generators, and outlets hot and cold. When the electricity works it is often in only part of the house and so it is your task to find the hot outlets and run enough extension cords to them to power what you need . . . usually a laptop and maybe a space heater.

But when the electricity is totally out . . . as it is during most daylight hours . . . we must use a generator, which involves even more extension cords. There is only so much power to go around, so if you want hot water or to flush the toilet you have to unplug your space heater or maybe the satellite TV (which seems to mainly show the Romanian Home Shopping Network and repeats of Italian indoor soccer matches). But our two small generators have not been powerful enough to run even the most minimal of equipment, so this week we sprang for a shiny new red Sawafuji SH 6000 DX. And this baby does hum. 4.5 kilowatts of gasoline-fueled fun. We can even hook a car battery up to it, which has become necessary because the charger to our satellite phone is burned out and the only way to charge the phone is to plug it into the extra car battery sitting on the floor in my room (or drive around with it dangling from the cigarette lighter in the car). Naturally, the car battery drains down every day or two, so we have to schlep it outside to the generator and recharge it. I'll be very sorry to leave the SH 6000 DX behind when I depart. As a matter of fact, I'm looking into a special 4.5-kilowatt visa for her from the U.S. Embassy.

We recently discovered that if you get friendly with the local "electrician"—the person in charge of power in your immediate neighborhood—he can make sure that electricity always flows to your house. This afternoon a gnarly older gentleman in a brown turban came by to explain that he could guarantee us power all the time, all over the house. What could we do for him in return, he asked, noting that the government hadn't paid him in a very long time. We agreed upon a figure of fifty dollars a month, and our personal voltage regulator left with a smile. He warned us against turning our lights on during the day, however, so as to avoid arousing the suspicions of our electrically deprived neighbors. But tonight, alas, the electricity has gone off in half the house, and we're wondering about the honesty of a man who would renege on a bribe . . . maybe it's just a blown fuse.

In Bamiyan you don't have to worry about the electricity going off because it never comes on. We drove to this ancient place earlier this week to see what remains of the giant Buddhas destroyed by the Taliban last year. The journey there is a grueling, rattling eight-hour struggle over narrow, washboard, dirt roads clinging to icy mountainsides, plunging into dust-choked valleys and up and over the desolate Shebar Pass at about 10,000 feet. When a car comes the other direction, you scramble for a nook in which to pull over.

Along the route, you pass tiny baked-mud villages where the main occupation appears to be squatting and watching the very occasional car or truck pass by. There is a shop or two selling purple plastic shoes and oranges, and an inordinate number of pharmacies. We are told these places sell an array of mainly useless watered down medicines manufactured in Pakistan. Local people can't afford the real stuff, and doctors make a bit more profit by steering patients to the drug store owned by a relative.

Also en route you pass young kids and grown men throwing shovels full of dirt in the road as you approach, ostensibly to help repair the ruts, but mainly they're looking for a tip . . . a clever money-making scheme in a place where there is no work. Our driver occasionally obliges with a ten-thousand Afghani note tossed out the window. Sometimes, too, you pass a disabled tank with a kid playing on top, twirling on the turret.

But before you get on the dirt road on the way to Bamiyan you ride north out of Kabul through the Shomali Plain. This is a scene of complete devastation orchestrated by the Taliban to wipe out resistance. The place is littered »

**ABOVE**

The 175-foot-tall, 2,000-year-old
Buddha statue located in Bamiyan,
about 90 miles west of the Afghan
capital of Kabul, is shown here
in 1997. Taliban rulers ordered
the destruction of all statues
considered to be insulting to
Islam, including this one, in early
2001. It was the world's tallest
standing Buddha statue (AP photo/
Zaheeruddin Abdullah, FILE).

with the carcasses of tanks, destroyed vineyards, burned out houses and huge twisted metal shipping containers that people had used as shops or even homes. Once, the Shomali was a garden spot that people from Kabul visited for picnics. Then came the Taliban and the drought. Now, it's an empty series of ghost towns where the remnants of bombed-out mud homes look like giant anthills. We're told that the Taliban paid people from Kabul $3 a day (a lot of money here) to come out to the Shomali to cut down the trees and help destroy buildings.

As you drive through the plain, the stones on the side of the road tell you where it's safe to venture off the pockmarked blacktop. Rocks painted red mean land mines. White rocks signify an area that has been cleared. All over the region, you spot these markers along with the acronyms of the mine-clearing group that's done the work painted on a nearby wall.

We arrived in Bamiyan, our spines slightly compressed from the bumps, in the late afternoon. It is a dazzling place sitting at 7,500 feet. Snow encrusted 14,000- and 15,000-foot peaks stare across a valley at a giant sandstone colored cliff into which the Buddhas were carved almost two thousand years ago. Now, they've been blasted away so only the faintest outline exists like the spirit of some dead person that lingers because it doesn't know it's really deceased.

Within minutes of getting into town, we heard about a mass grave of Taliban victims that had just been unearthed. We sped to the scene, and, in a barren valley, found two old men with shovels standing over a now-empty hole. Beside them we could make out a skull, some vertebrae, a watch, a cigarette lighter and some decayed clothing. One man told us that four years ago he had been ordered by the Taliban to bury four people in this spot. They had been shot in the head, their hands tied behind their backs. Now he had unearthed them in order to give them a proper burial. The Taliban had also killed one of the men's brothers. He was seventy-seven years old when he was shot. The Taliban were particularly vicious in Bamiyan because it is the home of the Hazara people, an ethnic minority in Afghanistan. The Hazaras are known as fierce fighters, and they proved themselves against the Taliban.

With the sun setting and the temperature rapidly approaching single digits, we hunted around for a place to spend the night. There are no hotels in Bamiyan. Eventually, someone took pity on us and invited us to the guesthouse of the Hazara leader and warlord, Karim Khalili. Five of us slept in one big wood-heated room, dinner included . . . compliments of the warlord. I forgot to offer him an NPR pen.

The next day we checked out the Buddhas close up . . . scampered through tunnels and up decaying stone staircases to inspect the damage wrought by the Taliban and vandals. In addition to the two giant statues, there are countless portrayals of Buddha etched into the walls of the caverns surrounding the sculptures. The Taliban, whose distorted version of Islam banned all images of the human and animal forms, had scratched out the face on every single Buddha.

At the base of the cliff we came upon thirty-seven-year-old Mirza who had participated in the destruction of the Buddhas. We followed him up the cliffside to the 6-by-12-foot cave where he lives with his wife, mother, sister, and numerous children. The escarpment is dotted with tiny caverns where returning refugees have set up shop. It was cold in his cave, and everyone was coughing. Mirza had little food, no job, and no wood for his stove.

He said that four years ago when he was slow to vacate his cave on orders from the Taliban, they shot and killed his five-year-old son. Later, after his family did flee, he snuck back into Bamiyan to buy food. The Talibs nabbed him and forced him to unload dynamite for the Buddhas' destruction. While it's Buddhists and not Muslims for whom the statues were holy, this man respected them for their historical importance. Now, all he can do is shake his head and wonder what his family will eat today. We helped him out a little bit.

After an interview with Mr. Khalili, who insisted he is more than willing to work with the central government, we raced the sunlight back to Kabul, desperate to clear the dirt road before dark. We were forty-five minutes late on that count but made it back safe and sound. When we walked in the door to our house—dust encrusted and desperate for a shower—we were greeted by overflowing toilets and backed up pipes. Maybe we need to bribe the plumber. ∎

# RENÉE MONTAGNE
*Senior host,* Morning Edition

*Kabul February 6, 2002*

**In the late spring of 2002,** Afghans were coming home.

During twenty-three years of war, nearly six million people fled the fighting, and now they were flooding back. I had arrived in Afghanistan to create a series of stories about a country struggling to recreate itself.

One of those stories took me to the fertile countryside north of Kabul known as the Shomali Plain. It had once been a breadbasket for the country. But people there had fought against the Taliban so fiercely that when the Shomali Plain finally fell, the Taliban took their revenge. They torched its vineyards; destroyed its villages; and even, one farmer told me, "killed the birds in their cages."

The village we were headed for could be found on old tourist maps—noted, with a star, as Afghanistan's "Ceramics Bazaar." The pottery of Istalif was known, in particular, for a blue glaze that shone like lapis lazuli. A guidebook from an earlier time describes "a village cradled within lush orchards. In spring young boys stand by the roadside and offer wands of wild tulips . . ."

In the spring of 2002, the only things along the roadside were the charred stumps of ancient grapevines and fields dotted with the rusted ruins of Russian tanks. When we got to Istalif, we found the bazaar's long line of mud stalls turned to rubble. As we walked, we could hear beneath us the crunch of shattered pottery.

But we had come here to find some hope. Word was that a potter had returned, a single craftsman who was firing ceramics again. Yes, said a young girl, pointing up the hill. A man with a donkey directed us around the one remaining wall of a house. Up and up we went, until we saw him, perched behind his wheel under a lacy tarp of brown leaves, the golden valley far below, shaping wet clay into a pot.

Abdul Wahkeel was, indeed, the very first potter to come back to where his father and father's father had been part of a centuries-long tradition.

He'd spent the years of war pushing bricks in a wheelbarrow, longing for Istalif. He was in his thirties, caring for a wife and three small children, plus his brother's widow and teenage daughter. To survive here, he said, he needed a hotter kiln and a smoother road: to make stronger pots and to get them to market unbroken.

We spent an afternoon with Wahkeel. I went inside and visited with the women as well. They were filled with joy and trepidation. Peace, it seemed, was at hand. Now they needed a bit of prosperity to survive.

In my story for *Morning Edition,* Abdul Wahkeel appeared for less than two minutes. But that morning, the letters and e-mails started pouring in. Hundreds of listeners wrote, many of them potters themselves.

Typical was a card sent by Mary Fischer from Dripping Springs, Texas.

"I participate in an event called Clay Fest. About forty artists who work in clay gather to sell their work and have a good time. Part of the event is a raffle . . . and funds go to artists who are in need.

"I was hoping this year we could send the money to help the potter in Istalif."

Like others who wanted to send money or buy pots, Mary Fischer asked if they could reach Abdul Wahkeel by mail.

Ah, I thought: If only there were mail in Afghanistan, or phones, or paved roads, or commercial flights.

In the end, we found a way. A nonprofit group called Aid to Artisans, which specializes in finding markets for artisans around the world, took on linking our listeners to Abdul Wahkeel. It sent a representative to Afghanistan with money and information on the latest technology.

Aid to Artisans eventually adopted the entire pottery community of Istalif.

When I returned five years later, Abdul had two more children, his daughters were in school, and his stall in the bazaar was brimming with goods.

I found him up the hill, leaning down before his new, hotter, kiln.

When he saw me, he stood up, wiped his dusty hands off, and laughed, "Salaam! Where have you been?" ■

**ABOVE** Renée Montagne on a hill in Kabul, Afghanistan, in 2002. The boys surrounding Renée are kite runners (photo by Tom Bullock).

# I WAS
# SUPPOSED
# TO DIE
# HERE

By far, the most dangerous and costly story NPR has covered in the last decade was the Iraq War. NPR had covered international conflicts before—the first Gulf War and the wars in Bosnia and Kosovo, among others. But this was different. The Iraq War lasted far longer than those conflicts and cost many more American lives, including the lives of journalists.

"When we started covering this we thought it would be three to six months, then it would all settle down and go back to normal," says foreign editor Loren Jenkins. "That was 2003. We never thought we'd have to bear the brunt and the cost of covering it as intensely as we have." Jenkins spent his early career as a journalist covering wars for *Newsweek* and the *Washington Post*, and he won a Pulitzer for his work in the 1980s. He has overseen NPR's foreign coverage since 1996.

At times, NPR had four correspondents in Iraq at once. In addition, the network hired as many as a dozen Iraqi staffers—drivers, guards, translators, and others without whom NPR could not have functioned in the country.

It was an expensive undertaking, but Jenkins says the network never stinted. "When we told them it was too dangerous to drive around in a normal car—that we needed an armored car, they said, 'Go get one.'"

"The first one we bought had to be flown in to Baghdad," Jenkins recalls. "That cost us about $140,000. And when we needed a second one, we got a second one."

Despite the security precautions, there were some frighteningly close calls.

In January of 2005, hardly a week after the armored car arrived in Baghdad, correspondent Lourdes Garcia-Navarro was driving from the center of the city to the American military base near the airport. "And so we're speeding down the road to get to the airport, and all of a sudden we hear this kind of crackling," remembers Garcia-Navarro.

In that moment, Garcia-Navarro learned that bullets make a strange sound when they hit an armored car. "This sounded like we were going over gravel, and then we turned around and we saw that in the back window right near where our heads were, a bullet had obviously struck. We realized we were under fire. Nothing to do but keep going."

When the NPR team arrived at the American base, the guards said, "You're lucky you were

in an armored car, because someone just got killed on that road earlier this morning."

Garcia-Navarro opened the trunk to inspect the damage. "My laptop had taken a bullet to the heart and was smoking. Thankfully, that was the only injury we sustained."

The computer survived. It was a Panasonic Toughbook, and Panasonic wanted to use the computer for advertising, but NPR wouldn't give it up. Instead, CEO Kevin Klose displayed the laptop with the bullet hole in the center of his office for visitors to see.

Another near-miss took place in December 2008. NPR correspondent Ivan Watson and his team parked their armored BMW and a second "chase car" outside of a restaurant in western Baghdad's Rabiye Street. They went inside for lunch. About forty-five minutes later, the NPR team walked back to the vehicles. In an essay on NPR.org , Watson described what happened next:

*Suddenly, Iraqi soldiers ran up screaming "bomb" in Arabic and pointing at the parked BMW. They blocked oncoming traffic, and an Iraqi officer named Lt. Mohamed Jabbour physically pulled one of our drivers away from the parked car.*

*Seconds later, the BMW exploded and burst into flames some fifteen feet from us.*

*The bomb appeared to have been one of the so-called sticky bombs that insurgents have increasingly used to lethal effect in Baghdad over the past year. The bombers use magnets to attach the explosives to the underside of parked vehicles.*

*The device was placed underneath the driver's side of the vehicle. The force of the blast blew out the vehicle's armored floor plates. There was no sign of the steering wheel. Looking at the twisted wreckage of the interior, it is hard to imagine how any passengers seated inside could have survived the attack.*

Moments after the assassination attempt, NPR videographer Ali Hamdani began filming the blackened hull of the armored car for a video on NPR.org. In the footage, Watson says to Hamdani, "This should have been our coffin." Hamdani then leans into the car and says in Arabic, "I was supposed to die here, but it seems my life is longer than this. I will be back, habibi."

# REPORTING IRAQ

**ABOVE** A statue of Saddam Hussein, later toppled in a scene broadcast throughout the world, stands amid a sandstorm in Baghdad during the bombing of the city by coalition forces in March 2003 (AP photo/Alexandra Boulat/VII).

# PETER BRESLOW
*Senior producer*

## Baghdad Confidential

**Scott Simon and I had it easy**. The bombing of Baghdad was over, the shooting had calmed down by the time we arrived, and the only thing nerve wracking about our ten-hour drive into the city from Jordan was the fact that our driver did it pretty much without his hands ever touching the steering wheel. He brewed coffee from his cigarette lighter. He thumbed through his journal. He made sandwiches. He combed his mustache. The only time the gas pedal wasn't mashed to the floorboards was when we had to cross a bridge that had been cratered by bombs. Our car was loaded with supplies we'd purchased in Amman. While I was scouring the supermarket shelves there for dried fruit and bottled water, Scott was checking out the Dead Sea Salt facial masques. And it struck me, I was headed to Baghdad with Frazier.

We pulled up to the infamous Palestine Hotel as the light was fading outdoors and nonexistent indoors. No power, no elevator, and a garbage-strewn trip up eleven flights of darkened stairs to the room that had been heroically inhabited for so many weeks by Annie Garrels. The remnants of Annie's presence helped tell the story of her time in room 1133: helmet, gas mask and flak vest in the corner, a satellite phone with a broken antennae from the time security police made a sweep and Annie had to stash the phone quickly, and a view from the balcony across the Tigris to the charred Planning Ministry that had been hit by a missile. It seems petty to complain about anything when I think of Annie holed up in that room.

The dim lobby of the Palestine was constantly humming with journalists running back and forth hauling flak vests on one shoulder and camera tripods on the other; also, the occasional self-important Iraqi surrounded by a retinue of staff people and uniformed followers.

In front of the hotel sat a huge fleet of vehicles all sporting duct tape "TV" insignias on their doors and hoods, as if those two letters give you some kind of immunity. There was CNN's humvee, ITN's fully armored car, the *Wall Street Journal*'s big white Mercedes and NPR's little blue Toyota (excellent gas mileage) with our driver Ahmed. Looking up to the fifteenth floor from the outside, you can barely pick out the balcony where two journalists were killed by an American tank shell.

Beyond the vehicles, concertina wire holding off a throng of desperate people: A man looking for news of his brother who disappeared in 1979, an out-of-work engineer who asks in perfect English, "What can you do for me?" All we can say is, "We'll tell your story to the American people." Others are asking if they can borrow a satellite phone to call a sister in England or a mother in France to tell them that they are alive. Almost all are passing notes explaining their situations to a little kid who's collecting them in a cardboard box. It seems doubtful anyone will ever read these short pleas.

The one bright spot is a young man named Annis who speaks English with a mild southern accent. He'd spent time in Tennessee and was looking for work. We just may have hooked him up with some reporters from the *Boston Globe*.

We've been here for a week, and every day things improve: running water one day, electricity another, hot water even comes on at some point. Gradually restaurants are opening, and you can actually buy something besides kabobs. Gunfire occurs almost exclusively at nighttime, and we've started leaving our flak vests in the trunk of the Toyota.

Stories throw themselves at you as you walk out of the hotel. We feel a little guilty. It's almost too easy. Go to an emptied political prison, and you bump into a former prisoner who came back to see the cell where he was beaten. Strike up a conversation with someone at a fruit stand, and they tell you a story that makes you teary. Go to a school and you find a group of teachers who have spontaneously gathered to clean up the smashed windows and toppled desks for their students. People complain about the bombing, complain that the United States didn't stop the looting, complain about thirty-five years of repression, but they are endlessly courteous and helpful and generous. Sometimes they are even a bit hopeful. ∎

## IRAQ

# ANNE GARRELS
*Foreign correspondent*

**As American soldiers flooded into Baghdad** in April 2003, my trusted driver, Thair, and I wept as we realized we had survived the U.S. bombing campaign and Saddam Hussein's thugs. Staying in Baghdad had been a gamble, but one that we both thought long and hard about and about which my boss Loren Jenkins had the guts to say "Do it." We wiped off the sticky oil and sand that had covered us like glue because of Saddam's futile efforts to confuse U.S. ordinance with smoky oil fires around the city.

By being on the ground, we knew that most Iraqis were not overjoyed at the arrival of the Americans, despite reports to the contrary. It was immediately evident that the troops and their superiors were not prepared to fill the void. As President Bush announced "Mission accomplished," we watched Baghdad burn. As one Iraqi told us in those first turbulent days, "The Americans need to take control, and we will resent them." The Americans could not control Iraq, and the resentment was even greater for this.

What the NPR team in Iraq could not know then was just how deadly the war had yet to become. In the ensu-ing years, Thair's neighborhood became a battleground between Sunni and Shiite extremists. He had to send his wife and children to Syria, where they remain refugees. Within months, journalists were living in ever-more forti-fied compounds.

Despite the restrictions on our movements because of safety concerns, we lived outside the cocoon of the Green Zone. We documented the rise of Muqtada al Sadr and his Mehdi Army as they emerged to confront the United States. We were witnesses to growing sectarian violence before the Bush administration would admit the reality. We visited much-lauded U.S.-funded projects only to find that many were illusory. We were embedded or not as need dictated, giving us access to many sides of the Iraq story.

We have been able to do all of this because of the soldiers who helped us see the reality of the conflict. And because of Iraqis, like Thair, who worked with us at great risk. Translator Abdullah Mizead was with me when a nearby car bomb went off. He immediately called his father to ask, in good Iraqi tradition, that he buy a sheep to feed the poor, in thanks for our safety. His father was kidnapped not long thereafter, never to be found. Our house manager, Vahram Epikian, was kidnapped, tortured, and released. Thanks to the efforts of many at NPR, Vahram, Abdullah, and their families have started new lives in the United States. ■

## 2007: LIFE IN WAR, JOURNALIST'S ASSIGNMENT IN IRAQ ENDS

# TOM BULLOCK

*Senior producer,* Morning Edition

**The first thing I saw in Iraq?** An American soldier lounging in a plastic lawn chair. He was manning a checkpoint on the Iraqi Jordanian border. I was speeding past in a Chevy Suburban, trying to get to Baghdad as soon as I could.

It was just after the invasion, and this was the golden era—or at least that's how it seems now.

We worked our butts off. But looking back now, what I remember most is how we spent our downtime.

I found time to swim, safely, across both the Tigris and Euphrates—though not on the same day. When I needed a haircut, I'd walk down the block to an Iraqi barbershop that looked like something out of the *Andy Griffith Show.*

At a pizza parlor not far from where we use to live, there was a piano and an Iraqi-Armenian who had an amazing ear for music. You'd walk in, and he'd hand you a dog-eared copy of the songs he could play and demand you make a request. He spoke almost no English, and the song titles showed it. "Fly Me to the Moon" became "Fling Me at the Moon." Whatever the name, the guy could play—and the pizza was great.

On a regular basis, American troops would show up there to buy dozens of pies to go, then throw them in the back of their armored vehicles and drive them back to their base—basically the world's most heavily protected pizza delivery service.

That world was brilliant, brief, and, is no more.

As the violence increased, everything in Baghdad changed. The Americans became isolated behind barriers in the Green Zone and U.S. bases. All of Baghdad turned into 12-foot high concrete blast walls and razor wire that spread through the city like kudzu.

Our reporting changed, too, dominated by stories of car bombs, insurgent attacks and then civil war, millions of Iraqis fleeing and thousands dying as Shiites and Sunnis cleansed neighborhoods and bombed markets.

Kidnappings became commonplace.

I became a prisoner in our bureau. To go out meant putting not only my own life at risk, but the lives of my translators and drivers as well. So we taught the Iraqis we work with our trade, and they became journalists.

Our entire Iraqi staff is now made up of refugees. Each one has been forced to flee his or her home and seek safety in another neighborhood. Not because they work with us, but because they prayed slightly differently than the militia on their street.

They're some of the most amazing people I've known. And through all of this, they come to work every day, and our bureau has kept running.

Working in Baghdad is a strange thing. You get accustomed to the long days and constant work. You learn to live with having nowhere to let off steam. The cycle is simple: wake up, work, repeat.

You weed through press releases and sit through press conferences, which seem at odds with the reality we—living the Red Zone, the real world—know all too well.

Some of my favorites: a series of statements from the Iraqi government saying reconciliation is at hand. Read the fine print and make some phone calls, and you find out there's been a meeting to agree on a more important meeting on some unknown day in Iraq's very unknowable future.

Or, the U.S. military saying Iraqi forces will be able to take over security in the country in twelve to eighteen months. I've been told that regularly for the last three plus years.

Some press releases are just plain strange: U.S. troops defuse an explosive device strapped to a donkey. I'm pleased to report the donkey was unharmed, by the way.

Have I been harmed? I've come close. But after twenty-one tours, my body and mind seem to have held up okay.

And while the marriages of a number of journalists and soldiers I know here have fallen apart, I managed to fall in love with and marry a beautiful bride.

I met Carrie just before I started coming to Iraq. She's supported me through four-and-a-half years of this.

My last view of Baghdad will be of the city by air. I will leave, frustrated by the death of that golden era of pizza parlors and barbershops; frustrated with Iraqis I've talked to who proudly say "We are all brothers," then take up arms against each other; frustrated with American military and civilian officials who stand up and say everything in Iraq is working, then when they leave write books about how everything in Iraq has failed and it's not their fault.

And I'm pained by the number of people I've personally known who've been killed here: journalists, Iraqis, and American soldiers. ∎

TRANSCRIPT EXCERPT
### *ALL THINGS CONSIDERED*

**SHOW DATE:**
*2006-12-04*
**CAT. TITLE:**
*Fort Carson Soldiers with Emotional Issues Given Little Support and Often Punished*

**MELISSA BLOCK:** From NPR News, this is *All Things Considered.* I'm Melissa Block.

**ROBERT SIEGEL:** And I'm Robert Siegel.

For soldiers serving in the war in Iraq, the emotional toll can be very serious. Tens of thousands of those soldiers have symptoms of serious mental health problems, including depression, suicidal tendencies, substance abuse, and post traumatic stress disorder (PTSD). That is according to the military's own studies.

**BLOCK:** Even before the war started, administration officials said they had in place extensive programs both in Iraq and back home to heal those soldiers, but an NPR investigation at one Army base, Fort Carson in Colorado Springs, Colorado, reveals those programs are not working. Soldiers who feel desperate and have tried to kill themselves have trouble getting the help they need. In fact, evidence suggests that officers at Fort Carson punish soldiers who need help and even kick them out of the Army.

NPR's Daniel Zwerdling has our story.

**DANIEL ZWERDLING:** One of the first soldiers I met at Fort Carson is a young man named Tyler Jennings. He looks like a football player, and he used to be on junior varsity. Jennings says when he came home from Iraq last year, he felt so depressed, so desperate, he decided to kill himself.

Jennings takes me to the second floor of the bungalow that he rents with his wife to show how he almost did it. As we pass the closet, I ask to see his uniform, pinned with medals. He seems embarrassed.

**TYLER JENNINGS:** The one on the very top is my most prestigious. That's my purple heart. And then the expert marksman badge.

**ZWERDLING:** Jennings says it was late at night, the middle of May. His wife was out of town, and he felt more scared than he'd felt in gunfights in Iraq. Jennings opened the window and sat on the ledge and he started swigging a bottle of vodka to get up the courage. He was twenty-three years old.

**JENNINGS:** I had like one of those big orange extension cords.

**ZWERDLING:** An electrical cord.

**JENNINGS:** Yeah. That was around my neck, like a military-style slipknot. And then the other part was just wrapped like a bunch of times through and around here. So I was just kind of setting here trying to get drunk enough to you know, either slip or just make that decision.

**ZWERDLING:** Five months before that, Jennings had gone to the medical center at Fort Carson. A staff member typed up his symptoms, quote, crying spells, hopelessness, helplessness, worthlessness, unquote. He was doing drugs to make himself numb. But Jennings says "You know what was even worse?" When his officers found out he was having a breakdown and taking drugs, they started to haze him, and they told him they were kicking him out of the Army. Jennings says that's when he decided to jump.

**JENNINGS:** You know, there were many times that, you know, I've even told my wife that I really wished I just died over there because if you just die over there, everyone writes you off as a hero.

**ZWERDLING:** Tyler Jennings isn't the only one who's felt desperate. I've talked to twenty soldiers who've come back from the war to Fort Carson, like Jason Harvey, Jonathan Duncan, Jeff Conley, Lawrence Keifer, Ron Backhouse, Adam Caplan, William Morris, Mickey Davis, Michael Lemke, and they say the way officials have treated them and other soldiers with problems makes them feel betrayed.

*SOUND BITE OF MUSIC, "REVEILLE"*

**ZWERDLING:** It's 6:00 A.M. at Fort Carson in Colorado Springs. The jagged tops of the Rockies are glowing pink. Soon soldiers fan out across the lawns and start morning workouts.

*SOUND BITE OF SOLDIERS COUNTING*

**ZWERDLING:** Top officials at Fort Carson refused to talk with me. So I contacted soldiers on my own. I also obtained Army documents and talked to witnesses. They corroborate everything you're about to hear.

*SOUND BITE OF SOLDIERS WORKING OUT*

**ZWERDLING:** Most of the soldiers I spoke with say they wanted to go to Iraq to avenge 9/11. They didn't know what to expect. Here are Alex Orum, Tyler Jennings, and Corey Davis.

**ALEX ORUM:** And it really pisses me off when people go around saying, "Oh man, I saw what you guys went through on TV." No one saw what we went through on TV. They can't show you little four-year-olds screaming because their leg just got blown off.

**JENNINGS:** One guy that always sticks out in my head, he had a hole in the back of his head, about 6" by 6," and I kept having to push his brains back up into his head and even after we got it bandaged up, brains are pretty heavy actually, and they were, like, seeping through, like pushing the bandages off.

**COREY DAVIS:** I'll probably never forget that day for the rest of my life. There's just body parts everywhere, you know. People crawling with no legs, no arms. I mean, and there were just screams that you could—I don't know what will go away in my head.

**ORUM:** But the worst smell in the world is something I can't seem to stop smelling; it's the smell of burning flesh.

**ZWERDLING:** Still, the soldiers felt proud to fight in Iraq. Many reenlisted. But then they came home to Fort Carson, and over the next few months, their world turned upside down. ∎

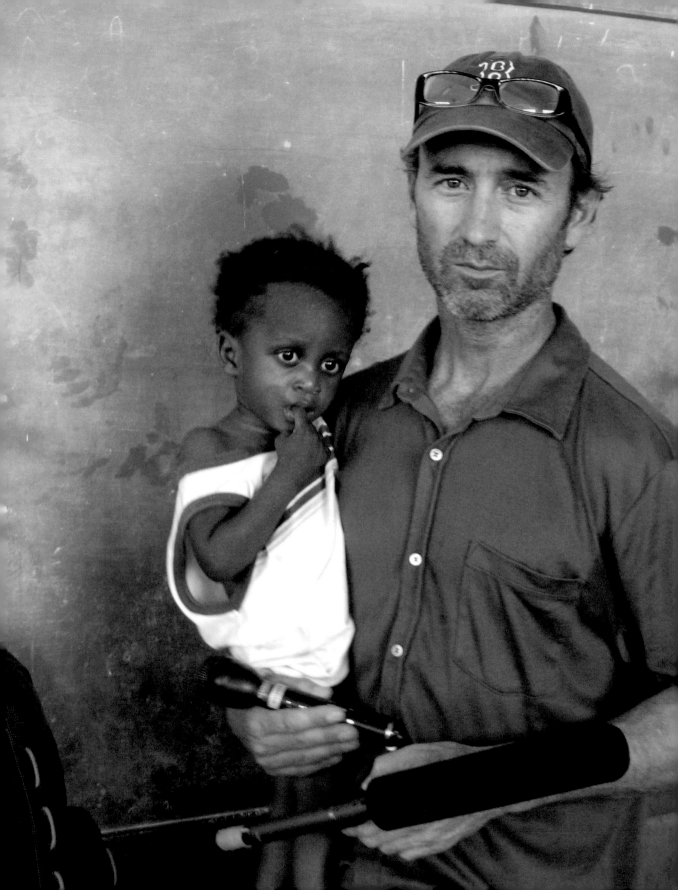

# JASON BEAUBIEN
*Foreign correspondent*

**This was on the border** between Chad and Sudan in 2003. It was the early days of the crisis in the Darfur region of Sudan. The government in Khartoum was making it almost impossible for journalists to get to this remote region. There were reports of ethnic killings and thousands of people fleeing through the desert. An Italian TV cameraman, Emilio, and I had managed to catch a flight with an aid agency out to the western edge of Darfur. People were telling us about Janjaweed fighters on horseback descending on their villages like vicious sandstorms and destroying entire settlements. Emilio and I were sleeping outside, filing our stories by flashlight and desperately trying to save the battery in my satellite phone because we had no idea where we were going to get it recharged.

**I was trying to record** a group of refugees who'd moved into a school in Port-au-Prince after four hurricanes hit Haiti in 2008. The room was packed with kids waiting for some biscuits and juice. This little guy was screaming his head off, crying, and, as I recall, had rivulets of snot coming out of his nose. He was just a little younger than my youngest son. I picked him up, and he immediately shut up, allowing me to record the distribution of the biscuits. I, however, was then obligated to carry him around for the rest of my visit. He wouldn't let me put him down. ∎

**ABOVE** Jason Beaubien filing by flashlight in Darfur, 2003 (photo by Jason Beaubien).

**LEFT** Jason Beaubien in Haiti, 2008 (photo by Jason Beaubien).

# INVESTIGATIVE REPORTING WAS ALMOST NONEXISTENT

If NPR's twenty-first-century goal was to become a powerhouse news source that could rival any in the world, the network already had some distinct advantages. Only NPR had the combination of deep local access to every part of America through member station newsrooms and far-reaching resources around the globe through overseas bureaus. But in other areas, NPR was seriously lacking. A top-tier news organization needs to consistently break stories and set the news agenda. Newspapers such as the *Washington Post* and the *New York Times* have a long history of investigative reporting, but that had never been NPR's strength, nor really part of its culture.

"In terms of storytelling, NPR was an A-plus," says former vice president of news Bill Marimow. "Investigative reporting was almost nonexistent."

Marimow remembers a few exceptions—Nina Totenberg's coverage of the Supreme Court, Barbara Bradley-Hagerty's reporting on religion, and Peter Overby on the lobbying beat—but otherwise, at the beginning of the twenty-first century, many NPR correspondents simply didn't see investigative reporting as part of the job description.

Marimow, by contrast, had won Pulitzer prizes for his investigative reporting at the *Philadelphia Inquirer.* As an editor at the *Baltimore Sun,* he mentored other reporters to do the same. When he re-entered the job market from the *Sun* in January 2004, he says, "I was getting literally hundreds of calls." One was a voicemail from NPR president and CEO Kevin Klose. "I thought he was a reporter, and I always return reporters' calls," says Marimow, "so I called back."

Marimow reached Klose's secretary. "I thought it was very odd for a reporter to have a secretary, so I asked—what does Kevin Klose do? Well it turned out he was the president of NPR."

A few months later, Marimow came to NPR as managing editor. "There was almost a mono-maniacal focus on getting access to newsmakers, because you needed their voices," recalls Marimow. He taught reporters to focus on getting information from documents and sources rather than holding out for an interview with the person at the top of the food chain.

"For me, working with Bill was an incredible education," says Ellen Weiss, who succeeded Marimow as vice president of news. "I thought I knew what my yardstick was, and I thought I

knew where I was on my yardstick. It became immediately clear that my yardstick was much longer and I had tons to learn."

Marimow, Weiss, and other senior news managers agreed that if NPR was to improve its journalism, the newsroom would need to emphasize beats—specific subjects that individual reporters would own and master.

Within a year, the network hired new correspondents to cover labor, the environment, media, technology, the White House, and police and prisons.

"Every corner of my office was filled with resumes," Weiss recalls, "because I had six jobs I was hiring for, all reporters."

The hiring blitz coincided with a downturn in the rest of the news industry. More than ever before, NPR had its choice of some of the best journalists in the country.

## 2006: BABY SCREAMING IN BACKGROUND

# MARY LOUISE KELLY
*Former correspondent*

NPR installs broadcast-quality lines in correspondents' homes, so we can do live updates in the wee hours. For new mothers, this can be a mixed blessing. One early morning, bleary eyed after hours pacing with my newborn, I got a call from *Morning Edition*: Could I do a quick live interview to lead the 6 A.M. feed? So there I am in my pajamas, trying to sound authoritative about the latest intelligence on Iran's nuclear program, and in the middle of the interview, my son starts to screech. I am mortified: a couple of million listeners nationwide are being subjected to my son's tantrum. But Steve Inskeep, never one to miss a beat, deadpanned, "Mary Louise, sounds like anxiety about this nuclear issue has really got folks riled up at your place." I had to grin. "Steve," I replied, "I gotta tell you; it's kept us up all night." ∎

# DAN GEDIMAN
*Executive producer,* This I Believe

**It was March 2003**. I was home sick with the flu, desperately bored and hungry for something to read. I found a book on my wife's bookshelf that I had somehow never seen before. It was called *This I Believe,* and it was based on a radio series of the same name hosted by legendary broadcaster Edward R. Murrow.

At first glance, I thought a fifty-year-old book filled with "the living philosophies of 100 men and women in all walks of life" might be dry and dated. But I was wrong. It was as timely as could be. Not only was the content on these pages fascinating, but the idea behind the pages captivated me as well: that all these writers had dug deeply inside themselves to discern what they truly believed—and then had the courage to share it with the world.

*This I Believe* was the result of a lunch meeting in 1949 between Murrow, Philadelphia advertising executive Ward Wheelock, and CBS founder William S. Paley. The men bemoaned the spiritual state of the nation in the face of economic uncertainty, discrimination, the threat of nuclear war, and the rise of McCarthyism. To help counter this trend, they created a five-minute daily radio program in which the famous and the unknown would speak about the guiding beliefs by which they lived their lives.

The series launched in 1951 and quickly became a national phenomenon: the radio program aired on nearly 200 stations, including WHAS in Louisville. The *Courier-Journal* and more than ninety other newspapers printed *This I Believe* pieces, usually as a weekly feature. Simon and Shuster published two best-selling compilations of essays, and Columbia Records released a popular two-disc set of *This I Believe* statements as read by their authors.

In introducing the series, Murrow said, "We hardly need to be reminded that we are living in an age of confusion. A lot of us have traded in our beliefs for bitterness and cynicism, or for a heavy package of despair, or even a quivering portion of hysteria. Opinions can be picked up cheap in the marketplace, while such commodities as courage and fortitude and faith are in alarming short supply."

Those were the words that inspired me in 2003 to re-create *This I Believe*, nearly fifty years after Murrow's series ended. The country was deeply embroiled in the Iraq War to fight the terrorists "over there" so they wouldn't attack us "over here." You could easily substitute the terrorists of today for the Communist threat of the 1950s. And we were facing the Patriot Act, also eerily reminiscent of the McCarthy era.

In four years of weekly *This I Believe* broadcasts on NPR, listeners heard from corporate executives, two former U.S. secretaries of state, a presidential candidate, Nobel laureates, and leading figures from the arts and sciences. We also featured the wisdom of Americans whose names you wouldn't recognize: a librarian in West Virginia, a social worker in New Orleans, an attorney in Chicago, a factory worker in Utah, and an airline baggage handler in Alaska. The more than 200 people broadcast on NPR were selected from some 60,000 essays submitted to our Web site, www.thisibelieve.org. Nearly a third of those statements have come from students in grades ranging from middle school to college.

For an individual to write of his or her most firmly held beliefs and then earnestly present them to the world takes courage, especially in an age when fist-waving shouting matches erupt at public forums, and the president is heckled before a joint session of Congress. Yet thousands of Americans continue to write and submit their statements of belief, and thousands more read and hear the results on our Web site, in our podcasts, and in our books.

The popularity of the exercise stems from its simplicity: Write in the affirmative—say what you do believe, not what you don't believe. Speak in the first person, not the editorial "we." Limit the essay to 500 words so as to truly focus on the belief that is central to your life experience. The *This I Believe* essay-writing exercise has been used in coffee houses, adult literacy programs, hospices, churches and synagogues, hospitals, retirement homes and prisons. The experience is transformative, both for the individual and often for their communities.

As I have learned again and again, the power of *This I Believe* goes beyond writing down one's belief. It is the acts of sharing and listening that provide us opportunities to better understand one another and come to respect beliefs that are different from our own. ∎

**OPPOSITE** CBS News broadcaster Edward R. Murrow smokes a cigarette on a CBS set (AP photo).

# IT CHANGED THE DIMENSIONS OF HOW PEOPLE THOUGHT ABOUT THEMSELVES

One woman bore almost total responsibility for the dramatic expansion of NPR's reporting staff, and most NPR employees never met her.

Joan Kroc was the widow of McDonald's founder Ray Kroc. She was also a devoted public radio listener.

In 2002, Stephanie Bergsma was the associate general manager for member station KPBS in San Diego. She was also a personal friend of Joan Kroc.

Bergsma told NPR CEO Kevin Klose that a "very generous supporter of the station" might be interested in contributing to NPR. Bergsma invited Klose to a breakfast in San Diego with the potential donor. When she told Klose the woman was Joan Kroc, Klose recalls, "I almost fell out of my chair."

What followed was a year-long professional courtship between Klose and Kroc. Almost no one at NPR knew that the two were in contact. Even Klose did not know that Kroc had been diagnosed with inoperable brain cancer until shortly before her death.

In August of 2003, Kroc invited Klose to attend her seventy-fifth birthday party. It was an intimate luncheon at her home for family and fewer than thirty guests. Kroc sat in a wheelchair, Klose recalls. "She looked like she'd had a stroke."

Klose had brought Kroc a birthday gift—a hand-painted box from Russia, with a picture of two swans flying into the twilight. As he gave her the gift, Klose recalls, "She takes both my hands in her hands. She looks up at me with her piercing blue eyes and says to me, 'Oh we're going to do such wonderful things together.'"

Two months later, Kroc died. Klose read about it in the news on the night of Sunday, October 12. Four days later, he received a call from Richard Starmann. Starmann was a former senior vice president at McDonalds, and he had been a consultant to Kroc on her charitable giving. He had visited NPR to review the network's financial records, and, in the ensuing months, Starmann and Klose had developed a friendship.

Klose remembers the phone call word for word.

"Starmann says, are you sitting down? I say, yeah. He says, do you have something to write

"

## She takes both my hands in her hands. She looks up at me with her piercing blue eyes and says to me, 'Oh we're going to do such wonderful things together.'

*Kevin Klose on his last meeting with Joan Kroc*

with, like a pencil? I say, yes. He says, you have something to write on, like a piece of paper? Starmann is clearly trying to drag this out as long as possible. He says okay, put down a number two. And I write down two. Now write another two. And we go through it number by number."

Starmann remembers, "I get to 222,000 and said—that doesn't seem right, Kevin, throw another 2 on there. Then I said, throw another 2 on there. Eventually we got to 22 million dollars. And when I told him about the last 2, which took it from 22 million to 222 million, then I think he was surprised."

Starmann told Klose, "At one of the rallying points close to Joan's death, she looked up at me and said with a big, big smile, 'Oh I just wish I could be there to see Kevin's face when he learns the numbers, she said. It's gonna knock their socks off.'"

At the time, it was the largest gift that had ever been given to a cultural organization. Before the bequest, NPR's foundation had around $30 million.

The gift "gave us a sense of arrival," says Klose. "We can now take ourselves much more seriously

in what we're doing. Not to say how smart we are, but just to say—we can do this job."

As much as the money changed NPR financially, it also changed NPR psychologically. It made staffers appreciate that we were no longer just scrappy underdogs—we were worthy of respect. Kroc "was basically saying NPR is a national treasure and worthy of all this investment," says former vice president of programming Jay Kernis.

I remember the day Klose announced the Kroc gift at an all-staff meeting. Susan Stamberg, one of NPR's founding mothers, stood in the front of the room with Klose. She had tears in her eyes.

## YOU CAN'T SPELL FUND-RAISING WITHOUT THE F-U-N IN FUN

# P.J. O'ROURKE

*P. J. is a contributing editor at the* Weekly Standard *and the author of many books, including* Driving Like Crazy.

**I like to think of myself** as the only wholehearted, full-throated, money-donating, tote-bag-carrying supporter of NPR in the entire GOP. And I'm not an NPR booster simply because I am one of the rotating cast of panelists on *Wait Wait . . . Don't Tell Me!* (Although, since I'm a selfish Republican, this helps.) I've been a fan of NPR since *WWDTM*'s prize offering was "Win Carl Kasell's Voice on Something That Hasn't Been Invented." Contestants had to invite Carl over to their house for a drink to get him to answer their phone. Nor am I deaf to NPR's liberal bias. As a friend of mine who's a little to the right of Karl Rove said, "If Congress is debating labor legislation, NPR will get a balanced story by interviewing the AFL and the CIO." That's harsh, but I take his point. I still love NPR because, whatever the organization's human failings, it tries like hell to tell the truth.

NPR tries to tell the truth both qualitatively and quantitatively. That is, NPR gets the facts but then takes the time to give us those facts in detail and provide us with some detailed perspective. Other radio news operations get the facts, too, and you'd think their all-talk formats would give them scope to do something with the facts. But either they just repeat a fact every ten minutes, or they turn some big-mouth commentator loose on the fact, and smoke is blown up microphones for three hours.

However, I believe I'm supposed to be recounting an anecdote about working with NPR, and the above doesn't qualify. One year I endeavored to make my Republican pro-business tendencies useful by helping my local NPR member station raise money. I've never understood why those fund drives have to be more painful to listen to than even the loudest and most mendacious paid radio advertisements. "You can give WEDU a dollar a day, and that would be just (pause as liberal arts major does math) seven dollars a week!"

I could do better than that. I went on, live, with the host of a popular news program about state and regional issues. "Give us a million dollars," I said, "and we'll stop all bird noises on NPR for one month. No more cheep-cheep-cheep sound bites to establish that the reporter is outdoors, no more quacks, honks, and loon calls as stand-ins for the visual grandeur of nature, no more to-whit to-woo background ambience for experts on climate change." The public affairs show host tried to say something, but I was too fast.

"Speaking of climate change," I said, "give us $10 million and we'll walk right out of this radio station and stop global warming personally. We'll go house to house turning down thermostats, we'll plant trees in coal mines, and we'll stuff potatoes up the exhaust pipes of every SUV we see." The public affairs show host attempted to interrupt. I was not daunted. "And give us $100 million, and [I named an NPR national correspondent on whose melodious voice I've had a crush for years] will broadcast the news in the nude!"

The host's jaw dropped. The engineer's jaw dropped. The producer's jaw dropped, and so did the intern's. There followed a long, deep silence such as you can hear only on live radio. It wasn't that I was being sexist. It wasn't that I was being disrespectful. It wasn't even that I was being Republican. It was just that . . . I wasn't telling the truth. ∎

FIGURE 6

# WHO LISTENS . . . AND DOESN'T CONTRIBUTE?

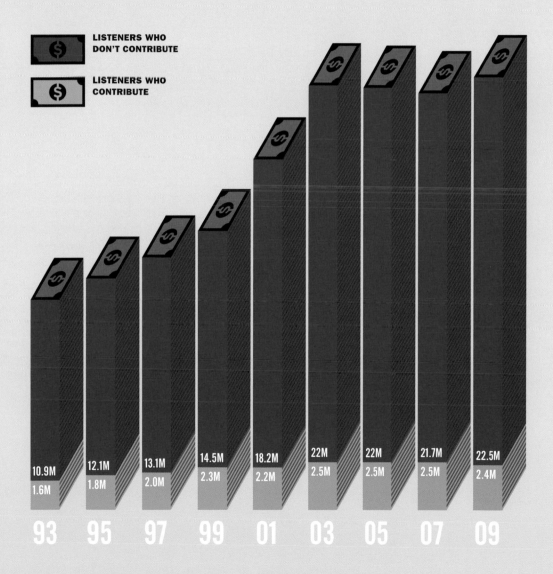

LISTENERS WHO
DON'T CONTRIBUTE

LISTENERS WHO
CONTRIBUTE

| 93 | 95 | 97 | 99 | 01 | 03 | 05 | 07 | 09 |
|----|----|----|----|----|----|----|----|----|
| 10.9M | 12.1M | 13.1M | 14.5M | 18.2M | 22M | 22M | 21.7M | 22.5M |
| 1.6M | 1.8M | 2.0M | 2.3M | 2.2M | 2.5M | 2.5M | 2.5M | 2.4M |

**SOURCE:** *Corporation for Public Broadcasting Annual Financial Reports; 1993-NPR Arbitron; 1995–1999, RRC/Arbitron; Fall 2000–present Arbitron/Act 1. Persons 12+*

# TOM THOMAS AND TERRY CLIFFORD

*Co-CEOs, Station Resource Group*

**"Why, that was Mom's station,"** says the young waitress at an Iowa diner, smiling at the mention of WOI, the NPR station in Ames. "She had her radio up on a shelf in the kitchen. Listened to that station every day."

"And you know," she added, refilling a coffee cup, "it's my station now, too."

WOI-AM, broadcasting from Iowa State University, preceded National Public Radio by a generation. It was one of America's "educational broadcasters," most based at Midwestern universities, that offered school-of-the-air instructional programs, recipes for the homemaker, rural extension service advice for the farmer, and uplifting selections of classical music and drama.

In the 1960s, WOI added an FM station and, in 1970, was one of the ninety charter members that launched NPR.

Forty years later, WOI has long since dropped the classes, built up a wide-ranging schedule that speaks to contemporary Iowa, and added more stations to extend its reach. The WOI stations have joined with colleagues at the University of Iowa and the University of Northern Iowa to create Iowa Public Radio, which each week reaches more than 220,000 listeners across the state with multiple services including full-time news, full-time classical music, and news and adult alternative music mixes.

"It's a connecting station to the whole country," is the way one listener describes the twenty-first-century WOI. Another captures enduring themes, "Good information, serious in-depth news . . . coming home."

**Stations are the crossroads** of the public radio enterprise. Trusted selectors, creators, integrators, and presenters of quality content—from their own studios, across their communities, and from far beyond. Stations are the link through which an international correspondent reaches your kitchen, some of the world's greatest music finds its way to your office, and the *Car Talk* guys join you on Saturday errands. Public radio stations are the pathway between network and listener and the reflection of a community back to itself.

While they share their NPR connection, public radio stations are a diverse lot. They are owned and operated by scores of state and local organizations—colleges and universities, independent nonprofit groups, state agencies, and others. Each station makes its own programming decisions, hires its own staff, and manages its own budget. As the ownership of commercial broadcasters has been increasingly consolidated in the hands of national corporations, public radio stations remain emphatically rooted in the local communities and regions that they serve.

Stations are the backbone of the public radio economy. They raise most of the money: the dreaded fund drives; business sponsorships; allocations from university budgets; and funding from federal, state, and local governments. All told, public radio stations generate nearly a billion dollars every year, the majority of which is spent on creating, broadcasting, and providing information about their national and local programming. Stations are the largest source of funding for NPR, providing four out of ten dollars that fuel the network.

The mix of programs on stations' schedules has always been a combination of network shows and local efforts. In addition to choosing from NPR's powerful lineup, stations also select programs from American Public Media, Public Radio International, and the Public Radio Exchange—and the multiple networks help stations shape distinctive services for their communities and increase choices in the growing number of cities served by more than one public station.

Many stations today have a greater capacity than ever to create their own content that resonates with public radio's core values and realizes the highest standards of quality. They are working with more skilled staff, more robust technology, and more knowledge of the audiences they serve.

And they are using the Internet and new digital channels to expand and enrich their services and extend the life and value of their program investments. Stations are eager to find innovative, compelling, and effective ways to put this growing capacity to work in pursuit of their missions.

**In October 2007**, wildfires spread with devastating speed around San Diego, engulfing over 800 square miles, destroying more than 2,000 homes, and forcing millions to evacuate. Public radio station KPBS swung into full emergency mode, quickly becoming the community's source for vital information and providing some eighty hours of continuous crisis coverage.

KPBS complemented its broadcast coverage with an array of new media tools. The station's Web site featured a continually updated fire map tracking the situation and news headlines summarizing official information and station reports. The headlines were in turn distributed via Twitter feeds, reaching citizens displaced from their homes as text messages on their mobile devices.

**At NPR's fortieth anniversary**, local public radio stations are reaching the largest broadcast audiences in their history. In the near term, public radio's greatest opportunities are in broadcasting—terrestrially based radio signals that are omnipresent and freely available to everyone. At the same time, public radio has extraordinary opportunities—created by the tools of the new network age—to make its great content more broadly and easily accessible, to engage with people in new ways, and to enlarge its public service offerings in ways that go well beyond broadcasting. These efforts will, in turn, reshape the character and focus of the broadcast service.

For a decade or more now, public radio's most inspired stations, both large and small, have been becoming something more—public service media companies, defined by the character of their content, their commitment to public service, their trusted relationships with their audiences, and their capacity to move across multiple channels to achieve their missions.

America's public radio stations give their listeners better lives—more thoughtful, joyful, and useful; more fulfilled in the pursuit of understanding, challenge, and personal growth. Public radio stations work for the health of their communities across many dimensions of public life—education, arts and culture, economics, the environment, and the sense of connection and responsibility to others. Public radio stations keep our democracy vital—providing the free flow of ideas that sustains a free society, accountability for those who govern, and information that helps citizens make good decisions for themselves, their communities, and their nation. ∎

"
**Many stations today have a greater capacity than ever to create their own content that resonates with public radio's core values and realizes the highest standards of quality.**

# MAKING THE DEMOCRACY BETTER

The expansion of NPR's news division was part of a larger reorientation away from music programming over the last decade. In 2002, NPR overhauled its cultural programming. Murray Horwitz, a Tony-award winner who served as NPR's vice president of cultural programming, left the network that same year. A few years later, NPR stopped producing the most listened-to classical music program on the radio, *Performance Today*, and gave the show to American Public Media.

Jay Kernis was one of the driving forces behind the reorientation away from arts programs. "The coming of the Internet meant listeners really didn't need their public radio station to be everything—news, classical, folk music," Kernis recalls. "During this decade there were many other sources of classical music. So the question was, what was public radio's future? And many of us felt public radio's future was in making the democracy better and helping citizens become smarter."

Part of that project involved creating new shows.

There were some listener-driven reasons for creating new programs. *Day to Day* was designed to create a midday "tentpole" at a time of day when listeners tended to tune out public radio.

*The Tavis Smiley Show* (later *News & Notes*) and *Tell Me More* were intended to build ethnic diversity in NPR's listenership. *The Bryant Park Project* tried to appeal to a younger audience and establish a stronger foothold for NPR in the digital world.

But there were other reasons for the creation of these programs, too. In the fall of 2002, NPR opened a spacious new production facility in Culver City, just outside Los Angeles. "We've got to be in California in a new way," NPR CEO Kevin Klose told NPR's managers. "We've got to reset how we report on California and the West. We have huge audiences out there, and they continue to grow."

*Day to Day* and *The Tavis Smiley Show* were both produced out of NPR West. Those programs helped fill the empty space NPR had acquired in California. But the radio dial was far more crowded. "Any time you create something new, something else has to be displaced," says Weiss. "So we had essentially four programs competing with each other for the same limited space on a public radio station. I think that represented at the time a very radio-centric strategy." It was a strategy that would ultimately prove unsuccessful, as three of the four new programs folded by the end of the decade.

# DAVE ISAY

*Founder and president,* StoryCorps

**StoryCorps has aired** hundreds of stories on *Morning Edition* since we began our Friday morning broadcasts in 2005. I'm always asked for a favorite story, and usually it's whatever we aired that week. But one story in particular embodies the values of public radio—encouraging thoughtful listening and ennobling the stories of all people—perfectly: the love story of Danny and Annie Perasa.

Danny worked as a clerk at Off-Track Betting; Annie was a nurse. Both were consummate New York characters, with storied lives and thick Brooklyn accents. When they came to our Grand Central booth, Danny told the story of their first date twenty-five years before, and Annie read aloud one of Danny's daily love letters. He told her, "I always feel guilty when I say, 'I love you' to you, and I say it so often. It's like hearing a beautiful song from a busted old radio—and it's nice of you to keep the radio around the house." Listeners loved it.

Danny and Annie embodied so much of what Story-Corps stands for—the grace and poetry in the words of everyday people and the idea that the lives of the people around us can be even more compelling than those of the rich and famous. They eventually became the unofficial spokespeople for StoryCorps, and we began traveling the country together, spreading the word about the project.

Danny and Annie never ceased to astound me with their kindness, humor, wisdom, and, most of all, their boundless love for one another. Danny was short, bald, toothless, and cross-eyed, but he had more romance in his little pinkie than all of Hollywood's leading men put together.

In January 2006, Danny was diagnosed with end-stage pancreatic cancer. In February, unable to travel, Danny asked us to come to his home to record one last conversation with Annie. That Friday's broadcast on *Morning Edition* came from their conversation, and it ended with Danny's ode to Annie:

> *She lights up the room in the morning when she tells me to put both hands on her shoulders so that she can support me. She lights up my life when she says to me at night, "Would you like a little ice cream?" or, "Would you please drink more water?" Those aren't very romantic things to say, but they stir my heart. In my mind and my heart there has never been, there is not now, and never will be another Annie.*

Danny passed away two hours after the East Coast broadcast. E-mails flooded into NPR's Web site. In all, Annie received upwards of two thousand condolence letters from listeners. At Danny's funeral, Annie placed a copy of these letters inside the casket to be buried with him. She keeps another copy at home. Annie continues to read one letter each day instead of her daily love note from Danny.

I have never been prouder to be part of the public radio community. ■

**LEFT** David Isay, the founder of StoryCorps, LeAlan Jones, and Lloyd Newman in 1996 (photo by Russ Berkman).

# WILCO DID IT

"

**That completely opened the doors. . . . After that, all you had to do was call a band and say, 'Wilco did it,' and they'd say 'That's fine.'**

Bob Boilen on the start of *All Songs Considered*'s live concert series at DC's 9:30 Club

As the growing news operation squeezed some music off public radio's airwaves, innovators within NPR found other ways to reach listeners who were curious to discover new recording artists.

Bob Boilen had been a director of *All Things Considered* since 1989. Each day he would choose the snippets of music to play between segments. "I knew from all the email I was getting that there was a massive audience out there who loved music and had not a clue where to get it," says Boilen.

Just before the turn of the new century, Boilen created a music show called *All Songs Considered*. His efforts to find space on the radio failed. So he debuted the show on the Internet.

The official launch of NPR's first Web-only program came in January of 2000. During the show's early years, slow Internet connections often made streaming the program a painful test of listeners' patience. But the show steadily built its audience, and in 2005, Boilen started offering live-streaming concerts on the NPR homepage under the *All Songs Considered* heading. The first was from the band Bright Eyes. "It was a question in my mind whether a band would say 'Yes' to this," Boilen remembers. "Back then the big question was, do I want to give away my content?"

A few concerts later, Boilen scored a coup. Wilco let him stream their show at the 9:30 Club, a popular concert venue in Washington, DC. "That completely opened the doors," says Boilen. "After that, all you had to do was call a band and say, 'Wilco did it,' and they'd say 'That's fine.'"

Recognizing the success of *All Songs Considered*, NPR decided to create a new online home for public radio music programming. "The challenge was to create a place where all of the material from our acquired programs, from twelve stations, from all the news programs that had to do with music, and original programming would sit together in a place and feel like it belongs together," says the Music Unit's executive producer, Anya Grundman.

The redesigned NPR Music page went live in November of 2007. "It turned the relationship between stations and the network on its head," says Boilen. For the first time, stations and NPR were collaborating rather than competing online. Traffic to the site immediately doubled and has continued to grow in the years since.

The new Web site propelled NPR's profile even higher in the music world. In 2008, Boilen's phone rang, and a representative from Sony Records was on the other end. "They told me there was going to be a new Bob Dylan record coming out," Boilen remembers. "They wanted to premier the record on NPR.org."

His first reaction was shock. Sony had been reluctant to give NPR access to its artists in the past, and Bob Dylan is not known for being generous with rights to his music. Boilen's response was equally shocking to the Sony people. "I said, 'Well, let's hear it first.' And there was real silence at the other end."

NPR.org posted the exclusive first listen to Bob Dylan's *Tell Tale Signs* on September 30, 2008. New albums from Neil Young and Paul McCartney followed soon after.

What made these and other NPR Music offerings so unusual for NPR is that almost none of them had any presence on the radio. In the realm of music, NPR had created a flourishing online universe that was more than simply a companion to the radio.

**ABOVE** The Swell Season (Marketa Irglova and Glen Hansard) play a *Tiny Desk Concert* in August 2009 (photo by Coburn Dukeheart).

# STEPHEN THOMPSON

*Editor, NPR Music*

**When I started at NPR** back in 2006, I assumed that a good chunk of any given day would consist of pressing my nose against the glass as my favorite musicians performed songs before my awestruck eyes. But it almost never happened; either the musicians we'd feature would perform at some other bureau, or else they'd show up unannounced and perform in secrecy. As delighted as I was to work for NPR, I'd overestimated the number of opportunities to see live music in lieu of doing actual work.

Cut to March 2008, at the South by Southwest Music Festival in Austin, Texas. *All Songs Considered* host Bob Boilen and I had agreed to meet at a club called The Thirsty Nickel, which had thoughtfully double-booked singer-songwriter Laura Gibson with an obnoxious, beer-swilling audience of nattering knobs. Each individual yahoo in the crowd was louder than Gibson, who seemed to sing into her own lungs in an effort to perform as quietly as possible. To be fair to the noisy dinks in attendance, Gibson could just as easily have been drowned out by the sound of my own breathing, or by the sloshing din of blood rushing through my veins.

Bob and I shrugged exasperatedly throughout Gibson's set, during which I added to the crowd noise by suggesting to Bob that we should give up on quiet concerts altogether, and instead ask Gibson to perform at his desk the next time she passed through Washington, DC. We could invite all our coworkers to watch, call it "Live at Bob's Desk" or something, and there'd be roughly half as many noisy drunks on hand.

This, friends, is what's called a "Eureka!" moment. Bob and I agreed that this was not such an idiotic idea, in spite of its source, so we waited around to chat with Gibson after the show. "Boy, it sure was hard to hear you," we said. "We were thinking it would have been better to just have you perform at Bob's desk the next time you're in Washington, DC!" To which she responded, "I'll be there in three weeks. I'd love that."

Which, in turn, is how the marvelous Laura Gibson became the Typhoid Mary of the Tiny Desk.

Gibson showed up, as promised, and played a mesmerizing four-song set while our assortment of recording equipment rolled on. Bob hooked everything up and stitched together the audio and visuals to look as professional as possible, and we gave the video away as part of our "Live

in Concert from *All Songs Considered*" podcast. The result was something I'd actually listen to voluntarily, even if I weren't on NPR's payroll, and a new series was born. Bob and *All Songs* producer Robin Hilton came up with the name *Tiny Desk Concerts*, as both a descriptive moniker and a sly reference to Bob's old band, Tiny Desk Unit.

For the first few months, we booked a succession of our favorite moderately well-known, acoustic-guitar-wielding mopes: Vic Chesnutt, Sam Phillips, Sera Cahoone, Lambchop's Kurt Wagner. And then Tom Jones's people called. Sure, the series was conceived as a way to showcase the quietest of the quiet, but could we maybe accommodate one of the biggest voices in the history of modern music? We said sure, because: Tom Jones—and *Tiny Desk Concerts* quickly became less tiny than we'd anticipated.

Jones showed up and blew the doors off the place, and he was followed by singers with voices both big (The Swell Season, The Avett Brothers) and small (Horse Feathers, Maria Taylor), as well as members of the Australian Chamber Orchestra, a jazz brass band led by Dave Douglas, Somaliborn rapper K'naan, harp-wielding Colombian Edmar Castaneda, soulful R & B throwback Raphael Saadiq, a cappella bluegrass legend Ralph Stanley, party-loving rocker Andrew W.K. (performing improvisational piano instrumentals, natch), and more beard-sporting folkies than you could possibly shake a stick at, no matter how tempted you might be to do so. The *Tiny Desk* tent gets bigger and bigger as I write this, to the point at which we've got no qualms about trying—and failing spectacularly—to book U2, Paul McCartney, and Bruce Springsteen, just in case they'd always yearned to perform at some dude's desk in a bullpen full of office drones.

To me, though I'm more than a little biased, the *Tiny Desk Concerts* have evolved into the very embodiment of NPR—and in particular the spirit of try-anything, gather-'round, why-not performance that produces magic and mistakes in equal measure. As long as the magic is the only stuff that winds up airing, what could possibly be better? ∎

**THIS PAGE**
Edward Sharpe
& The Magnetic
Zeros play a *Tiny
Desk Concert* in
October 2009
(photo by Coburn
Dukehart).

# STEPHEN THOMPSON

*Editor, NPR Music*

**Consider Our Dust, Jerks!** A trophy case in NPR's lobby tells the story of a journalistic giant whose courageous and tenacious reporters, editors, and producers have given a voice to the voiceless, spoken truth to power, comforted the afflicted and afflicted the comfortable. The Peabody. The Gracie. The National Medal of Arts.

NPR Music has won awards in its own right, but on the whiteboard near my desk hangs a symbol of what I consider our greatest achievement. There, a flaccid pink inflatable saxophone dangles majestically as a reminder of NPR Music's finest hour: the 2008 NPR Relay Race, in which four-person teams signed up to run around the Washington, D.C., city block that contains NPR, a bank and a sidewalk pockmarked with missing bricks and strewn with broken bottles. (Each team's baton consisted of an inflatable doodad of some sort; ours was the saxophone, for obvious reasons.)

The contest, held in late November in lieu of a holiday party, followed a protracted stretch of office-wide taunting: A team representing *All Things Considered*—thoughtfully dubbed "Consider Our Dust, Jerks!"—had made a good deal of noise, but none barked louder than NPR Music's own "Greased Cheetahs," so named because a greased cheetah was the only animal I could think of that would be faster than the world's fastest animal.

The Greased Cheetahs were and are a veritable murderers' row of lightning quick mofos: Lars Gotrich, whose majestically flowing blond mane proved impervious to wind resistance; Mike Katzif, also known as the Mike Katzif-shaped puff of smoke that appears when he's handed an inflatable pink saxophone, Patrick Jarenwattananon, who's crossed the finish line by the time you're done saying his name; and me. As the team's eldest member by roughly a decade—I like to think of myself as the Greased Cheetahs' creepy uncle—I had to take extra measures to keep up, so I wore my sleekest racing cardigan, which I'd coated with a space-age polymer to keep my torso from breaking up upon re-entry.

It took a while for our opponents to become fully aware of which team had won; at first, we'd only appeared to them as four indistinct blurs. But, oh, they heard about it. At this very moment, they may be reading about it in the book you now hold. It remains a high point of my career at NPR, and perhaps even a high point of my entire life.

You see, from the time I slid down a rope and racked myself in sixth grade to the time I coached *The Onion*'s softball team to a 10-3 defeat at the hands of a group of developmentally disabled adults, my own athletic life has been synonymous with dismal, nauseating failure. But this! This was a moment of actual, non-Pyrrhic victory. I'd spent the preceding thirty-six years scouring the earth for peers with whom I might be able to compete on a level playing field—bedridden dowagers, science-fiction chat rooms, the Washington Nationals—and all had proved my superiors. It wasn't until I was held to the drab, hemp-bedecked bosom of public radio that I actually got to win a race.

This book is surely packed with inspirational tales of NPR's greater meaning to the worlds of journalism, radio and politics. But let us never forget the network's meaning to the Greased Cheetahs' motley band of fleet-footed dreamers—and, now, to the annals of sport itself. ∎

> **"**
>
> **I had to take extra measures to keep up, so I wore my sleekest racing cardigan, which I'd coated with a space-age polymer to keep my torso from breaking up upon re-entry.**

**OPPOSITE** The Greased Cheetahs' motley crew. From left: Stephen Thompson, Lars Gotrich, Patrick Jarenwattananon, and Mike Katzif (photo by Katie Burk).

# YOU DIDN'T NEED TO DO A RADIO SHOW

> ## Ultimately the show demonstrated you could produce audio, text, video, graphics, animation in a place and people would find it, and it would go virally out all over. You didn't need to do a radio show.
>
> *Jay Kernis on* The Bryant Park Project

In 2007, the network tried to establish another multiplatform presence with a New York-based newsmagazine called *The Bryant Park Project*.

The day the show launched, Jay Kernis described his dream to the staff. Every public radio Web site would have a section with *The Bryant Park Project* heading. "Local, regional, and national material would all live there together under that banner," Kernis told the staff in New York. It would be a place for younger staff members at public radio stations across the country to contribute interesting and experimental text, video, and audio. That dream was never realized.

The show struck an off-the-cuff, quirky tone. It had a reputation for experimentation and seeing what worked. Although it picked up some followers on the Internet, NPR cancelled the program less than a year after its debut.

Kernis now says his biggest mistake with the show was thinking it needed to be a radio program at all. "Ultimately the show demonstrated you could produce audio, text, video, graphics, animation in a place and people would find it, and it would go virally out all over. You didn't need to do a radio show."

At the moment vice president of news Ellen Weiss was involved in cancelling *Bryant Park*, another opportunity fell into her lap. She was determined to learn from the lessons of *Bryant Park*.

**FIGURE 7**

# AUDIENCE GROWTH: TOTAL RADIO VS. NPR

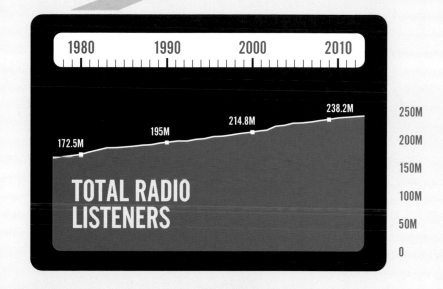

1980     1990     2000     2010

172.5M    195M    214.8M    238.2M

**TOTAL RADIO LISTENERS**

250M
200M
150M
100M
50M
0

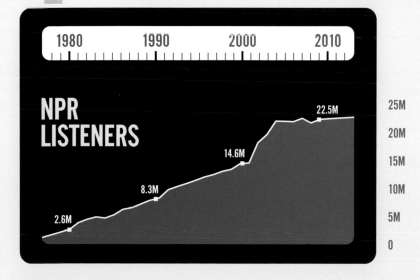

1980     1990     2000     2010

**NPR LISTENERS**

2.6M    8.3M    14.6M    22.5M

25M
20M
15M
10M
5M
0

**SOURCE:** *Spring Public Radio Nationwide/Arbitron (Spring 2000–present, Arbitron Nationwide/Act 1); 1980–1994,
NPR Arbitron; 1995–1999, RRC/Arbitron; Fall 2000–present, Arbitron/Act 1. Persons 12+.*

# THE WAY WE APPROACH TELLING THE STORY WILL BE DIFFERENT

In the summer of 2008, NPR's international economics correspondent, Adam Davidson, had completed a collaboration with Alex Blumberg of *This American Life*. Their report on the housing crisis was called *The Giant Pool of Money*. It aired on *All Things Considered* and *This American Life*, and the response was overwhelming. The *Giant Pool of Money* won a Peabody award, a duPont-Columbia award, and other honors. Davidson proposed spinning it into something larger.

*Bryant Park* had taught both Weiss and Davidson that a new radio show was not the way to go. "It seemed to me very possible that no one should ever start a radio show anymore," said Davidson. "I was really excited by the idea of figuring out how to be something that wasn't a radio thing that was then turned into an online thing or vice versa, but was all at once."

"I didn't want it to be contaminated by us," said Weiss. "I wanted to incubate it in a way that said, 'break the model.' We'll step on a few toes. Jobs will be defined slightly differently. The way we approach telling the story will be different."

*Planet Money*, as the project was named, would aspire to explain the economy to people who may not be literate in business terminology. It would tell good stories in a narrative way and make complicated concepts understandable.

Adam Davidson thought the timing was perfect. It would launch in the fall of 2008, the height of election season. "Nobody will care what's happening, so we can quietly make all of our embarrassing mistakes," Davidson predicted. "We'll have six months before we really have to put our game face on and figure out who we are."

**LEFT**
Alex Blumberg (middle) and Adam Davidson (right) of *Planet Money*, Brian Lehrer (left) on WNYC in October 2008 (photo by New York Public Radio).

## LIFE AS AN NPR BROADCAST LIBRARIAN

# JANEL WHITE
*Broadcast librarian*

**Working on the reference desk** in the Broadcast Library is always an adventure. You never know what type of audio a staff member will need. Sometimes you can find audio on the topic or person easily but then have to make a judgment call whether or not that audio will work with the angle of the story. Archival sound can help set the mood of the story or put an answer to a question in context. Once you do find audio that fits the story, the last part of the process is hearing that audio on the air later that day or the next day.

A recent request from the Arts Desk was for audio of the construction of the Empire State Building in 1930. I knew that an historical newsreel would be the best source of audio from that time period. During my initial searching, I found newsreels of the Empire State Building construction, but they were either silent films with a soundtrack or too generic to work for the story. I kept trying different combinations of search terms within Google and scrolling through multiple pages of results. Suddenly on page 5 of the search results, I found a Universal Newspaper Newsreel with pictures of construction workers on beams and good audio describing the process. That audio ended up being used briefly to establish the giant size of the Empire State Building before explaining the current steps being taken to make the building greener. ∎

*Planet Money* launched as planned on September 7, 2008. That day, Fannie Mae and Freddie Mac almost collapsed. "That was the start of the financial crisis," remembers Davidson, "and we've just had to play catchup every second since then."

Since then, *Planet Money* has created a unique niche in the public radio world. It is a podcast, a radio feature, and a blog. "We're able to pick a length that's right for every single thing, and that can be three minutes or an hour," says Davidson. "We can be *Fresh Air* one day, *This American Life* the next, and college radio the next. Or be them all in the same day. And I think that's really nice."

# THIS IS A TERRIBLE SITUATION

While NPR journalists covered the economic collapse, the network soon found itself part of the story. The financial meltdown led to one of the worst crises in the company's history. Madeleine Brand, host of *Day to Day*, explained the chain of events this way in an online video about her program's cancellation:

> *"You have a bunch of mortgages that go bad. The housing bubble bursts. That brings down a Wall Street firm, Lehman Brothers. That causes a ripple effect in markets worldwide. That causes a credit crunch. That means that people can't buy cars anymore because they can't get the credit. That means the auto industry is practically bankrupt. That means the auto industry isn't buying ads on NPR, and that means my show gets cancelled, and I lose my job. There it is."*

Brand was not the only one out of a job. NPR also cancelled *News & Notes* and laid off people in other departments, sixty-four in all. Roughly half were from the news division. People whose voices NPR listeners had grown to know over decades—Alex Chadwick, John McChesney,

Ketzel Levine, and many others—suddenly found themselves out of work.

Although the Joan Kroc gift created a cushion, her more than $200 million bequest was not enough to make up for the loss of income from investments and underwriting. NPR's annual budget at the time was more than $120 million.

"The cuts were extremely painful," says Ellen Weiss. It was she who decided the cuts would not be across-the-board, but rather targeted at specific programs. Weiss remembers telling managers at a budget meeting, "I want to put something on the table, and I want everyone to agree to this."

"Our audience wasn't going down. Our revenue was, but our audience wasn't. So I kept thinking, two years from now I don't want our audience to hear programs that are lesser quality. And it's a fine line, where does the audience notice?"

While *Day to Day* and *News & Notes* were eliminated, *Morning Edition* and *All Things Considered* were left relatively untouched.

NPR was contemplating these cuts just as the board was concluding a CEO search. The search team settled on Vivian Schiller of nytimes.com. Schiller remembers a board member calling her

# MELISSA BLOCK
*Host,* All Things Considered

**"Don't step on those meatballs!"**—those words of warning from my Yupik Eskimo guide on St. Lawrence Island, Alaska. At his urging, I was lowering myself into his underground meat locker, carved out of the permafrost centuries ago by his ancestors. Why did I agree? I wasn't sure. But I was quite certain it was an offer I'd never have again.

Down I went into the pit, six feet under the tundra. "I've seen this in *The Silence of the Lambs*," muttered my waggish producer, Art Silverman.

After a careful descent, I stepped into the meat cache alongside the "meatballs": a dozen giant pillows of fermenting walrus blubber. Months before, our guide and his crew had caught the walruses about 40 miles out in the Bering Sea. They had stitched the brown walrus hide around the blubber, which oozed forth as the meat aged, mottling the skin with gray-and-black patterns. The permafrost—as the name suggests—stays frozen year-round, so it preserves the meat.

As I looked around, I realized the chamber itself was quite beautiful: a circular space about 10 feet across, with whalebone ribs arching to form the struts of the earthen roof. I tried to imagine the Yupiks hacking this deep pit out of the permafrost ages ago, using the shoulder blade of a bull walrus as a shovel.

Underground, it was oddly peaceful and—to my surprise—didn't smell at all of fermenting meat. I caught a whiff of a wild herb from above. "I might want to stay down here!" I shouted up to my guide. He shouted back, "What you need is a cot!"

In my twenty-five years with NPR, I've had some great adventures. I've porpoised through the air inside the Goodyear blimp and ducked champagne sprays in the Yankee clubhouse as they celebrated winning the World Series. And I feel quite confident that I'm the only NPR host who has ever spent quality time under the Alaskan tundra among fermenting walrus meatballs. ∎

**ABOVE** Melissa Block in the walrus locker in Alaska (photo by Art Silverman).

before the hire was final to warn, "You're walking into a difficult situation."

NPR managers decided it was best to make the cuts before Schiller arrived. "We want you to come in with a fresh slate," the board told her.

Even so, Schiller's first few all-staff meetings were spent explaining drastic cuts and cost-saving measures. It was not an easy way to begin, "but I haven't been daunted by it," says Schiller. "I don't walk in there saying, 'I did a terrible thing.' I walk in there thinking this is a terrible situation, and I have a responsibility to lead this company out of it."

# THE GROUND IS UNDULATING UNDER MY FEET

On May 12, 2008, NPR journalists found themselves in a different kind of disaster. Hosts and producers from the staff of *All Things Considered* were working in Chengdu, China. Beijing was a few months from hosting the summer Olympics, and *All Things Considered* was about to host the show from a foreign country for the first time in the program's history.

Host Melissa Block was conducting an interview in a church meeting room in downtown Chengdu. This transcript of her recording describes what happened next:

> **Pastor Cai Lingyun:** *My position is to help my colleagues or my pastors—to pastor the church or to groom the church.*
>
> *SOUND BITE OF NOISE*
>
> **Melissa Block:** *What's going on? The whole building is shaking. The whole building is shaking.*
>
> **Cai:** *[Speaking in Chinese]*
>
> *SOUND BITE OF NOISE*

> **Block:** *My goodness. Oh, my goodness, we're in the middle of an earthquake? Earthquake. Pieces of—the top of the church is falling down. The ground is shaking underneath my feet, and all of the people are running out in the street.*
>
> *SOUND BITE OF PEOPLE SHOUTING*
>
> **Block:** *As we're standing here, birds are flying. The ground is undulating under my feet.*
>
> *SOUND BITE OF PEOPLE SHOUTING*
>
> **Block:** *The cross on the top of the church is waving wildly and bricks are falling off of the ceiling—falling off of the roof. People are huddled together here on the street. The ground is still waving.*
>
> **Block:** *The shaking seems to be slowing down. We can still feel vibrations underneath. Everybody has run out onto the street. There are crowds gathered. Somebody is naked.*

*All Things Considered* producer Andrea Hsu was holding the recording equipment when the earthquake hit. She and Block fled down several

flights of stairs and into the street. "I was still wearing the headphones," remembers Hsu. "I heard Melissa start talking through the headphones, then I realized—Oh, my God, Melissa's doing radio. She was narrating what was going on."

The 7.9-magnitude quake left about 90,000 people dead or missing. NPR journalists were the only western reporters on the scene.

But none of the staff in China realized that in the moments after the quake. Block and Hsu reunited with *All Things Considered* host Robert Siegel, producer Art Silverman, and translator Xiao Yu Xie at their hotel. They took a car to the area hardest hit by the quake, about thirty miles away. Block and Hsu went to a school that had collapsed. They arrived shortly before midnight.

"Most of it was just huge piles of rubble, heavy machinery, and floodlights shining on it," remembers Hsu. "When we first walked in, people were really eager to talk to us. Parents were showing us photos on their cell phones of what they thought was their child reaching out from under the rubble. They were saying, 'This photo was taken at 3:30 this afternoon, my child is here, and we can't do anything.'" After about ten minutes of interviews, Chinese police forced Block and Hsu to put away their recording equipment. It began to rain.

"That's when we noticed these makeshift tents all along the basketball courts," Hsu recalls. "Underneath were all these bodies that had been pulled from the school, and the families had wrapped them in shrouds of cloth. They were burning paper money, lighting incense, and setting off firecrackers." Hsu and Block watched as rescuers brought out one small body after another. There were dozens. Each time the crew would put a corpse on the tarp, "the families would rush in to see if it was their child, and then after a scuffle of a minute or so, everyone would disperse except for the family whose kid it was. It was awful."

The stories that NPR's team produced from Chengdu over the following days were picked up by nearly every major American news organization. NPR won national awards for the coverage.

"It was only when I got back that I realized the impact the coverage had," says Hsu. Although she played a major role in crafting NPR's stories from Chengdu, "to this day I still haven't listened to most of those pieces. I just didn't want to."

When NPR first decided to broadcast *All Things Considered* from China, the network's goal was to give Americans a sense of what the country and its people are like today—how we

**ABOVE** Art Silverman (with microphone) in Chengdu, China, after the 2008 earthquake (photo by Andrea Hsu).

are similar and dissimilar. "I think we ended up achieving that, but in a much different way than we'd originally planned," says Hsu. "It was, 'I can imagine what these people are feeling,' instead of, 'These are people who don't speak my language in this place halfway around the world.'"

# WE DID IT IN THE WORST WAY POSSIBLE

On many of NPR's most popular programs, the hosts who ushered in the twenty-first-century were gone by the middle of the decade. Melissa Block and Michele Norris replaced Linda Wertheimer and Noah Adams on *All Things Considered*. Neal Conan replaced Juan Williams on *Talk of the Nation*. *Weekend All Things Considered* scrolled through at least half a dozen hosts over ten years. But no single host replacement caused as much controversy as the replacement of Bob Edwards on *Morning Edition*.

"It was my baby," says Edwards. "I loved being the host of *Morning Edition* because of what we had there. It was the program everyone listened to."

Edwards had hosted *Morning Edition* since the show's debut in 1979. He was replaced just eight months before the twenty-fifth anniversary.

"We did it in the worst way possible," says Jay Kernis, NPR's then-senior vice president for programming. "We did it very, very badly."

NPR managers and stations wanted *Morning Edition* to be more nimble and responsive to breaking news. They wanted hosts who would explore the world, taking *Morning Edition* listeners with them. And they wanted a show that would frequently update to reflect news developments throughout the morning.

"We needed to ensure that drive time in Los Angeles and Seattle was every bit as fresh and newsy as drive time in New York," says executive director of news programming Ellen McDonnell. Like Edwards, McDonnell was part of the *Morning Edition* staff from the show's debut in 1979. When she had Bob Edwards replaced in 2004, she was the program's executive producer.

Edwards acknowledges that he was resistant to doing as many updates as the show producers wanted. The program's producers had also concluded that the show needed a two-host format—another proposal that Edwards was reluctant to sign on to. And there were other concerns, as well.

"I felt he was holding the show hostage," says Kernis. "I felt that he was phoning it in. I felt that he lacked the hunger and enthusiasm of those early years."

"I don't know what that means," says Edwards. "Did I sound laconic? Sleep-deprived, maybe. But, no, I was still very dedicated to what I was doing."

In March of 2004, NPR announced that Bob Edwards would be reassigned as a correspondent. The revolt from listeners was immediate and intense.

"Mornings are so special and so much a habit that I knew there would be concern among listeners," says McDonnell. "The extent of the concern? I probably underestimated that."

She describes the listener reaction as "an avalanche."

"My resident assistant from college in Penn State, who I had not heard from in twenty-some years, tracks me down, sends me an email, and says: 'Tell me you had nothing to do with this,'" remembers McDonnell.

Some people within the public radio community pushed back, as well. Minnesota Public Radio's senior vice president of news Bill Buzenberg, who used to be vice president of news for NPR, told the *New York Times*, "Bob was like Walter Cronkite. Let's do what we can on other parts of the show, change some things around him, but let's leave him there."

Edwards says he was prepared to take the job as a correspondent for NPR, but the relationship with managers at the network became so

**ABOVE**
Editors, including
Ron Elving (far
left) and Ken
Rudin (second
from left), in
the studio on
Super Tuesday,
2008 (photo by
Steven Voss).

poisonous that it was impossible. The breaking point was a *Times* story that described some of the complaints about him.

On the day that article ran, Edwards recalls, "I was just feeling so bad. I went home, and I was ranting to my wife, and she said to me—you got this FedEx letter." It was from Hugh Panero, then CEO of XM Satellite Radio.

The letter proposed that Edwards host a one-hour daily long-form interview program on satellite radio. It also included this message from Panero: "Maybe Jay Kernis doesn't want to hear you every day, but I do." Edwards accepted the job.

Five years after the change in hosts, *Morning Edition* still regularly receives email from listeners lamenting Edwards's absence. But by every measurable statistic, the program has grown during those five years.

Since Steve Inskeep and Renée Montagne took over in 2004, *Morning Edition* has broadcast from Afghanistan, Iran, and Pakistan, among other countries. Over five years, as radio listening plummeted across the rest of the dial, *Morning Edition* listenership increased 8 percent, to a weekly audience of 14 million.

McDonnell says she never regrets the decision, and *Morning Edition* is now what she always

# STEVE INSKEEP

*Senior host,* Morning Edition

**"I'm about as far away** from you, I think, as I could possibly be."

Those words by Anne Garrels, reporting from Afghanistan on September 30, 2001, serve as the refrain for years of news coverage after 9/11.

We heard many of Anne's reports via a high-quality satellite phone, a kind first widely used after the attacks on the Pentagon and World Trade Center. It brought us Anne's voice, increasingly raspy from the Afghan cold and desert sand. Never mind the words: the tone told a story.

As recently as the 1990s it typically required a truckload of equipment to broadcast from a war zone on anything better than a scratchy phone line.

In a new century, a backpack would carry everything necessary into Baghdad or New Orleans—a special satellite phone, or sometimes just a laptop.

In December 2001 I stood with a microphone in the ancient Afghan city of Balkh. I recorded a musician strumming a homemade instrument. Gunmen put down their rifles to listen. American listeners heard the same song.

In several thousand years of Balkh's existence I must have been the first person to broadcast in studio quality halfway around the world.

Eight years later I followed an elderly Iranian woman climbing five flights of stairs to her apartment. The microphone captured her labored breathing, a metaphor for a struggling people. Never mind the words: her tone expressed everything she could not say. ∎

**ABOVE** Steve Inskeep utilizes his laptop and satellite phone in Lashkergah, Afghanistan, in January 2002 (photo by Qudratullah Ahmady).

imagined it could be. "The first time I heard, 'This is *Morning Edition,* I'm Renée Montagne in Kabul,' or 'I'm Steve Inskeep in Karachi,' I got chills," McDonnell says. "I still get chills when I think of that."

Edwards continues to host his daily interview program on satellite radio. Every morning as he drives into work, he listens to *Morning Edition.* "It still sounds great," he says. "NPR still does the best reporting. No one else even comes close."

# STEVE INSKEEP

*Senior host,* Morning Edition

**Many people ask** what time I get up. Lately, it's been 2:41 in the morning. By about 3:45, I'm in the office. The show starts at 5 o'clock, Eastern Time, and of course we can never start even one second late.

People cringe when they hear this, as if I were confessing that I was slightly insane. The truth is that it's not bad. Renée Montagne and our staff in California work the same routine, only three hours sooner because of the time difference. As I've told Renée, that's insane.

It's okay to be up early. If I ever write a memoir, I might call it "Shaving in the Dark." I kiss my sleeping wife goodbye and walk downstairs and raise my hand for a taxi. It's Washington, DC, and the bars have not been closed very long. People are out.

You see little things at that hour—little signs of the world going around with its shirttail out. Morning after morning a rat scurries out of the same restaurant door. Somebody leaves a ceiling fan on the sidewalk in front of a beauty parlor. Now and again you meet people swaying, slurring words, working their way home.

On election night 2008, I went to work several hours early. It was before midnight, and I woke to a continuous roar, the sound you would expect to hear down the street from a football stadium.

Outside I saw the streets filled with people. The biggest crowds gathered a block from my house, on the corner where a riot began in 1968 after the assassination of Martin Luther King Jr. On that corner in 2008, thousands of people were celebrating the election of Barack Obama. The street was blocked. Traffic stopped. I found a taxi going nowhere, and the driver made a U-turn to get away. He had the radio on, and that was how I heard Obama's acceptance speech, in a taxi creeping through streets filled with people who seemed like they could float off the pavement.

Whenever I reach the office, I find producers, editors, and engineers who've been there for hours before me. Here's an editor who's writing a book in his daylight hours; there's a producer with a stamp on her wrist from a concert the evening before.

Many people work appalling hours, since *Morning Edition* is a twenty-four-hour operation. Even reporters and editors who don't regularly work the overnight know they're liable to get a call about breaking news at two in the morning. Scores of NPR employees have, at one point or another, done something important for this program at a ridiculous time of night.

A few people have worked for *Morning Edition* for decades. Ellen McDonnell, who's in charge of NPR programming, started on *Morning Edition* a few weeks before its premiere in 1979.

Ellen has always worked to bring younger people behind her. Some years ago, she arranged for me to spend time in Iraq with a producer named Cara Tallo who was, if I'm not mistaken, approximately eleven years old at the time. After several more years of effort for NPR, Cara received the reward of all rewards: coming in to work before midnight for a couple of years as the *Morning Edition* overnight producer.

Something about this program has attracted people from other media. Madhulika Sikka, our executive producer, previously worked at ABC's *Nightline*, which means that she went from working many late nights to being eternally on call for us. Somebody has to think on Sunday about what we put on the air for Monday.

We don't get a lot of sleep, but we can take pride in that. Somewhere in America a woman is brewing coffee at 7-Eleven, while an autoworker is finishing the night shift. A farmer is awake; a bartender is stacking chairs. A student is trying to get an online degree. An insomniac poet is hacking away at the keyboard all night like a latter-day Charles Bukowski. A soldier is lacing his boots.

For those of us at *Morning Edition*, it's an honor to be awake along with them. ∎

**THIS PAGE** Renée Montagne and Steve Inskeep in the studio, 2007 (photo by Stephen Voss).

# MICHEL MARTIN
*Senior host,* Tell Me More

I left the house at 4:30 A.M., still in the fog you have when you get up even earlier than you normally do. I was resisting the urge to be angry at the world, knowing how tired I already was and how tired, cold, and hungry I would be several hours later. I had covered four previous inaugurations; I was always assigned somewhere outside, and I was always cold. It wasn't quite right to say the thrill was gone—I reminded myself how many people around the world would love to have a peaceful transition of power in their countries, let alone be there to witness it in person. And how many people did I personally know who would have loved to be in my place, heading to cover the inauguration of this country's first African American President? And not just some guy, but a guy with an amazing story, born to a mother barely out of her teens, all but abandoned by his African father, raised in two worlds and overseas, the first black president of *Harvard Law Review*, an unlikely candidate, an even unlikelier success. Friends were bunking with relatives and hitching rides and packing up kids in long johns and blankets just for the chance to be where I was going.

Still, how cold was it going to be anyway?

By the time I got to my first location, my hands were already numb despite two pairs of gloves and hand warmers, and my feet felt like blocks of ice from the two-mile walk, despite two pairs of socks. The crew at the Canadian Embassy, where we were set up along the parade route, was still straggling in. Some had slept in their offices the night before in order to avoid the traffic. I was still fighting irritation. What was I doing here? Who's listening to the radio anyway at a time like this? Isn't everybody in front of a TV? What was I thinking? Why is it always so cold?

But then I started to see them . . . Them. The people who did NOT have to be there . . . who weren't assigned . . . the people who felt they HAD to be there. It's been said so many times that there's no interesting way to say it, but it was true . . . people of all ages, people of every race and color, mostly smiling, from what I could see under their layers of hats and scarves. They were wishing each other well, like they do in those movies set on a mythic Christmas morning in a small town you didn't know existed. They were all heading off, in the same direction, with the determination of a mission, yet with a lightness of step.

And they kept coming . . . and coming . . . and coming. Everywhere we looked, more people, more faces. Faces filed with cheer, with hope, and later, as the oath was taken, with tears.

I don't remember a single thing I talked about on the radio that morning. But I remember all those faces. Oh, and yes, it was a bit cold. But nothing to complain about. ■

**LEFT** Audie Cornish-Emery interviews a bystander at President Barack Obama's inauguration (photo by Kathie Miller).

**ABOVE** Vivian Schiller,
President and CEO, in 2009
(photo by Stephen Voss).

# VIVIAN SCHILLER
*President and CEO*

**Not long after I was named CEO**, I was invited to dinner by the founding mothers of NPR. They wanted to celebrate the fact that a "girl" was finally going to run the place. Over lunch, Cokie Roberts, Susan Stamberg, Linda Wertheimer, and Nina Totenberg—these women I felt I already *knew*, these magnificent *voices*, these titanic *journalists*—regaled me with stories from NPR's glorious past. After a while I think they forgot I was there as they laughed their way through tales from the early days. I leaned back and took it all in . . . and fell in love.

NPR is no ordinary media company. No one talks about shareholder value. There are no daily Nielsen ratings being picked over to drive decisions for the next day. Editorial meetings don't begin—as in some news organizations—with, "What are people talking about?" but rather, "What's interesting? What matters? How can we inform, inspire, surprise our audience today?"

The news business is going through a rough patch, and NPR isn't immune to tough economic times or the changing media landscape. But still—coming to work is pure joy. We dream. We plan. We argue. We challenge each other. We laugh—a lot. We continue our conversations into the wee hours on e-mail and pick up again in the early morning. For most of us, there's not much of a line between NPR and the rest of our lives.

I was asked not long ago by a reporter what motivates me. The answer is easy: I wake up to it every single morning—literally. Like millions of Americans, my alarm is set to NPR and it's a daily reminder of what we do and why. Wherever I go, I hear the same refrain: "Oh my god, I love NPR!" We are part of people's lives, part of their family. I feel that responsibility keenly.

Looking ahead, we are committed to step up our coverage, where other news organizations are stepping away; to continue to cover the sciences and the arts with rigor and imagination; to explore the subjects that directly touch the lives of our audience—like health care, the economy, and the environment. We will hold public institutions and individuals to account. We will bear witness to history. We will remain a place for civil discourse in an age where civility sometimes seems at risk. We will provide, in the words of a founding *father* of NPR, Bill Siemering, "the exchange of ideas between people with different values." And most of all, we will provide our listeners with the information they need to be active participants in a vibrant democracy.

We'll always be there on the radio, of course, but also on the Web, on the iPhone, on the android—wherever there is an audience hungry for information. It's a thrilling time to be in public media.

As my one-year anniversary as CEO approached, I invited the founding mothers for another meal—dinner this time—to celebrate an eventful year and to thank them for the courtesy they had extended to me before I began at NPR. As the wine flowed the stories began, but this time I leaned forward—not back—a participant in the events of the last year and a proud and full member of the NPR family. ∎

# EPILOGUE: NPR NEXT

by David Folkenflik

In the future, the prototypical NPR reporter will appear as a miniature hologram darting about your car dashboard, narrating a story accompanied by visuals in vivid color, pungent smells, and tactile texture.

Kidding, folks. Though I wouldn't put it past CNN to try.

The truth is, people who say they know how the news business will work in the future are misleading you, themselves, or both.

When I first arrived at NPR, I opened the top drawer of my desk and found a small cardboard box filled with single-edged razor blades. It had to be explained to me that these were not the keepsakes of a despondent producer but had once been vital tools for slicing and splicing tape on deadline. Now, reporters are expected to gather their recordings on digital memory cards and write their stories on computers from locations around the country. In what might sound like a joke, the nation's leading radio network has won a passel of major awards for news photography.

The public radio network has never been more highly valued than it is today; supporters prize above all else the breadth and nature of NPR's news coverage. NPR still provides an intimacy and even a sense of whimsy often lacking in its broadcast competitors, as people are given the chance to speak in their own voices. The increased global reach of NPR's reporting staff is a mark of its serious journalistic goals, and stands in contrast to the corporate media world, where budgets are being slashed and bureaus closed down. NPR provides refuge for civilized discourse as the cable news world fractures into constant contention. By most counts, the arrows are generally all in the right direction for NPR, and, sad to say, too often in the wrong one for its traditional competitors.

"NPR is the only independent, national, significant source of broadcast news," says Wyoming Public Radio general manager Jon Schwartz, a former NPR board chairman. "Everyone else is owned by some larger corporation that doesn't have a lot to do with journalism."

NPR strives to be a constant companion wherever you might happen to be, a nimble network that funnels programs or stories to you at your own pace.

## TECTONIC SHIFTS IN THE MEDIA LANDSCAPE

It's worth pulling back for just a moment to look at the broader picture as NPR enters its fifth decade. Major shifts are completely reconfiguring the media landscape.

Take newspapers, the traditional engine driving daily American journalism. In cities around the country, no one matches the size of their newsrooms. But these are weakened giants—stripped of classified advertising by free Web competitors and shorn of conventional ads by

OPPOSITE Media correspondent, David Folkenflik, 2007 (photo by Stephen Voss).

the declining economy. The corporate owners of the *Baltimore Sun*, the *Chicago Tribune*, the *Los Angeles Times*, the *Minneapolis Star-Tribune*, and the *Philadelphia Inquirer* are all, at this writing, in bankruptcy proceedings. Other newspaper companies are laboring under onerous debt.

The Hearst Corporation threatened to close the *San Francisco Chronicle* and did still the presses at the *Seattle Post-Intelligencer*, which became a Web-only outlet. The long-stable *Washington Post* is losing astonishing amounts of money, the New York Times Company took out a loan of more than $200 million from a Mexican billionaire and had been shopping around the *Boston Globe* until it won enough concessions from unions to minimize huge losses.

These financial problems are exacerbated by the current recession—but they are not caused by them.

Magazines are faring little better. *Business-Week* was sold to Bloomberg News at a bargain basement price, and of the three primary general-interest newsweeklies, one (*U.S. News & World Report*) has become a monthly; a second (*Newsweek*) has reinvented itself with a thinner publication relying on reported essays; and the original colossus, *Time*, has accepted a diminished publication and public impact, and no longer commands quite the same influence as it did in the past.

Unlike the print outlets, the big broadcast television networks and their local affiliates rarely cover their own plight—but they are seeing audiences decline and age. Meanwhile, cable news channels are generally continuing a retreat from serious news by plunging further into a world of staged polemicism.

For NPR, the tumult offers plenty to cause concern, but also astonishing opportunities—if it can figure out how best to play to its strengths, which include not only its journalists, but its audience.

## LOYAL LISTENERS

People in media circles have long envied NPR's not-for-profit model, which includes staunchly loyal followers who help to support member stations, instead of shareholders to please. After all, in the best scenario, we are entering into an age of patchwork media. Legacy media outlets are likely to survive by stripping down, constricting their ambition and reach, and picking several areas in which they choose to be authoritative. And they will inevitably cede much ground to the smaller, more nimble competitors that are springing up around the country, like *Minnpost* in Minneapolis, the *New Haven Independent*, the *St. Louis Beacon*, *Voice of San Diego*, and *Crosscut* in Seattle. *Pro Publica*, an investigative newsroom based near Wall Street, gets most of its funding from a pair of key donors, Herb and Marian Sandler. Many of the other newcomers receive key support from the John S. and James L. Knight Foundation and a handful of other philanthropies active in journalism.

But Joel Kramer, CEO of *Minnpost*, argues that such backing is seed money, not sustaining. He wants to develop a reliable base of advertisers, or underwriters, foundation grants, and, most important of all, contributors.

"When it comes to cultivating such sources, everyone looks to one organization for guidance: NPR," wrote the media observer Michael Massing in the *New York Review of Books*. "At a time when not only newspapers but also commercial broadcasters are struggling, NPR has thrived."

Yet as NPR and public radio stations can attest, a not-for-profit structure does not guarantee financial stability. Every year, public radio has to earn its support from listeners, underwriters, and foundations. And NPR has had to hustle to gain audiences on emerging platforms.

## FITS AND STARTS

By its own admission, NPR was a reluctant and relatively weak entrant into the world of media Web sites. For years, the NPR site was pretty much an archive of what had been broadcast on the air. The reluctance to delve in was understandable. It took most news organizations seven or eight years to turn a profit from their Web sites after establishing them fully around 1996. The *Washington Post* sank a billion dollars into washingtonpost.com, and the profits that have finally started to come in don't come close to replacing the money vanishing from the print edition.

By 2009, many news organizations had repeatedly rethought the relationship between their core platforms and the Web. NPR had already hired Kinsey Wilson, the innovative executive editor of USAToday.com, as its senior vice president and general manager for digital media. The newest redesign of NPR's Web site represents a very conscious effort to give people useful, engaging information through original content and complementary material. New blogs are guiding visitors to NPR.org to read not just NPR's stories, but material from other organizations. NPR.org is designed to be a trusted portal to the day's news as well as NPR's beloved stories and features. "What we need to deliver when they're in front of the computer is very different than when they're home making breakfast or when they're picking up the kids from school," Wilson says.

The new emphasis on digital media has grated on some radio professionals. Some jobs on the radio side went unfilled while candidates for digital jobs circulated through NPR at a brisk pace. Some reporters initially blanched at writing online versions of stories in addition to their other deadline duties. But recent moves to better integrate online and broadcast staff, including a weeks-long immersion in the digital world for hundreds of NPR's editorial employees largely underwritten by the Knight Foundation, has helped to blunt internal tensions. "Ultimately, the winning formula is content," says Ellen Weiss, senior vice president for news. "I don't think things become better or more interesting because they're online—just as I don't think something is better because it's on radio."

NPR has enjoyed some success in developing audiences for new online streams. For example, NPR is currently one of the nation's leading producers of news podcasts. Its expansion has been impressive. But those who see it as NPR's online salvation may prove disappointed. "My prediction for podcast use is that it has peaked but will stay steady over the next two to three years before it starts to shrink," wrote NPR analyst Matt Gallivan after pouring over Forrester Research's summer 2009 surveys. "Currently, podcasts do meet the needs of a certain set of media users, but . . . more and more, on-the-go media needs are being met by on-demand mobile usage."

"I'm much more likely to listen to podcasts and Internet radio streams than terrestrial radio, and increasingly want to listen only to the content and artists that I find interesting," says Michael Frederick, a software designer for Google who lives in New York City and is a self-described NPR fan. "In the past, radio was something that I tended to listen to when there were no alternatives. Now, I have the option to listen to relevant stories and programs when I want to. With the advent of smart phones, the content, time, and place can all be completely of my choosing." Frederick may be articulating the next media model.

On his own time, and for no compensation, Frederick is devising an NPR application for Android, a software platform for mobile devices meant to compete with the iPhone. He hopes that it will draw more listeners to NPR's programs and stories, more readers to the text Web pages, and more colleagues to design their own NPR applications.

Kinsey Wilson is among those making a similar point. Mobile devices represent the next wave of the Web, and they could help propel NPR from the pace of a gentle trot to an all-out canter.

"We have the potential to be at the forefront of mobile delivery—in text but also particularly with audio," Wilson says. Sound, after all, is what made Apple's iPod and more recently its iPhone seemingly indispensable for the digerati. Sound doesn't require you to stay still to read. Sound goes with you. And sound is NPR's indisputable competitive edge. Taken together with its radio broadcasts and Web site, Wilson says, "you have the ability for NPR to (attract) one of the top audiences during drive time, at work during the day, and when you're on the go."

## COLLABORATION NOT DOMINATION

NPR is well-placed to capitalize on the opportunity. But that won't matter if NPR fails to deliver on its promise to be a trusted source of news.

"Within the next five years, I think that public radio will be the dominant force for enterprise and accountability journalism in the country," says Ellen Weiss, the news chief. "I think it's our time to step up to the plate and make sure that kind of role not only grows but thrives."

NPR has done some sparkling investigative reporting over the past few years—for example, Danny Zwerdling's pieces on the mental trauma suffered by soldiers returning from the Iraq War and Laura Sullivan's work on the treatment of federal prisoners and the handling of rape allegations on American Indian reservations. On the other hand, when Bill Marimow, NPR vice president for news, left in 2006, the network lost his strong leadership in enterprise reporting. Noted newspaper investigative editor Brian Duffy joined NPR as managing editor but now lends his writing and editing expertise to NPR's development department.

NPR's leading news executives have made clear that they want to rebuild the newsroom's investigative muscle. In December 2009, veteran Canadian Broadcasting Corporation editor Susanne Reber was named NPR's deputy managing editor for investigations.

## 2009: NPR 2.0

# DICK MEYER

*Executive editor, NPR News and Information*

**So NPR is radio, right?** And radio is supposed to be, well, kind of twentieth century, right?

Not quite.

At the beginning of the twenty-first century, NPR is growing and flourishing when many of the other great American news and information companies in print and broadcast have been shrinking and struggling. Amidst a transformation in communications that has been likened to the Industrial Revolution, little old NPR held on to old world craftsmanship and values—and kept getting a bigger and bigger audience.

But hold on: NPR's listeners were also becoming NPR readers. They wanted NPR when *they* wanted it, around-the-clock and not just on the radio but on the computer, the cell phone, and all sorts of new portable contraptions. And we wanted to give it to them. After all, the mission of NPR goes beyond producing great radio; it is about providing the public with high-quality, noncommercial news and information programming.

In 2008 and 2009, NPR truly turned the digital corner. Prior to that, NPR.org had been primarily an archive for radio stories. Now, NPR produces a huge menu of stories and programming for all sorts of new platforms.

The first challenge was how to give NPR—famous for its sound—a visual identity. What does NPR *look* like?

The answer we came up with fit the simple NPR recipe: hire talented, independent-minded journalists and technologists and let them loose. So this old radio outfit started bringing on photography editors, graphic artists, and videographers. And radio folks were given weeks of in-depth education in digital production.

Next came the unveiling of a radically new NPR.org in July 2009. It was a light, airy site with sleek graphic design, fine still photography and careful attention to hard news. Increasingly, NPR.org has become a primary news source for the NPR community—not just a companion to the radio or yet another stop in the day's Web-surfing.

Among the new features on NPR.org, a suite of popular blogs with an especially "NPRish" feel, with names like *The Two-Way, Monkey See, Planet Money, Political Junkie, Shots* and even a fabulous blog about photography called *The Picture Show*. All NPR correspondents now routinely file stories for the Web as well as radio, many with elaborate multimedia elements such as information graphics, video, audio slide shows or photography.

A few weeks later, NPR revealed a new "app" for the wildly popular iPhone. The iPhone was an important step in the evolution of how consumers will get news. And it is technology especially well-suited to audio. The NPR iPhone app allowed NPR fans to get shows, stories, and podcasts whenever—and wherever—they wanted, and in the format they preferred—text or audio. Eventually, all major portable devices will have these kinds of tools. And folks who once just listened to NPR in the car or the kitchen will start *reading* NPR in airplanes and cafes or listening to NPR when walking the dog or raking leaves.

NPR has now merged its radio and digital newsrooms. You can hear an hourly newscast on the radio or a cell phone. You can listen to *Morning Edition* at night. You can talk back to the radio by posting comments and questions on NPR.org. You can find collections of NPR content curated and updated on Facebook, Twitter, and, we're sure, social media destinations that will be the next big things.

The American media landscape is changing at an astonishing pace. For many traditional news organizations, change will mean decline, disorientation, and an abandonment of quality. For NPR, it will mean more opportunities and more obligations: opportunities to serve a greater and more diverse audience, and obligations to do so with integrity, high standards, and serious purpose. ∎

"No other organization has the ability and the staffing and infrastructure and dedication to enterprise and investigative journalism to feed it downstream," Weiss says.

By "downstream" she means to the member stations for their own journalistic use. The system envisioned is based on collaboration, not domination. "If we build on computer-assisted reporting, yes, you can draw a national picture," Weiss says, "but the data we're mining can be developed locally (by member stations). Or you could post this information on your Web site and host a conversation around it."

NPR has seventeen bureaus around the country, including the headquarters in Washington, DC, and major presences in Los Angeles and New York. That's still far more than any other organization but the Associated Press. Given the budget constraints, however, this is no time to establish dozens of additional outposts.

And yet, if NPR can better leverage its relationship with its member stations, why would it need to? The hundreds of stations around the country represent NPR's "secret sauce," in new CEO Vivian Schiller's words—8,000 people in smaller newsrooms around the country operating independently but potentially in far greater concert than before. NPR would also be providing them more content, technical tools, and training to carry out their own reporting and analysis.

In this vision, and this is a key point, those stations would be better placed than ever to create indispensable local content. And this would answer the question of why people would rely on them when they could otherwise go directly online and through mobile devices

## THE FUTURE OF NPR

# KEITH JENKINS

*Supervising senior producer, Multimedia Desk*

**While I have been at NPR** for only a short time, I feel like I have already been steeped in the tradition of excellent, innovative journalism, delivered with the personal touch of the human voice. What I hope to add to that are the things that make twenty-first-century reporting so exciting—the ability to see your story unfold in pictures and video and to help our audience dive even deeper into the types of stories that have made NPR what it is today.

Trying to define a "look" for NPR has been challenging. We all know what NPR sounds like; its presence on the dial is so commanding that you know you've landed on an NPR station within a second or two of hearing it. How do you have that same impression in the visual space?

For me and the multimedia staff at NPR, the "look" must start with a foundation of the great audio storytelling tradition that lives within the walls of our building. Telling stories with pictures is, for us, an extension of telling stories with the human voice. We see our job as adding a visual layer of information to the editing timeline that ultimately ends up as an NPR story.

The NPR "look" must be as distinctive as its sound. Our visuals must be clean and unique, informative, and always contain an element of the unexpected. And while letting you "see" the story unfold is one goal, an even greater challenge is to immerse you in it with both sight and sound, so that you experience a story with all the depth that twenty-first-century technology can and will provide.

Personally, I have been amazed at what we have already been able to present to our audience. Colorful and majestic photography from China, beautiful and mysterious vistas from the Amazon, gritty scenes from the frontlines of war in Afghanistan, and the artistry of live music from here in our studios in DC. Photography and video, all created in support of the mission of NPR, to deliver the absolute best reporting possible to our family. As the history of NPR continues to unfold, that history will include a visual side, one that will help take NPR into the future. ∎

for more generic national content. It could prove a vital force to knit together the national news organization with its hundreds of local member stations. That relationship has been defined by distrust as well as mutual pride. Some stations are hesitant to accept NPR's promised embrace for initiatives, whether it involves Web site design, news coordination, fund-raising, or online music streams.

## THE RELUCTANCE TO WALK TALL

Those periodic fissures have in some ways stunted NPR's public profile. And NPR has never felt comfortable walking tall. As an institution created as a counterpoint to the corporate media, NPR presents stories on the air that aren't desperate bids for ratings or attention. This attitude is demonstrated in the way people at NPR think about themselves. NPR's hosts—don't call them anchors—make a fraction of the salary of their television peers, while carrying far heavier workloads. And the network would never hawk itself like its slickly marketed broadcasting rivals.

This first occurred to me a few years back when Tavis Smiley, then the engaging and peripatetic host of the eponymous NPR show, was feuding with the network over money—but not pay. He wanted the network to spend more to market his program. A lot more. NPR was walloped publicly for its reluctance to further fund the show's marketing, until an executive revealed that Smiley had sought $3 million for the publicity campaign. The marketing budget for the entire network at the time stood at just $165,000 a year. NPR, it turned out, was already devoting 80 percent of that amount to Smiley's show.

Most local television stations in the top twenty-five markets dedicate more to promoting their news teams. It's a reflection of NPR's values that it rejects the slick commercialism of its for-profit rivals and does not go in for intense promotion. But that sensibility also plays into NPR's frequent and strange marginalization in popular culture and the public consciousness, despite the vital role it plays in the media ecology.

In the 1998 movie *The Insider*, a real-life thriller about journalistic intrigue at CBS's *60 Minutes*, the lightly fictionalized Mike Wallace (played by Christopher Plummer) angrily explains why he yields to corporate pressure to squelch a story: "I don't plan to spend the end of my days wandering in the wilderness of National Public Radio."

In 2005, *New York Times* media critic David Carr described NPR as "the prissy, embattled bastion of the quiet left"—and that was in a column effusively praising the network's coverage of Hurricane Katrina.

NPR's decades-long tradition of self-restraint has developed into a problem, says CEO Vivian Schiller. That matters in winning more contributions, in drawing more underwriting and grants, and even in landing the next big charitable gift. (A more than $200 million bequest from the late Joan B. Kroc helped NPR redefine its ambitions and its reach—and also to weather the financial crunch that began in 2008 far better than most of its rivals.)

"Americans spend more time with NPR than any other source," Schiller says. "And yet, I feel that NPR is America's best-kept secret. We've got it all, but yet, somehow, we haven't penetrated the consciousness of a lot of people that we are an incredibly powerful—if not the most powerful—news organization in the country."

"We're not top of mind," she says.

And she says she will be judged in significant measure by how well she changes that. "I see NPR not only being, but recognized as, the most important quality news organization in this country."

For her part, Weiss promises that the values that defined NPR through its first four decades will endure.

"A couple of years ago, we branded ourselves NPR and NPR NEWS instead of National Public Radio," Weiss says. "We're not just national; we're international, and we have been for some time. We're not just radio. But we are public. And we always will be."

# INDEX

## A

Adams, Noah, *20, 28*–29, 66–67, *78, 119,* 128, 130–131, *147*
Adams, Rich, 37
Afghanistan, 203–208, 253
Afkhami, Mahnaz, 159
AIDS, 121–127
*All Songs Considered*.
   *See* NPR Music
*All Things Considered*, 13–15, 22, 25, 31–35, 46, 56, *74, 78,* 130–131, *145, 147,* 244
American Public Media, 230
Amos, Deborah, 104, 107, 135, *148,* 152
Anderson, Jim, 45
Ardalan, Davar, 157–160, *161*
*As It Happens*, 35, 73

## B

Baer, Jonathan "Smokey," *119,* 120
Banaszak, Brendan, *247*
BBC, 79, 104, 148
Beaubien, Jason, *218–219*
Beirut, Siege of (1982), 104–105, 107–109
Bergsma, Stephanie, 224
Berkes, Howard, 96–97, 121
Berlin Wall, 137
Berman, Doug, 172, 175
Block, Melissa, *245–246, 247,* 248, 250
Blount Jr., Roy, *177*
Blumberg, Alex, *242*
Board, Joseph, 44
Bodett, Tom, 99

Boilen, Bob, 87, 232–233, 235
Bornstein, Ron, 115–116
Bosnia, 152–153
Bradley-Hagerty, Barbara, 197, 220
Brand, Madeleine, 244
Breeding, Leslie, *78*
Breslow, Peter, *138,* 203, *204,* 205, 207, 213
*The Bryant Park Project*, 195, 230, 240, 242
Bullock, Tom, 214–215
Bureaus, 77, 97, 104, 138, 144, 148, 162, 195, 215, 220, 266
Buzenberg, Bill, 138, 148, 150, 174, 251
Byrd, Robert, 50

## C

*Car Talk*, 132, *172*
Carter, Jimmy, *52–53,* 54–55, 79, 94
Chadwick, Alex, 63, 134–*135,* 244
*Challenger* disaster, 121
Chaney, Renee, *14*
Charon, Scott, 184–185
Childs, Craig, 200–201
Chillag, Ian, 173
China earthquake (2008), 246, 248–249
*Christian Science Monitor*, 15
Clark, Ted, *131*
Clements, Maureen, 43
Clifford, Terry, 228–229
Clinton, Bill, *167,* 180, 184–185
Cochran, Barbara, 60
Cohen, Barbara, 82, 96–97, 115–116
Commentaries, 34–35, 76, 99, 120, 162, 164–165, 200–201, 226

Conan, Neal, 110, *138,* 148, 150, *151, 169,* 200–201, 250
Conley, Robert, 38–*39*
Conroy, Kimberly, *107*
Cornish-Emery, Audie, *257*
Corporation For Public Broadcasting, 21, 60, 97, 112–117, 120, 150, 166–167
Cranberry relish, 31
Cronkite, Walter, 52
Cullen, Michael, *181*
Czechoslovakia.
   *See* Velvet Revolution

## D

Davidson, Adam, *242–243*
*Day to Day*, 195, 230, 244
Dean, Richard, 182–183
del Aguila, Leo, *107*
del Barco, Madalit, *162–163*
Destajo, Vince, 101
Dickinson, Amy, *147*
Digital Media, 182–183, 232–235, 240, 263–266
Drummer, Connie, *133*
Drummond, William, 104–105, 108–*109*
Dudinska, Natasha, 134–135
Duffy, Brian, 264
DuPont Award, 154, 242
Dylan, Bob, 233

## E

Ebadi, Shirin, 159–160
Edwards, Bob, *46,* 56, *57,* 60, *78,* 196–199, 250, *251,* 252–253

Edward Sharpe and the Magnetic
    Zeros, *236–237*
Eisenhower, Julie Nixon, 38–39
El Salvador, 104–105
Elving, Ron, *252*
Energy crisis (1979), 54–55, 78
Engineering, 45, 50, 101

# F

Federal funding. *See* Corporation
    For Public Broadcasting
Felber, Adam, *177*
Financial crisis at NPR (1983),
    112–117
Financial crisis (2008), 242–245
Fitzgerald, Ella, 45
Flatow, Ira, 29, 31, 174–*175*
Folkenflik, David, *260–264, 266–267*
Foreign desk, 104, 107, 144–145,
    148–150
Freelance and contract reporters,
    *77*, 96–97, 104, 107, 144, 152
*Fresh Air*, 23, 173
Friedman, Milton, 44
Funding, 150, 182, 190–191, 224–227,
    244, 267. *See also* Corporation
    for Public Broadcasting

# G

Gabor, Jolie, *113*
Gabor, Zsa Zsa, *113*
Garcia, Lou, *151*
Garcia-Navarro, Lourdes,
    210–211
Garrels, Anne, 144–145, 152,
    213–*214, 253*
Gediman, Dan, 222

Gibson, Laura, 235
Gingrich, Newt, 116–117, 166–167
Gjelten, Tom, 107, 110, *111*, 199
Gladstone, Brooke, 184–185
Glass, Ira, 76, 168–*169*.
    *See also This American Life*
Goodwin-Sides, Anne, *133*
Gordemer, Barry, 163
Gotrich, Lars, *238*
Grant, Neva, 120, 144
Gross, Terry, *173*
Grosvenor, Verta Mae, 84
Grundman, Anya, 232
Gudenkauf, Anne, 121–122
Gulf War (1990), 110, 148, 150

# H

Hain, Penny, 113
Hansen, Liane, *28, 132, 133,* 143
Harris, Richard L., *138, 169*
Harrison, Archie, 122–124, *125,*
    126–127
Hedges, Chris, 110, 150
Henderson, Gary, 50
Hilton, Robin, 235
Hochberg, Adam, *114–115*
Holmes, Jane, *33*
Hsu, Andrea, 246, 248–249
Hudson, Ched, 79

# I

Inskeep, Steve, 221, 252, *253,*
    254, *255*
Internet, 182–185
    *See also* Digital Media
Investigative reporting, 121,
    216–217, 220, 264, 266

Iran, 157–160
Iranian hostage crisis, 56, 90, 94
Iraq War (2003– ), 210–211,
    213–217, 222
Isay, David, *231*

# J

Jarenwattananon, Patrick, *238*
*Jazz Alive!,* 45
Jenkins, Keith, 266
Jenkins, Loren, 210
Jones, LeAlan, *231*
Judd, Jackie, 44, 46

# K

Kamen, Jeff, 14, 26–27
Kasell, Carl, 60, *61, 78, 176*
Katzif, Mike, *238*
Keillor, Garrison 74, 102, *103,*
    131, 177
Kelly, Mary Louise, 199, 221
Kernis, Jay, *31, 47,* 56, 62, 78, 113,
    118, *119,* 120, 132, 196, 225,
    230, 240, 250
The Kitchen Sisters, *63*
Kling, William, 73, 102, 130–131
Klose, Kevin, 211, 220, 224–225, 230
The Knight Foundation, 263–264
Koch, Christopher, *138*
Kosovo, 186–87
KPBS, 224, 229
Kroc, Joan, 224–225, 244, 267
Kuralt, Charles, 22
Kurcias, Marty, 104–105
KUSP, 63

## L

Labor disputes, 97
Layoffs, 114, 116, 244
Ledbetter, James, 185
Lehrer, Brian, *242*
Leiderman, B.J., 62, 120
Lennon, John, 84, *86–89*
Levine, Ketzel, 244
Lewinsky, Monica, 180–181
Liasson, Mara, *167*, 180, *181*
Libraries, 43, 243
Listeners, 139, 150, 190, 241, 264
Loewenstein, Peter, *33*
Loomis, Henry, 60
Low Smith, Margaret, 181
Lyden, Jacki, *77*, 97, 152, 157–160, *161*, 199

## M

Magliozzi, Tom and Ray.
    *See Car Talk*
Malesky, Bob, 132, *133*
Malesky, Kee, 43
Marcus, Greil, 88–89
Mandela, Nelson, *143–144*
Mankiewicz, Frank, 48, *49*, 60, 62, 68, 82, 102, 112–115, *117*
Marimow, Bill, 220–221, 264
Marketing, 267
*Marketplace*, 68
Martin, Michel, 256
Marton, Kati, *14*
McChesney, John, 74, 96–97, *101*, 104, 107, 110, 138, 244
McCullough, David, 51
McDonnell, Ellen, *11*, 250–253
Member stations, *15*, 75, 116–118, 120, 150, 166, 183, 190, 228, 266–267. *See also individual stations by call letters*
Meyer, Dick, 265
Minnesota Public Radio, 73–74, 102, 130–131
Mitchell, Jack, 115–117
Molpus, David, 98

Montagne, Renée, *142*, 143–146, 208–*209*, 254, *255*
Montiegel, Robert, 44
*Morning Edition*, 31, 56–60, 62, 64, *74*, 76, 78, 96–97, 118, 120, 163, 244, 250–254
Mortensen, Kris, *14*
Mount St. Helen's eruption, 96
Murrow, Edward R., 155, 222–*223*

## N

Nafisi, Azar, 158–160
National Desk, 74, 96–97
Neary, Lynn, *135*
Neighmond, Patricia, 122–123, 126–127
Nelson, Davia. *See* The Kitchen Sisters
Newman, Lloyd, *231*
*News & Notes*, 195, 230, 266
Newscast, 46, 60, 64, 112
Nicaragua, 107, 110
Nixon, Richard, 33–34, *36*, 37–39, 60
Nobel Award protest (1976), 44
*NPR Music*, *232–239*
NPR West, 162–163, 230

## O

Obama, Barack, 164–*165*, 254, 256
O'Connor, Sandra Day, 90, *92–93*
O'Rourke, P.J., 226
Overby, Peter, 220
Overseas Press Club Award, 134

## P

Panama Canal Treaty debates, 48
PBS, 60, 166–167
Peabody Award, 22, 152, 168–169, 242
Perasa, Danny and Annie, 231
*Performance Today*, 179, 230
Pirro, Toby, 101
*Planet Money*, 242–243
Poggioli, Sylvia, 107, 134, 144–*145*, 152–153
Poundstone, Paula, *177*

Powell, Adam Clayton III, 138
*A Prairie Home Companion.*
    *See* Garrison Keillor
PTSD, 216–217
Public Broadcasting Act of 1967, 21
Public Radio International, 102, 169

## Q

Quayle, Don, 25

## R

Raz, Guy, *202*
Reagan, Ronald, 78, *80–81*, 82, 90, 93–95, 112, 137
Reber, Susanne, 264
Reiner, Steve, 115
Richards, Michael, *11*
Roberts, Cokie, *8*, *64–67*, 82–*83*, 152
Rockefeller, Sharon Percy, 114
Rosenbaum, Marcus, 104, 138
Rudin, Ken, 94–95, *252*
Russell, Jim, 29, 68
Rwanda, 154

## S

Sagal, Peter, 175–*176*, 178
Satellite distribution, *23*, 31, 44, 46, *49*, 56, 102, 112. *See also* Technology
Scaggiari, Stef, 132
Schaefer, Jack, 184–185
Schiller, Vivian, 244–245, *258–259*, 266–267
Schlesinger, Maury, 79, *138*
Schorr, Daniel, 120, 137, *155*
Schwartz, John, 261
Sedaris, David, 76, 170–*171*
September 11, 2001, 196–201
Shapiro, Ari, *194*, 196–*197*
Shortz, Will, 132
Siegel, Robert, 29, 46, 104, *106*, 116, 118, 120, 130–*131*, *169*, 180–*181*
Siemering, Bill, *13*, 15, 22–23, 25, 43, 56, 68, 73–74

Sikka, Madhulika, 254
Silva, Nikki.
    *See* The Kitchen Sisters
Silverman, Art, 42, *98, 138, 147, 249*
Simeone, Lisa, 179
Simon, Scott, *32, 77, 104–105,*
    *107,* 113, 118, *119,* 120, *150,*
    *172,* 186–187, *189,* 195, *204–*
    205, 213
Skoler, Michael, 154–155
Smiley, Tavis, 267
South Africa, 143–146
Stamberg, Susan, *12,* 13, 22,
    *30–31,* 33, *34,* 35, *46,* 52, 54–56,
    76, 79, 99, 112–116, 128, *129,*
    130–132, 179
Starr, Kenneth, 93
Starrman, Richard, 224–225
*StoryCorps,* 231
Strout, Richard, 37
Suarez, Ray, *173,* 250
Sudan, 219
Swell Season, *234*

**T**

*Talk of the Nation,* 174
Tallo, Cara, 254
*The Tavis Smiley Show.*
    See *News & Notes*
Technology, 46, 98, 145–146, 219, 253,
    261. *See also* Satellite distribution
*This American Life,* 168–169,
    242–243. *See also* Glass, Ira
*This I Believe,* 222
Thomas, Tom, 228–229
Thompson, Stephen, 235, 238–239
Three Mile Island disaster, 64–67
Tiananmen Square protests, 132
Tillotson, Drew, *124–127*
Tiny Desk Concerts.
    *See* NPR Music
Totenberg, Nina, *11,* 82, *90–91,*
    93, 220
Turpin, Chris, 195

**V**

Van de Geer, Richard, 40–42
Velvet Revolution, 134–135
Vietnam War, 14, 25–27, 40–42

**W**

Wahl, Bruce, *21*
*Wait, Wait . . . Don't Tell Me!,*
    175–179, 226
Walker, Leslie, 185
WAMU, 13, 50
Wasser, Fred, *133*
Waters, Mike, 29, *34*
Watergate, 33–39
Watson, Ivan, *211*
Watson, Walter Ray, *133*
WBEZ, 169, 175–176
WBFO, 22–23, 29
WBKY, 28–29
WBUR, 172
Web site.
    *See* Digital Media
*Weekend All Things Considered,*
    44, *133,* 250
*Weekend Edition Saturday,*
    118, 120, 137
*Weekend Edition Sunday,*
    132, *133*
Weiss, Ellen, *147,* 197, 220–221,
    230, 240, 242, 244, 264, 266–267
Wertheimer, Linda, *14,* 15, *32,*
    48–50, 82, *83,* 88-89, *131,* 141,
    *167,* 250
Wharton, Ned, *133,* 182
White, Janel, 243
Wilco (band), 232
Williams, Kim, 35, 76
Wilson, Kinsey, 263–264
WOI, 228
Woods, Ralph, *69*
Wonder, Stevie, 45

**Y**

Ydstie, John, *72,* 73–74

**Z**

Zwerdling, Danny, 121, 216–217, 264

# ACKNOWLEDGMENTS

Numerous people contributed their time, talents, and resources to the creation of this book. NPR would like to thank its employees for their help and enthusiasm; in particular, Leslie Sanders, Jo Ella Straley, Kee Malesky, Mary Glendinning, Susan Stamberg, Art Silverman, Barbara Sopato, Kathie Miller, Kerry Thompson, and the entire staff of librarians, who have contributed immense amounts of time and effort to this project.

Thanks also to our editor at Chronicle Books, Emily Haynes; Editorial Assistant Emilie Sandoz; and the rest of the Chronicle Books team—Jake Gardner; Beth Steiner; Becca Cohen; April Whitney; Hannah deBree, and Valerie Ruud.

Finally, NPR would like to thank the talented designers at Design Army.

NATIONAL PUBLIC RADIO, NPR, the NPR logo, ALL THINGS CONSIDERED, MORNING EDITION, PLANET MONEY, TALK OF THE NATION, WAIT WAIT . . . DON'T TELL ME!, and WEEKEND EDITION, are trademarks of National Public Radio, Inc. Reg. U.S. Pat. & Tm. Off.

A PRAIRIE HOME COMPANION is a registered trademark of Garrison Keillor.

CAR TALK is a registered trademark of Tom and Ray Magliozzi and Tappet Brothers Associates d/b/a Dewey, Cheetham, And Howe.

THIS AMERICAN LIFE is a registered trademark of Ira Glass and The WBEZ Alliance, Inc.

THIS I BELIEVE® is a registered trademark of This I Believe, Inc.

Library of Congress Cataloging-in-Publication Data
This is NPR / [Cokie Roberts . . . et al.].
  p. cm.
ISBN 978-0-8118-7253-9 (hardcover)
1. National Public Radio (U.S.)—History. 2. Public radio—United States—History. 3. Radio journalism—United States—History. 4. United States—History—1969– I. Roberts, Cokie. II. Title.

HE8697.95.U6T45 2010
384.540973—dc22
2010013793

Manufactured in China
DESIGNED BY DESIGN ARMY

10 9 8 7 6 5 4 3 2

CHRONICLE BOOKS LLC
680 Second Street
San Francisco, California 94107
www.chroniclebooks.com

KYUK KUAC KNAU KUAZ KAWC KUAF KUAR KASU KHSU KCHO KV
KSUT KPRG KHPR KBSW KEMC KUFM KNPR KUNV KUNR KANW KU
KUT KVLU KAMU KETR KEDT KTEP KMBH KOHM KSTX KWBU KUSU
WSIE WIUM WGLT WCBU WQUB WVIK WUIS WILL WFIU WVPE WNI
WNKU WUKY WFPL WMKY WKMS WEKU WRKF KRVS KEDM WWI
KBIA KCUR KXCV KMST KSMU KTBG KUCV KIOS WVXU WCBE
WVUB KBAQ KJZZ KUSC KPCC KPBS KALW KQED KCSM KCRW
WBEZ WNIJ WFYI WBST WEAA WYPR WBUR WGBH WUMB WUOM
WCPN WKSU KOPB WHYY WRTI WDUQ WQED WYEP WRNI KERA KU
WTSU WUAL WNPR WHDD WGCU WQCS WUFT WJCT WFIT WKG
CLWT MDWF CRWI CNWU RCWJ SUWM PNWP RLWE VOWN JTWA
WCQS WFAE WDAV WNCU WRVS WFSS WTEB WNCW WCPE WH
WUTC WETS WUOT WKNO WMOT WPLN WVPS WMRA WHRV WC
KASU KHSU KCHO KVPR KZYX KRCB KXJZ KXPR KVCR KCBX KUS
KUNV KUNR KANW KUNM KCIE KRWG KENW KCND KCCU KGOU
KOHM KSTX KWBU KUSU KPCW KCPW KUER KRFA KWSU KPB
WVIK WUIS WILL WFIU WVPE WNIN WBNI WLPR WBAA WOIK KWITK
WEKU WRKF KRVS KEDM WWNO KDAQ WKAR WGVU WIAA WM
KTBG KUCV KIOS WVXU WCBE WOSU WGTE WYSO WYSU WLS
KPBS KALW KQED KCSM KCRW KCFR WSHU WAMU WLRN WM
WYPR WBUR WGBH WUMB WUOM WDET WEMU KNOW KWMU WI
WDUQ WQED WYEP WRNI KERA KUHF WETA KEXP KUOW KPLU WXP
WQCS WUFT WJCT WFIT WKGC WUWF WFSU WXEL WUGA WJSF
WMPN WPRL WEVO WNJT WAMC WSKG WBFO WNED WSLU WR
WFSS WTEB WNCW WCPE WHQR WFDD WSNC WOUB WDIY WO
WPLN WVPS WMRA WHRV WCVE WVTF WVPN WWFM KYUK KUAC
KXPR KVCR KCBX KUSP KCUI KAIX KRCC KUNC KSUT KPRG KH